I0489087

MINIMUM VIABLE STRATEGY

WINNING IN BUSINESS INCH BY INCH

JOHN L. CHILDS

Table of Contents

To Ben. You were right about everything. *

*I sat down to write this dedication the morning of November 9th, the day after the 2016 US Presidential election. I lost a bet I made in September of that year to a friend of mine, Ben. I, a Hillary Clinton supporter, agreed to dedicate the book to him if my candidate lost and he, a Donald Trump supporter, agreed to dedicate a brick in my name at a building at the university we both attended.

At the time I made the bet, I was confident and did not consider the consequences or implications of the bet as the data at the time suggested that victory for Clinton was a sure thing. It would prove to be hubristic thinking, and in the process of making the bet I succumb to a number of the faults I've laid out for strategists in this book and have spent time warning against succumbing to.

The first fault was not seeing things as they are but as I wanted them to be. I, along with probably the rest of society today, live in an echo chamber, surrounded by the facts that fit to our hypothesis or by the opinions that meet our pre-conceived notions of a situation. Not once during the campaign did I seriously consider spending time reading those projections of what the opposite side was seeing, and thus I did not see things from a broader, more holistic point of view. This is one of the detriments of the society we live in: a post fact society with "Big" data and "enough" data to fit any particular hypothesis you choose to own. We call facts that don't mold to our agenda fake and seek those alternatives that do.

In fact, the data-driven website FiveThirtyEight wrote post-Trump election that:

> *The failure to see Clinton's vulnerabilities in the Electoral College reflected a lack of attention to detail. It was easy to make a superficial case along the following lines: Democrats had won two presidential elections in a row, the minority population was growing, and states such as Arizona were becoming more competitive. Therefore, Advantage Clinton in the Electoral College. By contrast, the flaws in the argument required a pencil and paper — or a spreadsheet — to work out. If you weren't being careful, you might have missed that the Midwestern states moving away from Clinton had a lot more electoral votes than the ones like Arizona that were moving toward her, or that polls showed her substantially underperforming Obama in middle-class states such as Pennsylvania and Michigan... Because journalists were predisposed toward the assumption that the country was too diverse to elect Trump, they didn't probe it for flaws as much as they might have otherwise. The "emerging Democratic majority" was reasonable-sounding argument, but it didn't hold up well to scrutiny and it didn't get enough of it[1].*

The second was that I did not consider the implications of one candidate having a clear, concise, easily explainable strategy that goes unchecked by one grasping for a pointed meaning. For all the faults of Donald Trump, it cannot be denied that he made clear *where to play* and *how to win* choices: focus on a particular segment of voters that feel left behind and turn traditionally Rust Belt blue states red. The strategy worked brilliantly as both Pennsylvania and Wisconsin, assumed to be "in the bag" by the Clinton camp, turned red. Wisconsin was all but ignored by Clinton, with the false assumption that the trusty blue state would hold strong for the general. This, however, did not play out as expected.

But hindsight is inevitably and will always be 20/20, and 20/20 doesn't help the strategist in the moment because losing, in hindsight, has already taken place. It is my hope that this book, which outlines a particular type of strategic construct for a particular set of circumstances, will help avoid the need for some individuals to look back and say "How did this all happen?" I, too, hope that in my own life I listen more to folks like Ben who warned me for months about what he observed and what his side of the argument was instead of making false assumptions and living in my own echo chamber.

-John Childs

PROLOGUE

I began to write this book, not as a student of business, but as a student of war. Having served in combat and as a lifelong student of history, I wanted to crystallize the idea of avoiding war. This idea was impressed upon me by my reading of *Thirteen Days*, an acute account of the Cuban Missile Crisis by Robert F. Kennedy, who served on the team that handled the crisis first hand.

About halfway through writing and researching for this book, a feeling of malaise began to settle upon me, or, as Winston Churchill once described the process of writing, "Writing a book is an adventure. To begin with it is a toy and an amusement. Then it becomes a mistress, then it becomes a master, then it becomes a tyrant. The last phase is that just as you are about to be reconciled to your servitude, you kill the monster and fling him to the public."

The book had become a tyrant. I struggled endlessly with the thought of being lost in the noise, and there was plenty of noise to research. Between the daily business news cycles, monthly editions of the *Harvard Business Review*, and the regular releases of books on tape, self-published books, and books released by the *Harvard Business Press* on strategy, it became difficult to see how this book might in any way say anything remotely unique on the topic of strategy. The theories were abound, the books on the subject diverse. There was no shortage of supply of "strategists" who were seemingly more than willing to put words on paper to justify charging $200 an hour to save your business from demise.

In the end, however, it often feels that many of these theories and ideas on strategy written by these self-proclaimed strategists often feel forced, as if the authors were, instead of seeking to provide value to readers, were instead looking to advance their own credentials as strategists. Many, some quoted and others not quoted in this book, have taken already pre-existing notions of strategy and rebranded them in a typical way as a new method of considering how to win. This is especially true in business strategic thought, as many business leaders want to be seen as thought leaders in their industry and as being "in-the-know" on the newest concept of strategy, no matter what degree of thought provoking it may be. These business books on strategy simply provide a very evident market need: to look smart at the office by having a business book on your desk, a fault which I am deeply guilty of myself as my collection of strategy books on my desk is often referred to as the office "library".

It is this author's hope that Minimum Viable Strategy does not present itself in this way. It is, indeed, a labor of love that is intended, not to advance a personal cause, but to help organizations avoid catastrophe, not just in business, but in geo-politics as later case studies will vividly articulate. But perhaps getting categorized into the same bucket as the rest of the mass-market business strategy books is unavoidable, and that to write an enduring book about strategy in the modern era is impossible in an age where the publishing world produces more new products than any other industry in history, with new works, professional published and self-published, are set upon a release tempo, not by weekly, but by hour.

It is almost impossible to compete, therefore, with the noise that is the publishing world and to write something that will stand the test of time. But with this aim I will move forth with purpose.

This book will attempt, not just to present a unique perspective on strategy, but also attempt to conduct a modern re-alignment of strategic thought on the whole. As you will learn in later chapter, the history and breadth of the topic is wide and deep, ranging as far back as Sun Tzu and the Art of War in 512 BC and certainly within the unrecorded human mind far before that.

But we live in a different world today. Modern science has brought the scientific method and "Big Data" (I'm still trying to figure out what Big Data actually is, although I know I'm perpetually in need of it). We must, therefore, reconcile historical strategic thought with modern day analytics to bring about a way of approaching strategy using these statistical techniques and data-centric approaches to management versus the gut-feelings and human inspired temperamental choices made by "bold" leaders at the top, though this, too, is still required in modern society.

It is this reconciliation of the old with the new that I hope to advance the cause of Minimum Viable Strategy. By preserving the best methods of the past and integrating the best methods of the present, I hope to develop an idea that can be useful for those few of us who respect all that history has done to bring us to this day and all the power of modern tools at our fingertips.

Finally, this theory is not a dictum. It is not written from the voice of someone who sees himself as an authority on strategy, pronouncing to the world a superior means of thinking about it and how to go about winning with it. On the contrary, this book and the proposal of the Minimum Viable Strategy theory is a starting point, a place for people to begin thinking about the world differently in a way to stave off catastrophe in theory own organizations. It is a place for a discussion to start.

Indeed, as the author, I welcome feedback, criticism, or further investigation into the viability or unviability of the theory proposed here. This book is meant to be accessible to all, so complex financial or statistical models or equations are not present to further the research or validate the hypothesis. Instead, it is based on the fundamental principles I've learned from experience in the trenches of both business and war. However, I challenge readers to further the work, to bring additional quantitative analysis to the proposed theory in order to further justify the implementation of minimally viable constructual ways of thinking to their organizations.

- John Childs, Denver Colorado

INTRODUCTION

I first became introduced to the idea of strategy as a boy when my mother taught me how to play chess and I read books on winning "chess strategies" so I could improve and hopefully, one day, beat my mother at the game. She never let me win, even as a small child, as she thought that would do more harm to me than good as it would give me a false sense of myself and my own capabilities.

My interest grew on the subject in my high school years as I read books such as *The Art of War* by *Sun Tzu*, *On War* by Clausewitz, and others. I would read histories of World War II and the Civil War and try to understand the method of the masters like Lee and Patton.

As my interest in strategy grew even more as world events took a turn toward violence with the attacks on September 11th, and, as my considerations toward an application to the military academy grew to action, I found myself submitting essays and filling out forms to attend the institution. I was accepted, thankfully, and entered West Point in July of 2003, the summer after the Iraq invasion took place.

At the Academy, I would be exposed to the formal study of military strategy and tactics between the summer training sessions where we were taught how to execute "Battle Drill 1 A: React to Contact" in the field by leading a squad of 10 soldiers against those playing the role of enemy combatants and the formal classroom instruction in the science of military planning as well as the art of military execution. In the study of the art of military execution, we began with the study of the great Battle of Agincourt and moved through history with the tides of technological change, which brought us to the reign of Napoleon and all the advances he brought to the military arts. We moved in our instruction to the Civil War and then the bloody war that brought the intersection of technology with outdated tactics, the Great War, also known as World War I.

All of this instruction, with its historical significance, placed a tremendous weight on the shoulders of the Cadets of West Point as we progressed through our final year, called "Firstie" year at the Academy. We were preparing to go to war, to fight the battles that had been raging for at that time almost six years. The war began in 2001, and for us it was closing in on May of 2007. The tide of the war had shifted from one outcome to the other and the President and his generals doubled down on both fronts, placing their reputations and the nation's on their chosen strategies called "The Surge" in Iraq and, a few years later, in Afghanistan.

At that moment, as we stood as Cadets with all of America's history surrounding us through statues and paintings and living legends like Lt. General Moore, author of *We Were Soldiers*, speaking about his engagements in Landing Zone X-Ray in Vietnam to inspire us, we realized daily that everything was at stake and the outcomes of both fronts was still very much unclear at the time. But we studied on, not knowing what piece of information picked up from a lesson on Chancellorsville or from Napoleon's maneuvers at Toulon would, one day, help us in our quest for what we called "victory" in the Global War on Terror for, after all, we would fight in battles in or near structures constructed by the British Empire and the Soviet Union in Afghanistan, a situation that would leave anyone to weigh the significance of historical context.

Graduation would come, and we would earn the right, in time, to lead soldiers in combat in different parts of the globe. Some of us would go to Iraq, while others Afghanistan. Still others would be placed in other parts of the globe, defending the world in a struggle which, at the time, had no clear end in sight.

Despite all the classroom instruction, despite all the field training and lessons, nothing could have prepared us at the time for what was to come, especially those headed to Afghanistan. When preparing for war with our soldiers at home and seeking to find a greater vision to pursue during the year we had to execute on that vision while deployed, we were given grandiose, loose, and often intangible descriptions of what the end goal was for us and for the nation. Soldiers are trained in terms of objectives, to take and hold positions or to seek and destroy places and people. In the past, generals were instructed to "take Berlin" or to "capture Richmond", but the mission we were given, with a strategy to build and support the government of Afghanistan, was one that required tremendous imagination on behalf of soldiers trained, not to build, but to destroy. And yet we strove on, as good soldiers always do.

The vague strategy and the near impossible means given to achieve that strategy often left soldiers wondering what our purpose was and, often, soldiers would find themselves conducting combat patrols in the country not knowing the greater goal or the overall mission or how what they were doing was part of the bigger picture of the whole thing. It was like groping through the fog for these men without anyone or anything to guide their conscience as they struggled in their lonely pursuit of purpose in the war.

The lack of a strategy that could translate down to individual actions, for me, was a telling and educational experience that stayed with me my entire Army and business career. There is nothing worse than a soldier putting his life on the line who doesn't know exactly why he is risking his life outside of that he trusts his leaders to put him in a position to make a real difference in the war.

For example, there was much debate in the war about this very topic when my former West Point Platoon Sergeant, Emily Perez, was killed in Iraq in September of 2006. She was one of the highest ranking African American female cadet to ever attend the Academy and was an athletic powerhouse in track and field. On the whole, she was an All-American who gave her life for her country.

When this happened, magazines such as *Time* ran a story asking why in an age when such promising young Americans were giving their lives for a cause was there so little debate about the strategic value of that particular cause. Nathan Thornburgh said that in the presidential debate that was taking place that very year that, instead of blaming each other, we should be asking more strategic questions such as, "Do we have enough troops? Is the war winnable? Should we redeploy to safer bases or should we be a more muscular presence on the streets of Iraq?"[2]

It was clear then as it was to me much later during my time in Afghanistan when we, too, would lose good soldiers in the war, that not enough emphasis was placed on strategic formulation and communication in a clear, sharp, engaging way to the ground-level soldier. This in-cohesive messaging created a deep rift in the morale of soldiers who risked their lives daily and the poor messaging often made decision-making difficult in the face of an ever-evolving enemy.

In no place did the consequences of this rift between the decision makers and the executors come to focus more than at Arlington National Cemetery, where I spent two years conducting military funerals for service members, some of whom fell in combat. One Lieutenant I had the honor of conducting military funeral services for, Tyler Parten, an Academy classmate and fellow soldier in the 4th Brigade, 4th Infantry division during deployment, exemplified just how much trust our generation was placing in the hands of those sending us to war and just how much we had lost because of it.

The strategy became reality on those hallowed grounds of Arlington National Cemetery. It was there, more than anyplace else, that taught me just how impactful strategy can be on the lives of those that execute the strategy, something I would carry with me throughout my Army and business careers.

And so my academic and personal exposure to strategy and the importance of its formulation and execution began with war but soon turned to business after I had decided to leave the Army and pursue a career in the private sector. My first job out of the Army was with a company who, although did not have a stated strategy as a company, had flourished for more than 100 years, had survived the calamities of national economic crises, and had executed to near flawlessness what was clearly their sustained competitive advantage over the long-run. The company I would join is called McMaster-Carr, an industrial supplies distributor that is family owned and is little-known in popular culture but highly regarding in both the engineer and distribution industries for their gold-standard of service.

McMaster-Carr delivers 500,000 different industrial supplies parts to customers who desperately need those parts to finish an engineered prototype or to repair equipment in their facility. The McMaster-Carr sustained competitive advantage is speed, selection variety, and accuracy above all else. With their top customers as engineers, it is important that McMaster delivers parts that are what the customer expects every single time. While some companies may find it difficult to distinguish the pitch between a screw 1.25-inch-long versus one 1.3 inches long, this is a normal process at McMaster-Carr that is well refined and practiced.

The second sustained competitive advantage is speed, where they receive orders and have them sitting on a truck to ship out of the warehouse in less than 15 minutes on average. This is incredible service and sometimes frustrating to customers who call to change their order but are surprised that it has already shipped. "How is it possible," customers would say "that I cannot change my order and that it is already shipped out? I just placed it 10 minutes ago."

How do we measure their success and what makes McMaster-Carr a successful company? As a family-owned business, it is a very private company that shares little to the outside world and does not conduct traditional marketing campaigns. However, when comparing their compensation to employees and to frontline managers, they deliver more value to their customers and, in return, share that value creation with their employees in multiples more than their competitors do.

How did McMaster-Carr achieve this level of sustained competitive advantage? The first answer is that they hire the very best, paying much more in salary and benefits than their industry counterparts to front-line employees and front-line managers, hiring graduates from Harvard Business School and MIT to act as floor supervisors in a warehouse, which is almost unheard of in the warehousing and distribution industry. These students, hired to run warehouse operations, construct incredibly detailed and complex models based on data sets from the operation's mainframe system in order to articulate exactly how many functional hours of capacity they need to accomplish their given work for that specific day. To be off in one's calculations even by 15 minutes or so could spell gross incompetence in a manager's ability to run his or her respective department as was expected at the time.

The second means is that they give these employees a set of business principles to act aggressively upon to pursue operational excellence, which they strive to achieve relentlessly on a daily basis with a rigorous regimen of self-study and self-criticism. Regular meetings are held daily to review even the smallest transactions that did not go as the customer would expect. These transaction reviews are in painstaking detail and no PowerPoint is ever used to present. Users are expected to present in the same processes a typical frontline employee would to show how actual processes work in the warehouse, not high-level descriptions of nebulous theories and principles. No acronyms are ever used, and everyone presenting is forced to assume no one knows what they are talking about, so every detail of the operation being explained needs to be elaborated upon so that anyone from any department across the company should be able to fully understand what is being described.

The third means that McMaster-Carr achieves a sustained competitive advantage is through data-driven decisions. Having now worked for a startup that often makes decisions based on emotion because of the kind-hearted nature of the company culture, in retrospect it was refreshing to have decisions made in an emotionless way based on the story the data tell, not only what the opinions of some of the highly-regarded employees are. This makes for a much clearer means of conversation when discussing business strategy or when it comes to making tough business decisions.

The final means that McMaster-Carr has sustained a competitive advantage over time is the culture of making decisions based on data, which is key to this book and key to understanding what it means to pursue a *Minimum Viable Strategy*. At McMaster-Carr, some data was available through database queries that you could then use to interpret for your specific means. But much of the data used for decision making was not capable of being captured in database queries, so it needed to be derived through a series of tests used to collect information and quantify processes that often had no quantifiable metric attached to them in the past. It was this pursuit of data and, consequently, truth that truly set McMaster apart from other operations I have seen.

It was my first exposure at McMaster-Carr to strategy in the private sector (not war) and the translation of that strategy to day-to-day execution that influenced my thinking later when I would move on to the startup world of chaos and a world without the 100 years of experience under its belt where smart people have spent formulating and translating strategy into execution.

After McMaster-Carr, I would be fortunate enough to join a startup called *The Honest Company* founded in Santa Monica by actress Jessica Alba. The company at the time had grown considerably and was just over two years old on my first day. It had and still has ambitious plans for the future, but at the time it wanted to grow from startup phase to implementing the building blocks for what could one day make it a product powerhouse, and there I was right in the middle.

My specific role at the company was concerning operations strategy, which many folks do not necessarily know what "operations strategy" really is. That is fair. My team primarily focused on projects to facilitate the company's scaling efforts, specifically when it came to operations' physical and software infrastructure. We also looked at ways to cut costs in our operating expenses in order to improve margins and, henceforth, company profitability. We were, in effect by doing this, increasing the gap between the willingness to pay bar and the cost bar in classical business strategy to improve the value created by the Honest Company versus our competitors to ensure we had a lasting competitive advantage (See Chart 1).

CHART 1: Value Creation Chart

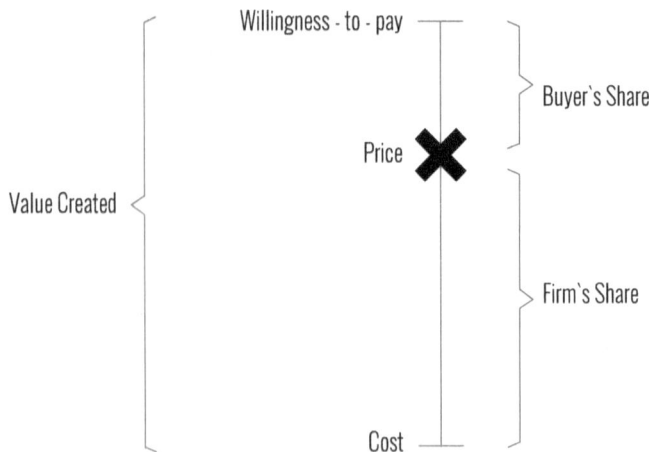

http://www.slideshare.net/IDGnederland/voisey-cio-of-the-future-2012-master-class-the-gap-between-business-and-it-slides

The thing about operations strategy in particular that many growing companies do not realize is that it truly needs to be two to five years ahead of planned company expansion plans. The reason behind this is because the lead-times to implement long-term operational projects such as warehouse infrastructure procurement or software implementation are long and take years of design, development, and testing before they are production ready. This is hard to do and the need is difficult to think about, especially in a startup where just getting to the next week is often the objective. This is why Honest has made a conscious effort to have a team (the team I was a part of) focused on those longer-term projects to ensure operations isn't the limiting factor in helping the company to scale.

But, despite the fun, Google-like atmosphere of the company and the celebrity involved with working for an actress, the company faced at the time deep, significant challenges that needed to be addressed. There were major decisions regarding infrastructure investment that needed to be made that could cost the company a significant amount of capital. There were decisions regarding international growth options that were being pursued and explored. There were yet more decisions about moving into our own retail stores that required vetting and execution.

With all of these efforts came questions about investments required to pursue these endeavors and the risk involved in committing to a China strategy or an aggressive retail growth strategy. Many of these questions often came with "all-in" decision points, where we came to a particular point in our discussions and planning that required the company to pull the trigger on an endeavor that would cost the company millions and had no guarantee of a return. We will call these one-way door decisions since, once you commit, you are "all-in"[3].

The one-way door decision versus two-way door decision is one made famous by a former COO at Honest and one that is harped upon to empower lower-level decision makers to execute upon. The term comes from Amazon, so we won't take credit for it, but it's a good way to provide a rule of thumb for employees to formulate and execute business strategy rapidly.

A one-way door decision is one, as described earlier, where you reach an "all-in" point that requires a significant investment and cannot be easily reversed. One example of this type of decision is choosing to purchase your own one-million square foot distribution facility and to outfit that building with millions of dollars of conveyor and software as still a growing startup with an unclear forecast ahead, experiences and decision points I've had personal experience with in startup-land.

Startups often make these large investments (one-way door decisions) that end up costing significant amounts of capital with little ROI actually realized because they don't understand how error in forecasts increases over time (Chart 2), and they extrapolate current growth projections without truly understanding how their assumptions affects their real-world decisions today in a meaningful way (more on this and Silicon Valley missteps in later chapters). This inability to see clearly into the distant future is what I have termed to be the Fog of Forecasting, adapted from my military experience from what was called the "Fog of War", where leaders can confidently state what they simply do not know about a situation given current intelligence capabilities.

CHART 2: Forecast Error Over Time

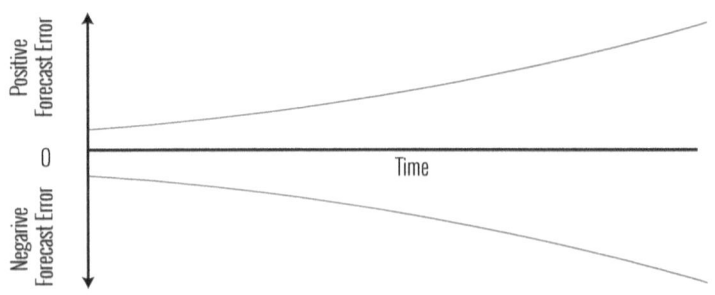

http://www.supplychainmusings.com/2010/10/postponement-as-supply-chain-strategy.html

This is a lesson that Honest learned early on by making small but meaningful and impactful capital investment decisions in material handling automation and software with major assumptions baked into the modelling that did not pan out and, thus, did not allow for the company to see the return on the investment it had hoped for. The lesson was small enough not to affect the company's future (so a two-way door decision), but big enough to have a significant impact on myself and my team's decisions on how we approached our strategic initiatives and future one-way door decisions and, consequently, helped formulate this theory of *Minimum Viable Strategy*.

The concept of forecast error increasing over time is nothing new to strategists. The Prussian military in the 19th and 20th Centuries "appreciated uncertainty - they had invented board games with dice to introduce the element of chance missing from games like chess."[4] Helmuth von Moltke, a German Field Marshal, believed that plans were never any good once they made first contact with the enemy and, therefore, improvisation was essential to military success.[5]

This uncertainty, however, requires planning for adaptability to friction, for planning for unforeseen circumstances when looking beyond the so-called "forecasting horizon."[6] Plans, as President and one-time Supreme Allied Commander during World War II Dwight Eisenhower said, are useless, but "planning is indispensable."[7] Plans are useless in the sense that they never are able to be executed against perfectly, but the process of planning allows for one to plan for events unforeseen beyond the "forecasting horizon" where the probability of forecasting error increases exponentially. The implementation of one-way and two-way door decisions allow for the hedging against the changing forecasting error over the forecasting horizon.

In addition to the faulty small but impactful capital investments we made during my time at Honest, another anecdote that stuck with us as we sought to scale the Honest Company by reducing risk was the story of One King's Lane, an online furniture retailer that was at one time valued at $900 million.

When looking to find warehouse space near one of our East Coast facilities, we were introduced to a space occupied by One King's Lane, a company whom had recently purchased a lease on a large facility and had expected to grow into the space over time because of their growth patterns and aggressive forecasts. However, in short time, growth stalled (it was bought for $30M) and the company was left with a large empty space and a large monthly overhead cost to contend with[8]. This story imbued upon our team the mantra: Don't be One King's Lane.

Thus, as a rule of thumb, as an operations strategy team and a company we often favored two-way door decisions to navigate our way through the heady times of hyper-growth startup land where the dreams of a fantastical future can often overshadow the harsh realities of today's and tomorrow's operational problems and challenges. Thus, an alternative two-way door decision against a one-way door decision for us at Honest Operations during growth periods would have been to outsource fulfillment to a third-party logistics provider that can scale with the company and, thus, reduce upfront capital expense as an alternative to acquiring our own space as One King's Lane had done. Such a decision might, in effect, increase short-term variable cost but reduce overall expense in the short-term because of the lower upfront startup capital required. It is, thus, short-term pain for long-term gain.

Thus, was my introduction to strategy, not just in the private sector, but in startup land. I'd seen strategy from the mother-ship perspective of a large company such as McMaster-Carr, and then witnessed what it was like to actually being a part of strategy creation and execution at Honest, an entirely different, wholly unique experience than simply having it handed to you as it was done at McMaster-Carr.

But my strategy education was not complete just yet (it never will be), and my final introduction to business strategy was in the world of academics at *UCLA Anderson School of Management* where I pursued my MBA. One of the core principles of business strategy I learned there is that companies with the largest gap between a customer's willingness to pay and the cost structure of the company will win in the long-run (See Chart 1). Companies with the largest gap between these two factors will create the largest value over time and, hence, will beat out their competitors because they are capturing that larger value more than the competition.

In order to obtain that value, current strategic business thought, much of which I learned while at *UCLA Anderson*, leads businesses to consider a series of questions to formulate a strategy. Those questions are as follows and in order[9]:

1. Where does our company want to play?
2. How does our company want to win?

At the Honest Company, we often considered these questions when formulating our strategy to compete for the long-run. It is an important and valuable exercise to go through in order to understand the direction that you want to go in, but a limitation of this thought process is that it can easily lead to an organization committing to unproven strategies with "all-in" decision points, which can often be fatal and catastrophic, especially for a young and growing company with poor unit economics and limited capital resources.

Another limiting factor of these strategic formulation exercises is that they happen once or twice a year. This is often too much of a delay to consider if your strategy can and will work in the real world. How can we leverage these important questions of *where to play* and *how to win* while also searching for the appropriate strategy that will provide flexibility and not an "all-in" type decisions?

Additionally, while strategic formulation is vital to an organization because operational decisions and implementations can often take years and decisions around that direction often need to be in motion in advance of a greater overall company strategic execution, *Minimum Viable Strategy* ensures those strategic decisions are tied to operational realities. For example, if a company wants to sell in China through an e-commerce platform, there are months of thoughtful planning and testing just on the fulfillment section of the operation alone before a trigger can be pulled on a trading partner in addition to inventory considerations. In effect, then, because of these operational realities, strategists cannot and should not "live in a cloud" and dictate strategy from ivory tower conditions. Strategic execution is real, and often painful for those laying the groundwork, especially in the realm of operations where the theoretical often meets the physical.

The *Minimum Viable Strategy* approach, we believe, helps to keep strategy and strategists indelibly tied to operational considerations because of the iterative approach to strategic formulation and the testing of strategic hypothesis. This is important because it means that strategy won't stray too far from operational realities, which is vitally important as a company should be realistic with itself and its own capabilities and competencies.

In this book, I will explore a principle I designed during my time at the Honest Company called Minimum Viable Strategy that can be used to reduce the risk of strategy formulation and execution as well as provide a faster means of validating the strength or weakness of one's formulated strategy. While strategy is important for an organization to formulate because it allows everyone in the business to be aligned on a single direction, thus affecting all decisions that cascade down from strategy (in the Army, this principle of war is called Unity of Command), a Minimum Viable Strategy, the theory presented in this book, helps to mitigate the risks that come from traditional strategy formulation for organizations.

Pawns

Finally, we choose the pawn to spread the cover of this book for important reasons. Most books, especially strategy books, would never be bold enough to choose such an insignificant piece to idolize their means of thinking. They choose much more respected pieces such as the bold and nimble knight, able to move over and around others and in "strategic" ways such as the L shape.

Sadly, in the great Western strategy game of chess, the pawn is often overlooked by amateur players as a dispensable piece and that it is believed to be better to trade them early with your opponent to clear the board for more "impactful" pieces such as the rook or the queen. More experienced players, however, know the value of the pawn. Indeed, the master Philidor said two hundred and fifty years ago that "Pawns are the soul of chess."

Pawns move slow, one space at a time. They can often be weak when located along the same file together, or when in isolation. They can only attack diagonally, and remain "stuck" when an opponent's pawn gets in its direct line of movement.

Pawns can, however, be extremely powerful when used together. They can interlock, protecting one another from would be adversaries. This dichotomy of strength and weakness can be seen in the game depicted below, where black has isolated a pawn relative to its friends on C5 and whose only protector is the black bishop, who also faces a choice of protecting the pawn at G7 or C5. Alternatively, white's pawns are interlocked and protected, for the most part, in multiple ways with a few exceptions.

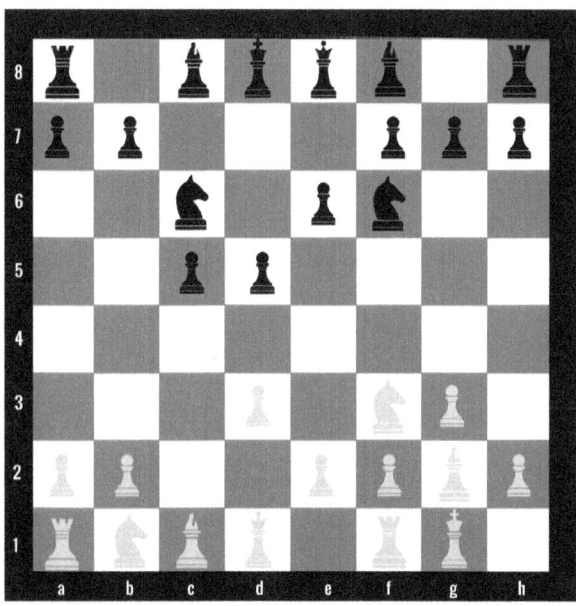

Pawns can slowly encroach on your opponent's space, allowing you to own more geography of the board to facilitate maneuvers that will enable more rapid deployment of pieces that work stronger in isolation. This slow encroachment of space across the board typically happens without notice to the opponent, as it happens slowly over time, single move by single move. Then, your opponent suddenly realizes what has happened after it is too late, that your pawns have given you effective control over large swaths of the board and all are in an interlocking defensive position, making an extremely powerful position for both attack and defense.

Such is the game of Minimum Viable Strategy. Each move singularly seems small, or smaller than the whole for sure. Each is not an all-in bet for the game, as moving a queen hastily into enemy territory early in the game would be.

Thus, Minimum Viable Strategy is the slow and deliberate march toward victory, board space by board space, with interlocking defensive and offensive capabilities that work seamlessly together to reinforce their overall position. Then, before the market or the opponent knows what has happened, you've won before the battle has truly begun.

To begin our journey into Minimum Viable Strategy, however, first we must look back at strategy and how it came to be what we know it today, but perhaps only briefly. By knowing the roots of strategy, we can know how far we've come and, perhaps, know how far we have left to go. With this, we move to a brief history of strategy for the reader.

A BRIEF HISTORY OF STRATEGY

Why do we choose to study and review the history of strategy? What purpose and benefit does studying that history provide to us as readers, as executors of strategy in today's modern world? What use do we have of knowing the constructs and foundations of strategy in ancient civilization for devising and executing our own organizational strategies in the 21st Century?

To not understand the history and foundations of our objectives and to construct a strategy to be executed upon by organizations is to not understand why it is we choose to devise our strategic objectives the way that we do. To not respect history at all is to find your way into the future as if groping in the dark without ever having seen the room you are trying to navigate in the light. We have no sense of self, of whom we are and how we got to where we are when we do not study history. We have no means of articulating what it is what we do and why it is we do it at all. To not respect and study history is to see yourself as a creature who exists in isolation whom was conceived in the present, without precursor events leading up to your existence. This is a fool's folly.

We must, therefore, understand the history of strategy, at least in brief, to understand the constructs we are attempting to build the same way an architect must understand the foundations upon which he is attempting to construct a home. One would construct a home differently in my home state of Louisiana than he would in, say, California or New York. The same goes for looking forward with new ways of articulating and developing strategy. We must understand what has succeeded and failed in the past in order to go forward to the future with strategies that work.

In the Beginning

It is difficult to say when strategy, or the thought of strategy, began. Where and when did people deliberately begin to contemplate the existence of means to specific ends? Perhaps it is with Sun Tzu's *The Art of War*, written in the fifth century BC, that gave us the first indication of deliberate strategy to achieve our specific ends.

Sun Tzu argues for the in-depth analysis of positioning in advance of battle. The famous *Art of War* line from the movie Wall St. quoted by Michael Douglas that "Every battle is won before it is ever fought" brought both Sun Tzu and the concept of competitive analysis using intelligence to the forefront of business, although this concept of competitor analysis had been developed by Michael Porter prior to Gordon Gekko's revelation to the public.

Certainly, strategy has likely always existed, but in ancient history it probably existed as something organic to our human nature. Early strategy, before the rise of the written word, is likely better termed as plans than strategy, for these plans were probably purely thought or spoken and more than likely used for short-term planning, such as surviving the brutal nature of the Hobbesian world that was pre-civilization.

But strategy, as Lawrence Freedman describes in *Strategy: A History, is not plans*, although many when discussing "strategy" often confuse the terms.

Strategy, he says, is the "ability to look up from the short-term and the trivial to view the long term and the essential, to address causes rather than symptoms, to see woods rather than trees."[10] Freedman claims, however, that strategy has been overplayed in our modern world. He says that "there is now no human activity so lowly, banal, or intimate that cannot reasonably be deprived of a strategy."[11]

Indeed, Lawrence is right. In the book *Your Strategy Needs a Strategy* (now there are books that offer strategic advice on your strategy as it seems) there is a chart (Figure 1) that describes over 70 business strategy frameworks that have risen from business literature to offer advice to business leaders on how to "win" in industry. And now this book, my book, seeks to offer yet another framework to the mix, as if plenty did not exist already for leaders to choose from.

Figure 1: Strategic Frameworks in Time

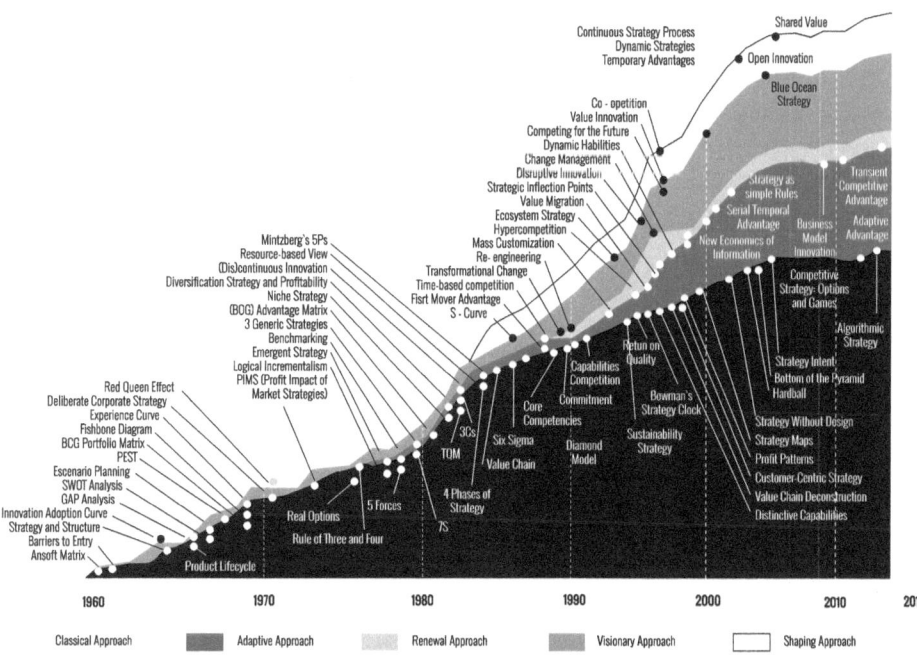

From *Your Strategy Needs a Strategy*

The word strategy itself comes from the ancient Greeks, who used the word "strategy" to refer to a military commander[12]. We can trace strategy to Pericles during the Peloponnesian War (431 BC – 404 BC) whom, despite portraying his "decisions on war as acts of necessity", likely made deliberate decisions based on strategic thought in war[13]. And so history played on, and military minds such as Napoleon and writers such as Clausewitz, author of On War, would make their mark on the topic of military strategy over the centuries, theories bending and molding as military means and political realities adjusted through the ages. Strategy evolved, with much due credit to Clausewitz, to a method of balancing "ends, ways, and means; about identifying objectives, and about the resources and methods available for meeting such objectives." [14]

Evidence of strategic thought is peppered throughout ancient history, especially when studying the choices of Ancient Rome and its adversaries during the Punic Wars (264 BC – 146 BC). Historians have contemplated strategic choices made by Hannibal during the First Punic War, especially the choice not to pursue the Romans after his victory at the Battle of Cannae.[15] Indeed, this era of ancient civilization highlights still other differences of strategy in ancient times amongst Roman generals whom were charged with facing Hannibal and the Carthaginians.

As Mary Beard describes in her book SPQR, "The eventual victory of the Romans highlights a much more down-to-earth clash of strategy and military style between, on the one hand Quintus Fabium Maxiumus Verrucosus Cunctator" and Scipio Africanus. Fabium, whom took command of the Roman Army after the Battle of Cannae, would rely on "guerrilla tactics", comparable to a strategy used by George Washington during the opening scenes of the American Revolution.[16] Africanus preferred a more energetic, direct approach, and the two differences of approach highlight just how much strategic thought had arrived in the ancient world.

The practice and study of strategy evolved as the world evolved and became more global, thus came the concept of "grand strategy". An entire book can and has been written (read *Strategy: A History*) to describe the execution and evolution of strategy over the course of human events, but for the purposes of this book we will just entertain the reader with a short description of the Romans and the name of a few famous military strategy authors in case there is interest in further reading. The point is that deliberate thought to achieve specific ends using desired means has existed throughout human history at various sizes of scope and scale.

As the industrial revolution took hold in the eighteenth century and the world became more interconnected through trade and transportation, strategy would elevate itself from the world of ground and battle level tactics or operational considerations of the Romans in the Punic Wars to treaties and global organizations contemplated by Woodrow Wilson during the Treaty of Paris after the First World War. It is this development of rapid advancement of men and material to and from the battlefield where the principles of Minimum Viable Strategy and their potential impact on history come to the forefront.

Because of the advancement of rail, of machineguns, of the advancements of chemistry, of machinery, and of technology, the First World War was a watershed conflict unlike the world had seen to that point. It was, indeed, the "War to End All Wars", but, as history had proved, that prediction, like many other optimistic predictions made of human civilization, has not come to fruition. What separated the Great War from its predecessors was the scale, not only of the humans and nations involved across the space of Eurasia, but the scale of the violence that would ensue.

And, indeed, this incredible violence happened rapidly, perhaps more rapidly than leaders who made such rash decisions to enter the conflict expected. As Barbara Tuchman in *The Guns of August* so eloquently argues, once the decision from the Kaiser had been made for Germany to advance to France and to execute the well-rehearsed Schlieffen Plan, there was no stopping the military machine that would be put in motion by that decision. Both the Kaiser's decision and the Schlieffen Plan were "all-in" decisions and strategies with existential consequences.

It is, therefore, as a result of the industrial revolution that we take a skeptical eye to "all-in" strategies that had been formulated and argued upon prior to their potentially disastrous results were realized. It is against such strategies that this book, as further chapters will describe, argues against and, consequently, argues in favor of a more flexible approach to strategic planning and execution.

Nevertheless, despite the world changing rapidly with the advancement of technology and the scope of strategy evolving from what was previously a tactical level of strategic thought to a global level of strategic thought, strategy and strategic formulation remained the same. Indeed, the principles of strategy did not change, but the scale at which they are contemplated often do over time. Strategy has been and always will be about answering a single critical question to success in an organization: *how do we win?*

Indeed, strategy for a city and a state on how to attract businesses is different than the strategy of a nation trying to attract businesses because the rules of the game are different and the space at which the game is played is different and the clientele one is trying to attract is different and the competitors are different, but the principles on how to get from no strategy to a winning strategy are the same. Therefore, even though the end result might be the same for these organizations, for example the end result might be to gain more top talent in a particular geography, the analysis that the organization must conduct to gauge its playing field will different significantly at different levels of scale of strategic thought.

Despite the scale at which leaders are considering strategy, however, they always consider what the goals or winning aspirations are and what are the means required to achieve those goals. These principles have been true from Fabium during the Punic Wars to President George W. Bush during the Global War on Terror. The principles of strategy, therefore, do not change with the situation or scale. Leaders can consistently have a logical, thoughtful approach when formulating and executing a strategy with the intent to win in various situations, industries, or periods of time. Indeed, the history of strategy has proven this to be true. While the means and the *how to win* have changed, the process as to how to derive a winning strategy has not. These principles will be discussed more in depth later in the book.

Strategy in Business

Evidently, as we have described, strategy amongst peoples, states, and ethnic groups has always existed internally and, eventually, externally in the form of written plans, treaties, and laws as the nation-state came of age through the millennia. Deliberate strategy in business, however, came to our modern consciousness and to the forefront of business thought only in the twentieth century.[17] It was, indeed, the rise of larger industry after the industrial revolution and the development of an interconnected transportation network through the spread of rail that brought the onset for the need of business strategy.[18] This was seen as a way to "control outcomes" and "tame the invisible hand" that was articulated by Adam Smith to be controlling economic factors.[19]

Business schools began to bring the world of strategic thought to the world of business academia with the coming of the Second Industrial Revolution, beginning with Harvard Business School, which began to design classes in "business policy" in 1912 which gave students "broader perspective on the strategic problems faced by corporate executives."[20] The global calamity of the Second World War brought about the early beginnings of quantitative analysis in relation to strategic planning due to the massive operational challenges brought on by the scale of the conflict.[21] The resulting work from this effort was *The Theory of Games and Economic Behavior*, which not only brought about logical thought processes and considerations around zero sum games, but also the concept of "learning curves", which describes how "labor costs tended to decrease by a constant percentage as the cumulative quantity of aircraft produced doubled."[22] The concept of learning curves becomes important later in this book as we describe how to mitigate risk with respect to strategic planning for systemic choice.

As war subsided and soldiers returned home to the United States, they brought with them the lessons learned from the war to business, especially with regards to operational and strategic thought processes and quantitative analysis. The most famous example is Robert McNamara, later Secretary of Defense under John F. Kennedy and Lyndon Johnson, who would bring the quantitative skills he learned during the war while working for the Office of Statistical Control to the Ford Motor Company as part of the group known as the "Whiz Kids". Although the quantitative measures would later be beneficial to improving Ford's operations and, thus, its successful pursuit of strategic objectives, this same reliance on pure data to make strategic choices would ultimately be the downfall of Secretary McNamara during his execution of the Vietnam War, a war which could not be won by brutal statistical outcomes but was more heavily reliant upon political considerations and how they affected the peoples of the South East Asian Nation.

An example of early corporate strategy was written by Alfred Sloan of General Motors (CEO of GM from 1923 to 1946), who analyzed the firm's strengths and weaknesses of its competitor, Ford, and developed a strategy based on that analysis.[23] These are early signs of competitor analysis, which would later be codified by the famous business strategist Michael Porter in his book *Competitive Strategy*, which is seen as the bible for corporate strategy in the 20th century, though some have seen it as outdated in a rapidly digitizing world.

Sloan would later articulate the strategy to execution method by stating that a general manager's job was to ensure the enterprise achieved its goals.[24] This, in another way, means that, as Kenneth Andrews of Harvard states in the 1950's, their objective is to ensure that the business stays on its chosen direction, which means to say that the business' managers are responsible for ensuring its units execute the business' chosen strategy.[25]

It is this strategic formulation to execution gap that has been perhaps the most prominent in recent decades amongst businesses seeking to re-define themselves and be competitive in new and existing markets. With new strategic constructs coming available to the fingertips of executives almost annually as it seems, a "strategy of the month" feeling began to take hold in business during the second half of the twentieth century and into the twenty-first as executives tried and failed to emulate the newest theory of strategy that had become popular in modern business.

For example, businesses whom tried to enter "blue oceans", or new business opportunities that are untapped by current competitors, suddenly realized that their current business capabilities were unfit for the needs of the new opportunity.[26] They pursued these opportunities, believing, as others have, in the rhetoric of the authors of *Blue Ocean Strategy* in combination with their business' perceived inability to compete or grow anew. Instead of looking inward for identity in their organization, they looked outward to fix existential problems.

Unfortunately, to the chagrin of these businesses who have failed in attempting to formulate and execute the "strategy of the month", much of strategic thought often looks good in hindsight, as those theories that are unsuccessful either in business or in war are not given the same modern coverage as those lauded by modern generals or business executives. Strategic recommendations are always anchored in cases of famous businesses whom have been studied and analyzed in tremendous detail (the examples always seem to be Apple, Southwest Airlines, or Google for some reason), but businesses often fail to find the capability to execute with similar success of those companies quoted in strategy books. This failure inevitably leads to further fruitless search.

This constant search for new meaning in a world of uncertainty, therefore, creates the gap of strategy to execution, a problem we will discuss more in depth later in the book in the chapter regarding leadership, as strategy is often set with high frequency at the top, but is just as often not translated to the every-day, to the mundane. It is this translation from theory to practice that is not only critical to success but is also core to the construct of Minimum Viable Strategy.

But, to close this gap, we must dilute strategy. We must simplify it from the 70 or so constructs that have arisen since the coming of age of business strategy to a few key, simple, easy to remember points. The authors of *Strategy That Works* and Michael Porter in "What is Strategy" attempted to bring calm to executives whom were lost in a sea of business strategy theories by asserting the following points, which can not only be applied to business but also multiple enterprises of different purposes. They are:

1. Operational Effectiveness Is Necessary But Is Not Strategy[27]
   a. The best operational effectiveness techniques can and will be copied by competitors and will largely, in the long-run, become industry standards as we have seen with Six Sigma practices.[28]

2. Doing Some Things Well Means Not Doing Other Things At All
   a. Strategy means not being all things to all people. It means doing some things very well while choosing not to do other things

3. Strategy Is Dependent On Your Value Proposition
   a. The things you do uniquely will affect how you deliver value over the long-run versus your competitors.

These definitions of strategy, however, aren't enough for the strategist. Strategies need, not just what strategy is, but how it can be developed. In the next chapter, now that the reader has been brought from ancient history to modern times from a perspective of the history of strategy, we will review applicable strategic constructs that will be helpful for the reader to be familiar with as we progress in the book. The reader should be aware of the various how to win options that have been quoted throughout time, which Chapter 2 provides in detail, in order to formulate a successful strategy.

STRATEGIC CONSTRUCTS

We have reviewed in the previous chapter a broad history of strategy from the dawn of time to the modern day strategic decisions of firms and the applicability of strategic principles to today's organizational problems. The history, while probably not very useful in figuring out just how to devise and implement strategy, does give the reader a sense for just how broad the scope of the problem is and how difficult it would be for this book to provide a complete history of strategy in a single chapter.

We have attempted to, at the minimum, provide a taste for the foundations of strategy in the modern world and its purpose: to devise a way for an organization to win. In this chapter, we will follow those foundations with basic strategic constructs that we have used in our thinking to create the Minimum Viable Strategy model. These constructs are the bricks from which we use to create the frame of our way of thinking.

Each of these constructs has some usefulness for the Minimum Viable Strategy model as they provide a glimpse into how we came about devising our strategic model and what the sources of inspiration where for this way of thinking. These constructs are useful in their own right as well for further research and analysis as Minimum Viable Strategy is just a single means of achieving a strategic end in a specific situation for a specific purpose. These other constructs may be more useful and beneficial in other situations in particular for organizations to use as a foundation for strategic thought as well.

Business Constructs

The following strategic constructs are utilized primarily in the business world to formulate and devise winning business strategies. Some are strategic initiatives used primarily to win in the long-run, though others are more discreet strategic constructs, such as the "pellets vs. cannonballs" theory that is more applicable to single decision points in time.

Playing to Win

The *Playing to Win* formula for strategy devising is the single most important construct that has influenced this book and is worthy of first note in this chapter amongst all of the strategic constructs we will discuss. It is the most important and most influential because it discusses strategy in the simplest terms. Strategy is simply, as we have said before and according to this book, a means for an organization to win. Its methodology for devising strategy relies on a few clearly articulated steps for organizational leaders to follow. Those steps are in order as follows:

1. What is the organization's winning aspiration?
2. Where will the organization play?
3. How will the organization win?
4. What capabilities must be in place for the organization to win?
5. What management systems are required for the organization to win?

Playing to Win is a business book, but its methodology and simple process for devising strategy can be followed by any organization, and we have used its constructs as a basic template to build the Minimum Viable Strategy theory upon. It is the opinion of this author that the best constructs are those that can be applied to multiple disciplines and not simply apply to business or war, which the *Playing to Win* model allows for.

For strategy is, inevitably, about how people clash with each other over competing resources in an effort to accomplish their desired objectives, or, to put it more simply, to win. The best methods for devising strategy must be boiled down to their most basic premises to apply to the core nature of our humanity. This framework, by cutting to the core of strategy, which is devising a way to win over the long-run, accomplishes that fundamental principle of bringing strategy closer to ourselves as peoples in struggle.

The beauty of *Playing to Win* is that it does not try to fit the model to the particular client engagements of the authors. Indeed, the authors were not management consultants looking to fit a particular model to specific experiences, the fault of other constructs discussed in this chapter, but rather they are business leaders in specific industries whom have used the *Playing to Win* model for devising winning strategies in businesses they ran.

One of the co-authors, A.G. Lafley, former Chairman and CEO of Procter and Gamble, describes his experiences at P&G in building the capabilities of managers to devise strategy using this model. It is this experience of Lafley, who brings to life, not management consultant experiences, but business leadership experiences that makes the *Playing to Win* construct stand out. It stands on its own merits, is easily repeatable and memorable, and can be taught as a construct without using P&G or other examples from the book at all, a far cry from other constructs that rely on specific examples in order to convey the true meaning of the strategic theory.

This book will go into more depth on the *Playing to Win* framework later. For now, however, we will leave the reader with a taste, as described previously, of its high-level pieces and applicability to the purposes of this book.

Your Strategy Needs a Strategy

This book, written by Martin Reeves, Knuts Haanaes, and Janmejaya Sinha describes six strategy options for businesses to choose from, depending on the industry they compete in and the winning aspiration of the business. The authors are leaders in the Boston Consulting Group, and the premise of the book is that it is rooted in client engagement analysis, thus basing the learnings on the experiences of the consultants with these businesses.

The fundamental problem, however, with fitting a model to a particular set of personal experiences is that often the models can be too specific, done so in an effort to fit a particular situation for each client engagement, which is especially true of this particular model of strategic thought. This is a typical problem of consultants, often seen as armchair generals in a world where commanders on the front-lines need something simpler to be able to formulate and execute strategy upon and turn that strategy into plans.

The consultants do not seem to take a stand on what strategy is and should be for organizations, nor do they try to limit the scope of the book to a particular strategic construct. Instead, they introduce a "strategy pallet" of options, which are meant to cover all of the examples from their client engagement at their disposal, which they use as examples.

It is difficult, therefore, to boil down their approach to a single sentence, which should often be the case for a successful construct in strategy. Understanding the principles of a strategic construct should be simple and transmittable in a single sentence, otherwise the strategy to execution gap becomes rather large and leaders, attempting to understand the construct, get lost in the details. This seems to be the limitation of Your *Strategy Needs a Strategy*, a drawback that *Playing to Win* does not have.

Regardless of these limitations, the book provides insight into the various constructs that a firm can consider when formulating a strategy, and a few of their constructs offer valuable building blocks for the Minimum Viable Strategy theory we are attempting to construct and utilize in this book. The *Your Strategy Needs a Strategy* constructs are:[29]

- *Classical Strategy* - for large businesses that have little year over year change in growth and business capabilities. These organizations focus on leveraging scale and winning in its core product categories. The "mantra is sustainable competitive advantage."[30]

- *Adaptive Strategy* - for businesses in unpredictable industries. They test a variety of different business opportunities and scale up the ones that are successful.

- *Visionary Strategy* - for businesses who want to compete in new, unexplored business lines with little to no current competition.

- *Shaping Strategy* - for businesses who believe their unpredictable environment can be shaped at an "early point" of the environment's development.

- *Renewal Strategy* - for businesses operating in a difficult industry who need to recreate their own businesses to continue to survive in the new normal.

The "strategic pallet", as the five strategic constructs devised by *Your Strategy Needs a Strategy* is called, was created to give businesses the options of figuring out which framework best fits their business's needs for strategy formulation. These five frameworks, however, seem more inductive from observed client engagements and business cases than deductive (starting with a general theory and then finding evidence to prove a hypothesis) as *Playing to Win* seems to do, and inductive theoretical formulation not done properly can often lead to frameworks that are often too specific to the case it was formulated around and, thus, not be beneficial to the user of the framework.

All of these approaches do, however, seem to be a step down from strategy. Strategy is, as mentioned before, the ability to look up from the trees to see the forest. The Adaptive Strategy framework, which promotes conducting multiple tests for new business lines and scaling those up as they succeed or fail seems to be a bit below what we would consider strategy. These frameworks, including the Adaptive Strategy framework, are more focused on operational and tactical level decision making, or "how to execute" strategy.

When businesses conduct multiple tests, resources are drained, and obvious questions are begged to be asked, such as: if we are conducting multiple tests, is the truth that we lack clear focus? Are we making up for our lack of focus by conducting multiple tests and, therefore, are we supplanting real strategy with hope that a test will work? Will conducting multiple tests facilitate our capabilities on the single objective of winning, or will we spread our capabilities across multiple losing objectives? What are the trade-off's and opportunity costs of spreading these resources?

Despite these questions, there are merits so the *Your Strategy Needs a Strategy* pallet, specifically with regards to the Adaptive approach. While testing new opportunities is the preferred method of execution, as it reduces risk for businesses moving into unchartered waters, multiple tests that don't seek to accomplish a single objective of winning through creating a long-term competitive advantage can be detrimental to an organization. The Adaptive method is, to put it simply, a product approach to winning when winning needs to be much greater than just a product oriented focus.

Instead of recommending that a business execute multiple tests to succeed in the marketplace, we will explore how we can instead first formulate a strategic hypothesis and an overall winning aspiration. Then, we will look at, with Minimum Viable Strategy, testing our capabilities while learning and reinforcing those capabilities over the long-run to achieve the single winning objective. As will be described later in the book, this is the essence of Minimum Viable Strategy.

Lean Strategy

This construct is intended for entrepreneurs to deliberately think about the strategy of their new venture and was developed by David Collins of the Harvard Business School. It is, as the author describes, the process that "guards against the extremes of both rigid planning and unrestrained experimentation."[31] Lean Strategy, as Collins describes it, is "both a screen that novel ideas must pass and a yardstick for evaluating the success of experiments with them."[32] This rigor ensures that employees, while still able to exert some creative decision making in the organization, stay in line with the company's priorities.[33]

This construct, while useful in terms of defining the impacts of what strategy does, does little to articulate the process of formulating a strategy. It also offers little novelty to the thought pool of strategic thinking, but rather combines the concepts of Minimum Viable Product, the Adaptive approach from Your Strategy Needs a Strategy, and with that of modern business strategy to formulate a construct to fit the author's purpose of writing an article about strategy called "Lean Strategy."

CHART 3: Lean Strategy

By combining traditional strategy with lean start-up practices, ventures can align employees around a common purpose, make the most of limited resources, learn from the market, and then adjust the strategy.

VISION	ANALYSIS	DELIBERATE STRATEGY	LEARNING	EMERGENT STRATEGY
Founders choose the business's reason for existence.	The organization examines its strengths, weaknesses, opportunities, threats, resources, and capabilities.	Senior executives agree upon the firm's objective, scope, and advantage	Managers at all levels make daily decisions and conduct experiments guided by the strategy.	Feedback and findings reshape the strategy.

THE PROCESS RESTARTS

https://hbr.org/visual-library/2016/03/the-lean-strategy-process

One critical difference, however, of "Lean Strategy" from other constructs and even the Minimum Viable Product theory is that it warns against early signals of product success. The author uses solid evidence, such as using a case study from Groupon, to indicate that early success of a new product may not be enough to justify deep investments for a company and that deeper strategic analysis is needed to justify the change of a company strategy because of early product success. Such factors, such as low barriers to entry, make such successful products like Groupon's an example to where early success may cause a shift in a company's strategy. [34]

In addition, Collins proposes iterative learning through a concept he coins as "Emergent Strategy." It is this process that he describes which allows for field tests of products to iterate back to the company's strategic direction and that the results of tests will drive the strategic direction of the firm.

Amazon seems to do particularly well at executing this strategy. As Jeff Bezos, CEO of Amazon, describes the use of experimentation at Amazon,

> *"One area where I think we are especially distinctive is failure...I believe we are the best place in the world to fail (we have plenty of practice!), and failure and invention are inseparable twins. To invent you have to experiment, and if you know in advance that it's going to work, it's not an experiment. Most large organizations embrace the idea of invention, but are not willing to suffer the string of failed experiments necessary to get there."* [35]

Amazon, therefore, embraces the idea of experimentation from both the product end of strategy and the capability end of strategy. We know this as they have not only brought to market products completely outside of the realm of their core business, such as Amazon Video and Amazon Web Services, both wildly successful products in their own right, but also because they have circumvented typically business norms by creating vertically integrated capabilities to streamline their operations. Such capabilities include owning delivery to customers from their fulfillment centers, thus circumventing FEDEX and UPS, a major cost center for the business.

Amazon did not, however, buy a large fleet of vehicles for all DCs and go "all-in" on owning delivery themselves. They did small tests in large geographies and will slowly expand this capability across different geographic regions. As the Motley Fool reported in February 2015,

> *"Amazon has been quietly testing its own delivery service since 2014 when it launched same-day delivery, but it appears ready to ramp up the program, listing logistics providers as competitors in its recent 10-K report. On its earnings call, management stressed that the company was not intending to replace FedEx or UPS, but just complement their services, especially when the company is confronted with high sales volumes like during the holiday season."* [36]

It is clear that Amazon both pursues and does not pursue a shade of Adaptive, Lean, and other strategic constructs. It both experiments with products and strategic capabilities. It does not seemingly fit nicely into a particular set of strategic construct categories where we can analyze its process for going from point A to point B on a business development curve. It has grown and evolved in ways no one could have predicted, and yet its categorical leadership is worthy of note and its willingness to go in directions thought impossible before are beneficial for the strategist to dissect.

We can see that experimentation in the Lean Strategy methodology has benefitted Amazon through experimenting with products and capabilities. Therefore, it has, from a product experimentation standpoint, executed a shade of the Lean Strategy construct examined above quite successfully.

But Amazon has significant resources at its disposal to experiment in many ways and at many times, reducing the aggregate existential risk of experimentation. The key is focus, and those topics Amazon has chosen to experiment with have been keenly focused on multiple vertical integration strategies as well as new product line strategies tangential to those they currently operate in. It is this keeping of focus, not the lack of resources, that is key to the approach for larger companies.

Bullets Then Cannonballs

The beloved business author, Jim Collins, who wrote *Great by Choice* brought us the idea that many great companies he observed through his intense research did not come about their success through profound product innovation. They did it, he claims, through disciplined innovation. Indeed, Intel, one of the companies highlighted in Collins' research, claims, "Intel's founders believe that innovation without discipline leads to disaster."[37] We will discuss this concept further in our Lego case study.

It is this disciplined innovation that Collins coins as firing "Bullets Then Cannonballs". It is the logical, systematic, structured approach to productive testing and development that drives innovation. It is the classical scientific method that Collins codifies in his firing analogy in essence.

One telling quote from Collins' coverage of the Intel strategy follows:

> *Adhering to Moore's Law was a discipline game, a scale game, a systems game, not just an innovation game. As Leslie Berline wrote about the early days of Intel in her authoritative and well-written book, The Man Behind the Microchip, "What Intel needs going forward was not the courage to take great leaps ahead but the discipline to take orderly steps in a controlled fashion." Andy Grove said during this era, "We have to systematize things so we don't crash our technology," in an article that compared Intel's approach to making semiconductor chips pumping out high-tech like jelly beans.* [38]

Collins' Bullets then Cannonballs, like other strategic frameworks quoted here, is primarily focused on disciplined product innovation through measured approaches and empirical studies. Companies must be disciplined, not only at taking this approach, but also conducting the disciplined "20 Mile March" as Collins describes it to eventually see the positive results of this measured approach. The "20 Mile March" is simply the daily measured discipline of pursuing the end goal in mind through executing daily activities, collecting data, and slightly changing approaches as needed.

Both the "20 Mile March" concept and the Bullets Then Cannonballs approach are about companies not getting ahead of themselves, about disciplined innovation through measured tests of a product's market potential. Collins has three characteristics of bullets. Bullets are:[39]

1. Low Cost
2. Low Risk
3. Low Distraction

These are, again, characteristic of product innovation tests. He quotes that companies that take this approach learned that "you can only know if something will actually work if you gain empirical validation, no matter how many slide decks support the idea."[40] Indeed, in one example with Progressive insurance, Collins states that "In the face of instability, uncertainty, and rapid change, relying upon pure analysis will likely not work, and just might get you killed. Analytic skills still matter, but empirical validation matters much more."[41]

Similar to the Lean Strategy framework, Collins' Bullets Then Cannonballs construct take the disciplined innovation approach to strategy, but goes a step further to emphasize the daily grind and grit in the "20 Mile March" it takes to achieve innovation. His main point here is that empirical data matters, and doing the daily, mundane work to innovate is what separates the winners from the losers. This is a point that will not be lost on this author in further analysis and recommendations for Minimum Viable Strategy.

Strategy That Works

The book by Paul Leinwand and Cesare Mainardi of Strategy&, the PwC strategy consulting business, is a highly influential work on the importance of defining and building capabilities to drive the closing of the strategy to execution gap. As they describe the importance of capabilities for companies, "It's not just their skills and talents that matter, it's the way they weave those individual skills and talents together with larger-scale infrastructure, operations, and technology to produce something that no other enterprise can match."[42] This author could not agree more.

Strategy that Works focuses on the importance of capabilities and how that will drive the successful execution of strategy. Key to note is that this book is in agreeance with this author on how difficult building or changing capabilities can be:

> *"But there is a second reality, just as powerful: distinctive capabilities are inherently slow to change. The capabilities system in any large, coherent enterprise involves hundreds or thousands of people as well as embedded investments in technology and specialized skills. These capabilities have been built up slowly, decision by decision, and thus they are sticky: they take time to update and replace. If the capabilities system could be changed easily, it wouldn't be worth very much, because anyone could build something similar. It is impossible to shift identify and build new distinctive capabilities on a dime.*

Strategy that works helps us understand how difficult it is to build capabilities (hence the existence of learning curves) and why it is important to take a minimalist approach in building these as firms often fail to do because they overwhelm themselves with doing too much too fast. *Strategy That Works* reminds us that, whether changing current capabilities or building new ones, we must remember that these are ingrained in a fundamentally human organization made up of people, and habits and instincts are difficult to build and change.

Blue Ocean Strategy

The essence of the Blue Ocean Strategy construct is fundamentally simple to understand: companies should stop competing in "overcrowded industries" or "red oceans."[43] Profits in these industries are tight and ever diminishing over time, while in "blue oceans", defined by authors W. Chan Kim and

Renee Mauborgne to be "uncontested market spaces where competition is irrelevant", profits are high and growth fast.[44]

The authors consider Cirque de Soleil, which invented a new category of entertainment by combining elements of theatre with elements from a "traditional circus". Their core argument is that Cirque was able to grow to revenue levels that comparable shows, such as Barnum & Bailey, took over 100 years to achieve, an indication of the speed to which growth was allowed for in the Cirque's self-created blue ocean market.[45]

Many of the Blue Ocean markets studied by Kim and Mauborgn have been generated by market "incumbents" such as IBM, AMC, and others. Thus, Blue Ocean creators do not necessarily need to be new entrants to the market. Further, they acknowledge that Blue Oceans do not need to be in "distant waters" but can be categorically created within red oceans themselves, such as Dell with the advent of a new supply chain and business model within the computer industry.[46]

So confident are Kim and Mauborgn in their construct, written during a time of high confidence in the MBA graduate's ability to bring deep strategic thought to companies and industries, that they boldly proclaim that, "So powerful is Blue Ocean strategy that a Blue Ocean strategic move can create brand equity that lasts for decades."[47] Indeed, they cite that the brand equity benefits can last from "10-15 years" as was experienced by companies such as Southwest Airlines and CNN.[48]

As we will learn with Lego later, the fault of this construct is not in its stars, but in ourselves. Those that attempt to sail uncharted oceans will often find they lack the experience in that ocean to stay afloat. They change course too quickly or, perhaps, too frequently, or, worse, they do both. They make fundamental market assumptions about Blue Oceans that are wholly untrue and make big bets on the assumption that, because they were successful in red oceans, they will be equally successful in their newly created Blue

Oceans. But, as they come to learn, past success is rarely indicative of future success when looking at new markets.

Finally, as we will discuss later, the authors underestimate how difficult innovation and "doing new things" actually is for a company and underestimate the value of doing what a company is doing today only better. These are questions and problems that this book will attempt to address in later chapters.

Learning Curves

Minimum Viable Strategy, as will be defined in later chapters, is a strategy formed around the acceptance of the fact that organizations, when attempting to perform new functions, enter new markets, or adapt new capabilities, will not perform those functions, compete in those markets, or execute those capabilities efficiently in their initial go a them. They will probably fail and, over the long-term, improve their capabilities over time. This is a process now referred to as the learning curve of organizations.

This learning is defined as

> gaining experience with products and processes, achieving greater efficiency through automation and other capital investments, and making other improvements in administrative methods or personnel. Productivity improvements may be gained from better work methods, tools, product design, or supervision, as well as from individual worker learning.[49]

The concept of the learning curve was formed during World War II in the aircraft production industry when those in the industry realized that, over time, production costs consistently declined as less labor was required to produce more aircraft, a common occurrence even among different aircraft manufacturing facilities, companies, and various airframes, such as fighters and bombers.[50] Interestingly, this same concept was also concluded to exist during World War II when analyzing the accuracy of night bombing of German cities by the allies (see Chart 4). The accuracy rate early in the war was abysmal, and the "GEE" system used by the allied to aid in bombing were ill equipped for the task at hand.[51] Throughout the war, better technologies were developed to aid the accuracy of night bombing, dramatically increasing the accuracy of these missions.

CHART 4: Accuracy of Night Bombing of German Cities (Excluding Berlin)

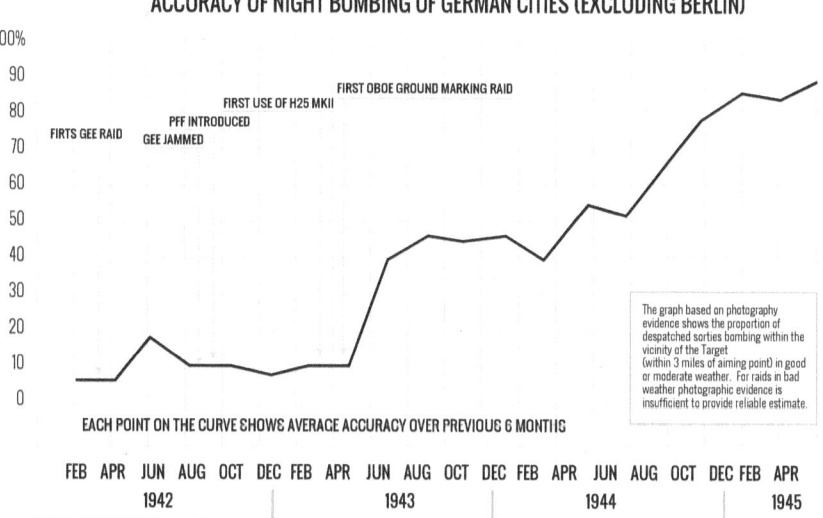

ACCURACY OF NIGHT BOMBING OF GERMAN CITIES (EXCLUDING BERLIN)

http://www.nationalarchives.gov.uk/education/worldwar2/theatres-of-war/westerneurope/investigation/hamburg/sources/docs/7/

Learning curves have been used by strategists to forecast a drop in overall unit production costs over time in a predictable manner (see Chart 5). The existence of learning curves brings favor to initial entrants into markets because "first companies in the market have a big advantage because newcomers must start selling at lower prices and suffer large initial losses."[52]

CHART 5: Reduction in Production Costs Over Time

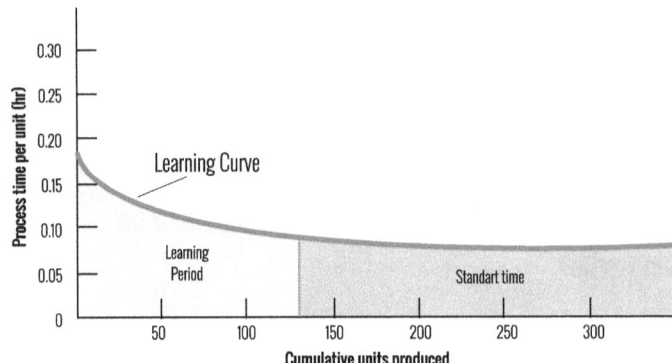

http://wps.pearsoned.co.uk/wps/media/objects/8970/9185376/65767_30_Suppl.pdf

Learning curves can also be seen in the average list price of the Ford Model-T. As volume and production experience increased, Ford was able to cut the price of the Model-T dramatically between 1909 and 1923 (Chart 6).[53] Intuitively, we know that this is true in our own experiences in the modern world as prices for electronics and other previously expensive goods have dramatically declined in the last two decades.

But as William Abernathy and Kenneth Wayne point out in "Limits of the Learning Curve", published in the Harvard Business Review in 1974, predictability of improved performance over time is predicated on certain conditions. In their insightful piece, Waye and Abernathy explain that "management cannot expect to receive the benefits of cost reduction provided by a steep learning curve projection and at the same time expect to accomplish rapid rates of product innovation and improvement in product performance."[54] The authors pointedly conclude that innovation and cost reduction are competing strategies that cannot be obtained simultaneously.[55]

Thus, the challenge to organizational managers is to balance innovation and deep-rooted learning. While deep-rooted learning and efficiency gains improve business metrics like margins or war-performance metrics like night bombing accuracy, the focus on efficiency gains assumes that the status quo of the competitive playing field does not change and, thus, investments in capital and labor are being allocated to performing those unchanging tasks highly efficiently.

But what if things were different? What if the Axis developed counter-technology only after the allies, hypothetically, invested heavily in executing night bombing raids with what they perceived to be effective technology? Or, as Ford Motor Company saw after assuming customer tastes would be static in the long-run, what if General Motors plays in the automotive industry and tailors its product to focus on quality versus price, cutting into Ford's volume and consequently their margins by increasing Ford's product costs. What use do learning curves have at that time?

Such are the questions addressed by Minimum Viable Strategy, specifically in our chapter covering strategy implementation, investments, and testing strategic hypothesis. These are the fundamental issues, those having to do with the incredible challenge of confronting the Fog of Forecasting and the Fog of War that the strategic construct of Minimum Viable Strategy attempts to reconcile.

CHART 6: Model T Price Reduction Over Time

Exhibit I - Price of model T, 1909 -1923 (Average list price in 1958 dollars)

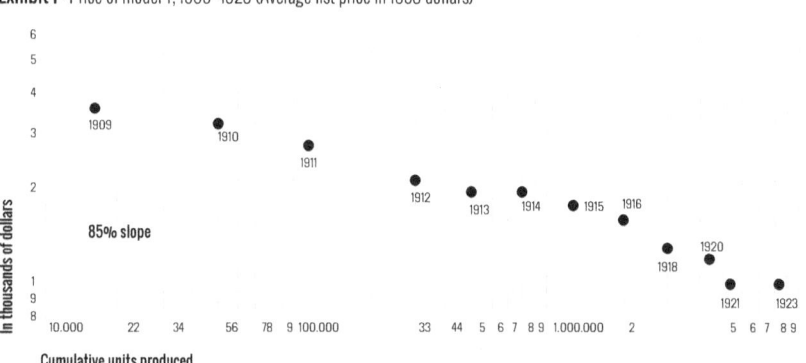

From "Limits of the Learning Curve" Harvard Business Review William J. Abernathy and Kenneth Wayne

Investing Constructs

The Theory of Base Rates

As I mentioned in the opening dedication to this book, during the 2016 election many prognosticators had the eventual victor, Donald Trump, at below 10% probability of winning the election after an already unlikely rise through the Republican primary process. What this represents, and other strategic constructs such as *Moneyball* identify, is the fact that human beings are often susceptible to their own biases based on their unique experiences, ignoring the larger universe of experiences and, consequently, the data around those experiences.

As human beings, we constantly express over-confidence, or simply irrational optimism, in the future and are susceptible to base-rate neglect, as Daniel Kahneman points out in his groundbreaking book *Thinking Fast and Slow*. Base-rate neglect is looking at experience and making decisions in a particular situation based on your individual experiences, which tend to lead to over-confidence in forecasts as the entire universe of experiences comparable to your own are neglected. Or, as Daniel Kahneman puts it, "People who have information about an individual case rarely feel the need to know the statistics of the class to which the case belongs."[56]

In an attempt to discount lofty forecasts and ground corporate thinking in the realm of realty, "Michael Mauboussin, a strategist at Credit Suisse, has taken that hint and compiled base rates for all sorts of corporate measures, so investors can readily check a company's projections against reality."[57] A simple example pointed out in Mauboussin's work is frequent overconfidence in sales-growth estimates. In Chart 7, one can see how, according to Mauboussin's work, over 1000 firms have averaged a highly confident sales growth forecast (dotted line) versus the historical universe (thin line).[58] This forecast represents a 3-year CAGR.

A base rate is simply context for the typical. It is what is what has happened, on average, for a particular situation throughout a particular set of time (1950 forward for Chart 7).

As we will learn later with Lego, overconfidence can lead to dismal decision-making processes. We look to base rates, or historical narratives of what is typical for the universe, to ground our expectations in reality and, consequently, make decisions that allow for overly ambitious forecasts to have room to fall short without betting too much of the house on its success. For, as plans and decisions are made, we must "must weigh not only the alluring probabilities of being right, but the dire consequences of being wrong."[59]

Chart 7: Sales Growth

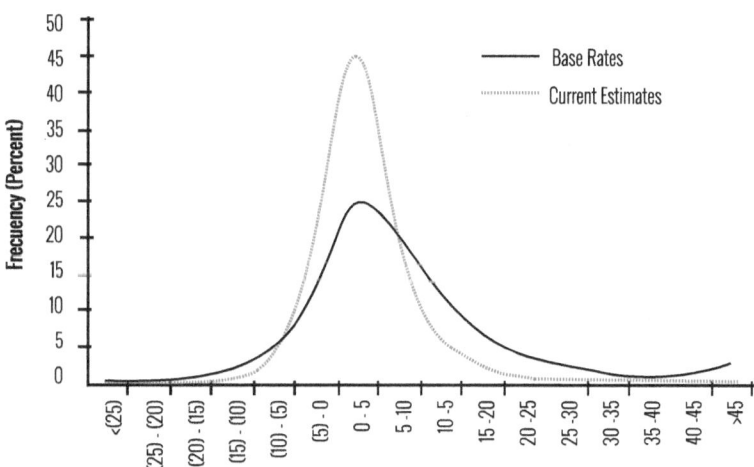

Credit Suisse Base Rate Book pg 19

Margin of Safety

Benjamin Graham, author of the seminal work *Intelligent* Investor that details core principles of investing that have been long adopted by value investors such as Warren Buffet, describes a principle which he coins as the "margin of safety". The essence of the "margin of safety" is that the "price paid for a stock or a bond should allow for human error, bad luck or...many things going wrong at once."[60]

From a technical perspective, according to Graham, the "margin of safety" is described as:

> *This past ability to earn in excess of interest requirements constitutes the margin of safety that is counted on to protect the investor against loss or discomfiture in the event of some future decline in net income.*[61]

When tasks to describe the "margin of safety", Warren Buffet used the analogy that for bridge building, you build bridges that can hold 30,000 lb truck loads but require only 10,000 lb trucks be driven across. Therefore, you have significant safety margins where it counts and where you expect there to be volatility, especially where there are a lot of unknowns such as in the world of investing.[62]

Both the margin of safety concept and the core principles of value investing are critical in understanding both the world of business volatility, the difference between business speculation, exuberance, and sound, logical business judgement. Graham, through conveying value investing principles, attempts to detach the notion that speculators are investors and quantifies what it means to buy quality investments versus speculative investments, which are largely driven on feelings of exuberance.

The "margin of safety", which allows for volatility in future business performance, allows for the investor to hedge their bets a bit by ensuring that a lot of things can go wrong of the business without systemic loss that would be incurred otherwise.

As minimally viable strategists, this core concept of baking in room for error, for loss, and for things to go wrong is critical and has shaped the thinking around the strategic construct of Minimum Viable Strategy. If the fault, as both Graham and Shakespeare put it, is not in our stars but in ourselves, then we must believe, as Graham did, that we are imperfect beings that make poor choices. Knowing that, Graham pushed for investors to bake in margins of safety in their investments to account for this imperfection. So, too, must we do the same for our strategy.

Military Constructs

Multiple constructs are covered here in this section. As with business, war has had more than its fair share of strategic innovators. As the human condition has a propensity to conflict, so does it have a propensity to hubris in the notion that anyone can be a great general if they study the great strategists, and many have put themselves forth as such as described below.

Scarcity & The French Way of War

In the modern era, where the national appetite for high defense budgets has waned, not only because of historical events such as the two World Wars fought on the continent and the preference grows for social spending over defense spending, but also because of the long wars that seemingly drag on to eternity in the Middle East, many European nations are learning to fight their battles with limited resources. France, for example, utilizes limited military resources to achieve its strategic objectives by leveraging "small but lethal operations, often behind the scenes."[63]

This lack of resources results in a few unique aspects of the French military and its capabilities. These aspects, which highlight the US and French military differences starkly, are 1) it's limited mission objectives and 2) utilizing the smallest force required to achieve a singular, limited objective. Thus, the French "aim low and strive to achieve the minimal required."[64]

The French are also extremely realistic about their military's capabilities. The military is good at "violence" and, thus, the nation does not give missions to the military that doesn't specifically require "violence", providing a stark contrast to the US that in recent decades has leaned on its military to achieve a wide array of political objectives in the Middle East.[65]

The French, therefore, are starkly aware of their capabilities and tailor their objectives to those capabilities. They will not, as Politico states in their article "The French Way of War", defeat ISIS alone (it is likely that no Western power could without neighboring Arab nation support). This is both a virtue of self-awareness and a fault of limited means. But, given that the French are making a deliberate strategic choice not to have comparable military means to the United States, they are able to tailor their how to win strategies specifically to achieve the desired objectives with their limited means.

This example is of benefit to this book as it highlights a source of inspiration for Minimum Viable Strategy. Later in the book, we describe how the goal of the MVS strategic construct is to test and build strategic capabilities. We must, therefore, be self-aware of our own capability limitations in order to build a realistic roadmap for how to eventually obtain more robust capabilities to achieve larger goals in the future. The French offer an example of how that self-awareness and tailoring of objectives due to limited capabilities works in practice.

The Obama Doctrine

The United States of America has had a number of Chief Executives that have brought their own personal style of foreign affairs, their own vision of grand strategy, and their own methods of executing that strategy. Some examples, not discussed in-depth in this book, are the Monroe Doctrine, issued by President James Monroe to ward of European interference from Western Hemisphere affairs, and the Teddy Roosevelt expansionist strategy, which sought to broaden America's influence in the world by successfully constructing the Panama Canal and displaying American naval strength by touting battleships in foreign national harbors through his Great White Fleet.

In the modern era, where political sensitivities are heightened, the backlash for a poor political and military maneuver could potentially be harsh and destructive. Consequently, President Barack Obama, 44th President of the United States, sought during his tenure to employ a more minimalist version of his predecessor's theory of American grand strategy doctrine. Obama's theory was been coined the "Obama Doctrine" as he has truly owned America's changes in foreign policy execution that have been so drastically different from his immediate predecessor, George W. Bush. Thus, he gets the credit, both for better and for worse.

The doctrine can be summed up in a classic statement by the President made both in jest and in seriousness. "Obama would say privately that the first task of an American president in the post-Bush international arena was "Don't do stupid shit."[66] Obama was aware of American military might and has sought to use it sparsely and wisely. The President was constantly taking "measure of our interests against the need for action."[67]

The premise for this belief, that a President should consider consequences heavily, which likely leads to more hesitation versus brash action, was anchored in his central belief about the world and humanity. The president believes that:

> *"the world is a tough, complicated, messy, mean place, and full of hardship and tragedy. And in order to advance both our security interests and those ideals and values that we care about, we've got to be hardheaded at the same time as we're big hearted, and pick and choose our spots, and recognize that there are going to be times where the best that we can do is to shine a spotlight on something that's terrible, but not believe that we can automatically solve it."* [68]

It is this core belief, the belief that the world is messy and complicated, that led the President to seek coalitions over unilateral action, to push those coalitions to be led by allies whom are regional influencers versus America taking the lead, such as the military action in Libya as well as Syria. By putting allies at the front of coalition efforts, the President by default reduced the risk America exposes itself through the use of direct, unilateral action.

By pushing allies to the forefront, the President was able to reduce America's ground-force presence where it is prudent. It is this minimalist approach to influencing world affairs that we draw inspiration from, along with Obama's core belief that there are core capabilities America has and those we do not have and that we should focus on executing on the capabilities we are good at versus those, such as nation building, we have struggled to succeed at.

Liddell Hart

Liddell Hart, born in 1895, was a military theorist whom, during the time after World War II, was an opponent of the mass retaliation military theories that dominated the Eisenhower administration's view of how to deal militarily with global Communist aggressions. Massive retaliation was, in essence, the use of large scale, powerful weapons in response to military aggression by a foreign foe. These powerful weapons were often assumed to be nuclear weapons which would, in the event of an attack by the Soviet Union, ensure immediate destruction of the enemy's attack capabilities as well as its civilian infrastructure and large cities.

The Eisenhower administration supported this policy of massive retaliation for two reasons. First, it allowed for lower expenses versus those required to maintain a large military force that would otherwise be required to have the same effect of enemy force destruction as nuclear weapons would perform. Second, it assured deterrence in a prisoner's dilemma scenario since it was clear that the Soviet Union would not initiate an attack on the United States outright as it was guaranteed that the United States would respond through nuclear attack. The same was true in reverse where the United States would not attack the Soviet Union as it was assumed that the Soviet Union would respond with a nuclear attack in kind. Thus, both were assured of their mutual destruction in the event of an attack of one on the other.

The theory worked, for the most part, as history has now proved that the mutually assured destruction guarantee allowed for a non-direct aggression policy by the United States and the Soviet Union against one another. However, this policy only worked with regards to direct aggression between the two superpowers. There were, however, unforeseen satellite wars on-going in Vietnam, Korea, and other parts of the globe where the United States and the Soviet Union competed for influence like foes on a chessboard. In these scenarios, where limited war and non-direct aggression was the status quo, massive retaliation was not a clear and comprehensible policy.

Liddell Hart believed that, in John F. Kennedy's words while writing in his synopsis of Hart's military thesis, "The West must be prepared to face down Communist aggression, short of nuclear war, by conventional forces."[69] Kennedy recognized that, despite the massive retaliation strategy, the United States was in fact dealing with Communist aggression by limited means through such programs as the Berlin Airlift.[70]

Above all, Hart sought to influence national leaders to avoid the type of all-in decisions of nuclear attack that would lead, eventually, to the destruction of the human race. The basis of his advice for national leaders is as follows:

> Keep strong, if possible. In any case, keep cool. Have unlimited patience. Never corner an opponent, and always assist him to save face. Put yourself in his shoes - so as to see things through his eyes. Avoid self-righteousness like the devil - nothing is so self-blinding.[71]

Hart is, thus, branded as a "minimum deterrence" man, focusing on the execution of limited war to avoid the provocation of the use of nuclear weapons by an enemy.[72] He believes in building the capabilities for *defense* as nuclear weapons do not, in a practical sense, provide the tools for such defense when their employment do not provide for a positive outcome for the employer. [73]

We are chiefly concerned with Hart's constructual thinking that all-in strategies are, on the whole, a guarantor of destruction as they do not allow for the flexibility of response as the situation unfolds in order to allow for cooler heads to prevail and, perhaps, better policies to be created and adapted over time. John F. Kennedy was a proponent of such thinking, as we will see in our case study on the Cuban Missile Crisis, and used it to his advantage greatly to avoid global nuclear war in October of 1962.

Clausewitz

Carl Von Clausewitz is the controversial and often quoted and misquoted granddaddy of military strategy (born in 1780) and author of the epoch *On War* (1832), a collection of Clausewitz's musings on military strategy. There are a few core concepts of the Clausewitzian way of thinking that are important to focus on, specifically that: 1) war is merely a means to political ends, 2) that the enemy has a "center of gravity" that is critical in defeating in order to be victorious in battle, and 3) that there is an existence of "friction" during strategy execution.

Indeed, Jack Welch, former CEO of conglomerate GE summed up the ideas best when he said:

> *"Von Clausewitz summed up what it had all been about in his classic 'On War'. Men could not reduce strategy to a formula. Detailed planning necessarily failed, due to the inevitable frictions encountered: chance events, imperfections in execution, and the independent will of the opposition. Instead, the human elements were paramount: leadership, morale, and the almost instinctive savvy of the best generals."* [74]

What Welch also understood was that strategy is "an art, not a science."[75] This, as was argued, meant shifting away from the mathematics of the business plans to that of concepts, ideas, and general strategic constructs.[76]

The idea of strategic planning being an art versus a science was also expressed by the "Prussian general staff, under the elder von Moltke."[77] Moltke was the Chief of the General Staff of the Prussian, later German, army who built the strategic and operational foundational thinking that would be the premise that the German Army of World War I would build off of.

The Prussian army believed that planning was useful until the plan came in contact with the enemy. In the contemporary Army, this concept is expressed in the saying: "the plan is only good until the first bullet is fired," which was a saying that I heard often as a young lieutenant in the United States Army while preparing for and fighting in a war.

Moltke's team, to overcome this friction, set "broad objectives and emphasized seizing unforeseen opportunities as they arose."[78] Strategy was not, therefore, something that could be executed with precision as an exact science simply because of the existence of friction with the enemy. It was something that evolved over time due to "continually changing circumstances," and the military leaders on the ground needed to be good enough to identify and seize opportunities as they arose in these changing circumstances. This strategic construct, thus, highlights the incredible need for thoughtful, trained leaders capable of making sound strategic choices.

Entire books can and have been written on Clausewitz and his strategic constructs. For the purposes of this book, it is important to understand, as mentioned above, Clausewitz's basic premise that plans are good, but friction exists and leaders must have the know how to react to that friction. What this book will present is, not only the assertion of the existence of friction but also a process for leaders to deal with that friction. This will be discussed in later chapters regarding leadership.

Sun Tzu

I will spend little time here outlining Sun Tzu as a quick Google or Wikipedia search will do far more justice to the author than I will be able to accomplish in this text, but it is worthwhile acknowledging this highly influential writer of strategy who, as can be argued, created the bedrock of strategic thought and strategic constructual thinking by writing *The Art of War*. In short, his influence can be described by quoting a text from The Economist on the strategist, listed in full below in order to capture the essence of Sun Tzu's influence:

"The search for a single strategy that can solve all the problems of a business is gradually being called off. Sun Tzu, all that time ago, emphasized the importance of flexibility, speed and timing in the successful pursuit of war. Only that way, he said, could unforeseen (and unforeseeable) opportunities be seized as and when they arose. The secret was not to have a specific plan to be put into action, but to be prepared to put almost any plan into action, depending on the circumstances."[79]

Preparation is critical to the central theme of Sun Tzu's text, and the most popular parts of Sun Tzu's texts quoted in business strategy decks (Honest Company has quoted these) are as follows:

- Every battle is won before it's ever fought (Made famous in the movie Wall St. by Michael Douglas).

- Know thy enemy, know thyself and you will be successful in a thousand battles.

Both of these quotes are strong proponents of preparation, study, and knowledge. It is the dedication to disciplined self that Sun Tzu proposes and that we take away from him in order to incorporate into our own strategic constructs.

Guerilla Warfare

Conventional warfare fought by armies of nations often consist of pitting well-funded militaries against one another in Clausewitzian style battles of decisiveness. I, however, during my time in war, experienced no such thing.

It was the insurgent, the Taliban fighter, who used guerilla warfare tactics that I came to know so intimately during my time as an Army Officer. The fundamental principle, or the basic underlying truth that one must understand to truly "get" what it means to understand the guerilla fighter, is their inherent necessity to do more with less.

Guerilla fighters historically have been those fighting much larger, sophisticated, and better funded military organizations. Max Boot, military historian, identifies historical examples other than modern military examples for us to consider when thinking about whom exactly are guerilla fighters. Some of these examples include "the struggle against Napoleon in the Iberian Peninsula; Greece's war for independence against the Ottomans; the wars of unification in Italy and various uprisings against colonial powers, such as the slave revolt against the French that led to the foundation of the Republic of Haiti."[80] More modern examples include T.E. Lawrence and Mao Zedong of the 20th century, both of whom contributed immensely to irregular tactical fighting theory in the modern era.

Because these examples of modern insurgencies have been historical David and Goliath matchups, the guerilla fighter could not realistically expect an immediate, decisive battle. The Clausewitzian approach to strategy of engaging in decisive battles with boldness is not an option as it exposes the guerilla too much to an enemy too capable in traditional methods of fighting.

A practical example of these irregular tactics is improvised explosive devices used to attack American convoys in Afghanistan and Iraq in order to choke off supply lanes, disrupt movement, and reduce morale with each loss of American life. These were all too common during my time in Afghanistan and were extremely effective at reducing the Taliban's risk of losing key personnel had we uncovered an individual planting the bomb. The Taliban's risk through employing these tactics are low compared to alternative frontal or ambush style assaults because of the lower number of personnel required to employ them successfully.

Thus, because these engagements are small but effective in each discrete instance against whom they are targeting, guerilla fighters require "patience, restraint and a good public-relations strategy."[81] This patience is the product of the need to chip away at the enemy's forces and morale slowly over time using minimal means for each discrete action, thus risking the least in each particular engagement and not putting it "all on the line" for a single defeat. By spreading out risk over multiple enemy engagements, and assuming probability of 50% success in each, it is thus more likely that over time success will trend toward the mean for each engagement and the enemy will see no end to the fighting as defeats are as common as victories and no decisive battle can ever be achieved. It becomes, for Goliath, whack-a-mole.

It is this incredible patience of the guerilla, to slowly build capabilities and support from the local populace and, thus, to build political capital and win the war through hearts and minds, that is the most applicable to Minimum Viable Strategy. When resources are scarce and the war being waged is one where the outcome is very much unclear, small engagements over time to reduce risk while building capabilities and support and slowly chipping away at the enemy is admirable and applicable to the methods of which we plan to propose our particular strategic construct.

Napoleon's Maxims

In the classic book *A Bridge Too Far* Cornelius Ryan tells the story of Operation Market Garden, the failed Allied operation to punch through German resistance in Holland in an effort to make a swift run for Berlin to end the war before year's end in 1944. The primary thesis of the book focuses on two key takeaways: 1) assumptions made by the British intelligence and high command on weakened German resistance despite many intelligence reports confirming the opposite: that German resistance was strengthening and 2) plans with significant "if's" built in, or a high number of dependencies with medium levels of success probability, were misinterpreted in terms of their overall probability of success (again, irrational optimism).

The second point of the book, that the probabilities of success were grossly overestimated by the British, is outlined by Cornelius Ryan when he quotes a British officer who, upon review of the operational plan for Market Garden, thought of Napoleon's Maxim, which is states that one should never fight unless you are at least 75% sure of success.[82] The other 25% is typically what is left to luck or "chance". This officer believed that the "British were reversing the process. We were leaving 75% to chance. We had only 48 hours to get to Arnhem, and if the slightest thing went wrong…we'd be off schedule."[83]

In the chart below (Chart 8), one can see how dependencies of medium risk level events can lead to an overall risk level for an event as a whole to be below 50% with just two medium level dependent events. In event A, the probability of success is 75%. For event B, the probability of success is 75% and so on for C and D. With each dependent event, probabilities need to be multiplies by the probabilities of discreet previous dependent events. Thus, event A (75%) multiplied by event B (75% chance of success) reaps an overall success probability of 56% [hence the equation P(A and B) = P(A) * P(B)]. This pattern continues with C and D as the overall probability of the sequence is reduced to 32%.

Chart 8: Dependency Probability

Overal Probability	75%	56%	42%	32%
Event Probability	75%	75%	75%	75%
	Event A	Event B	Event C	Event D

P(A AND B) = P(A)* P(B)

It is this understanding that the British officer quoted by Cornelius Ryan in *A Bridge Too Far* understood inherently without having to do the math. He understood that too much *had to go right* in order for the Allies to pull off success in a circumstance where friction in war played a large part of outcomes, which were turning out to be all too uncertain given the dependencies. In order to obtain Napoleon's Maxim from a mathematical standing, each dependency in an operation of 4 sequences events requires at least a 93% chance of success to have an overall probability of success of 75%.

This syndrome (to grossly overestimate the probability of success) is the reverse of gambler's fallacy, which is where people tend to believe that, for example, if in a Roulette table red has hit a dozen times that the probability of hitting red next is low and that one should bet on black (or perhaps the reverse). The truth is that each roll of the ball has discreet probabilities and there are no dependencies upon previous events; thus, gamblers have incorrect views of probabilities because they have insight into what they believe are dependent, previous events.

It is with this understanding of dependent probabilities that we employ the use of simple plans, easily explainable strategies, and the KISS method (Keep it Simple Stupid). It is also likely why one of the primary principles of war is Simplicity, as it reduces the likelihood that bright, ambitious commanders will try to bake in these complicated dependencies into an intricate plan like Market Garden. In these cases, too much can go wrong, and often does.

Minimum Viable Strategy seeks to reduce the number of these dependencies (and avoid gambler's fallacy) and avoid circumstances where *too much has to go right* for something to work. Alternatively, where it is understood explicitly that these dependencies exist, organizations should seek to reduce the existential level of investment in those ventures in order to allow for the organization to overcome the learning curves associated with those new ventures.

Finally, the first point of the book, that the British grossly underestimated German strength in the region, can be explained through a common heuristic of confirmation bias. In the book *The Undoing Project* by Michael Lewis, the author explains that when a scout observed players in baseball, they typically form "instant impressions" that they then find "other data" to justify that impression.[84]

This is critical in understanding why the British may have failed to come to grips with intelligence to the contrary. Ryan in *A Bridge Too Far* explains how the British were so intent on executing the mission that critical intelligence officers who attempted to bring up intelligence reports of gathering German strength in the region were ignored. Had they been heeded, the probabilities of success for each dependent event may have been adjusted and, thus, overall probability of success of the operation (if they had understood dependency probabilities) may have been re-looked. The operational plan could and indeed should have been re-thought through to heed these intelligence reports with more seriousness, or at least leaders should have sought to vet them more seriously.

It is the role of strategies and leaders to see things for as they are, not as they want them to be. It is with this unvarnished view of the world that leaders should make decisions for the organization, acknowledging that confirmation biases exist but that they make a conscious effort to seek out contradicting evidence to prevailing beliefs.

Sports

Moneyball

Moneyball, the book written by Michael Lewis, later a major motion picture film with star Brad Pitt, was a sensation that brought the concept of the use of data in managing baseball games and teams, or sabermetrics, to popular vernacular. Billy Beane, General Manager of the Oakland Athletics, was at the forefront of baseball managers for using data to make personnel decisions. The premise of the book and the strategy of the Oakland Athletics front office was to figure out a means to get the most bang for their buck in terms of paying for undervalued players who could return meaningful results.

Paul Depodesta, the whiz kid Harvard graduate who helped Beane crunch the stats and put quantitative capabilities behind the data-first strategy, was "fascinated by irrationality, and the opportunities that it created in human affairs for anyone that resisted it."[85] Paul had a number of influences that led him to be a disciple of the sabermetrics movement and to rely on data over traditional scouting reports to make personnel decisions. Those specific influences, in the words of Michael Lewis to reinforce its effects, were:

- *"The tendency for everyone who actually played the game to generalize wildly from his own experience. People always thought their own experience was typical when it wasn't."* [86]

- The *"tendency to be overly influenced by a guy's most recent performance: what he did last was not necessarily what he would do next."*[87]

- The tendency for a *"bias toward what people saw with their own eyes, or thought they had seen. The human mind played tricks on itself when it relied exclusively on what it saw, and every trick it played was a financial opportunity for someone who saw through the illusion to the reality. There was a lot you couldn't see when you watched a baseball game."*[88]

These insights offer to the reader valuable perspectives on how Paul and Billy approached managing baseball teams differently than other General Managers and baseball front offices. Rather than relying on a Scout's ability to sniff our talent through observation and vanity metrics such as the speed at which players can run certain distances, they used on-base percentages to calculate how much a player would contribute to the overall runs the team would acquire in a particular game, the only metric that matters when it comes to actually winning.

Moneyball the story is as valuable to us as strategists as is the strategic construct for winning baseball games. Sandy Alderson, a Harvard Law School graduate, Marine, and Vietnam veteran, who also brought the day-to-day discipline to Oakland organization and was an inspiration for Billy Beane, created a culture that facilitated the ability to execute organizational strategy. Alderson "created a new baseball corporate culture around a single baseball statistic: on-base percentage."[89] Alderson made the goal of winning a process, not an art, by breaking the goal of winning into its individual components.[90] It became, in effect, an organizational "routine" executed by managing a few critical player statistics.

This critical component of Alderson's leadership style, to derive the most important statistics that contribute to the overall success of the organization and manage those ruthlessly, is a testament to the team's later success. Being disciplined about holding individuals accountable to their own performance against the expectation also ensures that the metric becomes important and decisions for both individual and teams are made toward achieving the overall of winning. It is this dedication to and obsession with data that we take with us to our Minimum Viable Strategy construct.

Grand Strategy

China's 100 Year Game (Go vs. Chess)

Chess is the most popular board game amongst individuals in Western culture for matching brain power against brain power. It is a game of tactical maneuvers and strategic thought, where players must think ahead 3 or more moves before taking their next position. Each decision impacts the overall chances of a particular player winning, and games can be won in less than ten moves. It is, in summary, a game of frontal assault combined with intellectual prowess.

Chess, however, is a Western cultural game while in the East, particularly in China, a very different match is being played. "A 2,000-year-old board game holds the key to understanding how the Chinese really think—and U.S. officials had better learn to play if they want to win the real competition."[91] The game is called GO, and its concepts for winning are very different than that of chess. While chess involves frontal assaults, flanking maneuvers, short-term strategy of 3-5 moves in advance of current play, and piece for piece calculations made by players looking to reduce forces on the board and simplify the game, GO's rules involve enveloping a player's positions versus attacking them.

This Eastern game of envelopment versus attack requires much longer-term thinking, a much slower, progressive strategy played out over an average of 150 moves in professional games versus the 40 moves typically seen in professional chess. This key difference between Go and Chess highlights deep cultural differences between the East and West and their approaches to grand strategy.

"China deploys a long-term strategy in part because it has a very long memory, and in part because its ruling elite needn't bother too much about electoral constraints."[92] The lack of these constraints, in combination with its long-term thinking, has allowed China to make significant bets on capital infrastructure and military projection capabilities. Author Michael Pillsbury of The Hundred-Year Marathon argues that China has been seeking to achieve this since the Communist party came to power in 1949 and their goal is to be the global hegemon by 2049, or a 100-year grand strategy.

Some of these investments, capital and political, have been to claim rights to "small islands off the coast of Japan or the Philippines, or over oil exploration rights off the coast of Vietnam. Most recently, satellite images have shown Beijing building new islands in the South China Sea—islands that would presumably be used for new military installations."[93] Part of this slow encroachment, both economically and militarily, has been to avoid conflict in order to achieve global dominance, according to Pillsbury.

In 2012, during the commissioning of China's fist aircraft carrier, this desire to project power became evident and manifested physically in the form of naval power. The plan, however, in the short term is not to compete directly with US naval power, but to project its power to influence China's regional interests. It is ensuring China becomes an eminent regional player and can dominate its neighbors before bringing greater influence abroad.

Much of these differences of short versus long-term thinking has to do with the deep cultural memory that China retains as a people and their ability to think long-term. According to Pillsbury, "In the inner councils of the party in Beijing…Chinese scholars and strategists focus on how they can get the United States to go down easily—to step aside with some grace, as Great Britain did after World War II—rather than having to fight a war against it."[94] This is the genius and the curse of the 100-year strategy, to slowly supplant the West while it remains aloof to its own demise as a global power.

Whether one agrees with the premise that China's intentions are to be the global hegemon by the mid-21st Century or not, it is clear that they have employed a long-term strategy of growth and global influence. They have invested in capabilities to achieve this, such as investing in aircraft carriers, rocket launching capabilities, and a dense industrial manufacturing base. All of these are the beginnings of a new, global power eager to stand on the world stage as a real player.

This long-term thinking is important for practitioners of Minimum Viable Strategy, as the construct requires equal rigor and discipline to achieve long-term strategic goals. The Chinese, over the last half-century, have proven they have the discipline at least to move the ball forward toward their desired end, which is commendable for one of the most populous and complex nations and cultures on the planet.

In Summary

As you may have already concluded, each of these constructs is a shade of the other. All are important in their own right and stand on their own in terms of ways for strategists to approach problems. There are four critical points, however, that I hope the reader can both take away and appreciate from this chapter and which are things I have learned in both war and in the startup world:

1. There is no silver bullet.

As we research these strategic constructs, one realizes that no single theory can fit the mold of a single business, nor can a business rely on a single construct to solve all of its problems. It must look at all possibilities and choose the best and most applicable theories to apply to its own organization in the most sensible way.

The "no silver bullet mentality" is something that I've not only learned about strategy while researching this book, but also something I've learned in war and business. In my time in Afghanistan, we would often search for the critical piece of information, or the critical local Afghan ally that would turn the tide of the fight. These silver bullets often do not come in war. War, like football, is won by gaining a couple of yards at a time per play, not by throwing Hail Mary's. Like the "20 Mile March" described by Jim Collins, the daily grind to the final pursuit of victory is what separates great armies from mediocre armies

In business, while continually searching for profitability at The Honest Company, my team focused on projects would comprise of dozens of ankle biter initiatives that would save $20k here, $30k there, $100k here, or $150k there. Very few initiatives got us to the golden $1M mark for savings, although there were some opportunities there. What you learn, however, is that pennies equal dollars and that, totaling up those small savings opportunities equals big dollars of savings once they're all accomplished. Thus, it is important to keep in mind that often when looking to win, there is no silver bullet. It takes incremental gains over the long-run to gain a substantially defensible position as an organization.

2. Strategy requires grit.

Yet another lesson that can be taken away from these constructs is that strategy as a practice is difficult to pursue with vigor. It is hard because, while developing plans is easy, the grit it requires over the long-run to execute is mentally taxing. Angela Duckworth in her book *Grit* says that to have grit requires passion and persistence over the long-run, to keep at a problem despite its mundanity, to continue to pursue excellence, even at the margins, and to strive daily to complete Collins' "20-Mile March" toward success despite the obstacles that one might encounter along the way.

This grit is hard because it requires one to stare into the abyss of long-term thinking, to see the incredibly difficult challenges, the mundanity of the day-to-day painful work of becoming incrementally better over the long-run, and yet still aggressively pursue that excellence daily. It is this pain, this requirement for daily aggressive pursuit of excellence that precludes those intellectually gifted who develop strategy from actually executing it. But it is this execution over the long-run pursued with aggression daily that is required in a Minimum Viable Strategy approach.

3. Not going "all-in" allows you to fight another day.

Many of the constructs described in this chapter theorize on methods for approaching the question of "how to win" by reducing risk and minimizing investment capital. From guerilla warfare to *Moneyball* strategic approaches in baseball, we have learned that there are methods across different disciplines and activities for winning that reduce investment for those who simply can't afford it.

It is by not going "all-in" that these organizations, whether it's the Oakland A's or the Taliban, live to fight another day. By not betting all of its salary budget on a single player, the A's have capital to go around to other players if some investments in players don't pan out as expected. By not launching large-scale battles against American bases, the Taliban doesn't post existential threats to itself by trying to bring about a decisive victory. Both organizations can lose any single battle and hope, in the long-run, that they will win more battles than they will lose and, thus, will ultimately achieve victory.

It is this belief that, while each battle matters, no single battle should be decisive to the organization and, thus, pose an existential threat to it because organizations can't escape the "shit happens" syndrome that we translate to our Minimum Viable Strategy theory. Even in scenarios where something should only happen 10% of the time, it does happen 1 time of 10 and so existential threats, though low in probabilistic terms, *will* happen eventually. If an organization places a large bet and "shit happens" (i.e. Murphey's Law) unexpectedly in that 10% probability range of failure, then there will be no "tomorrow" to recover. It is this tomorrow that Minimum Viable Strategy hopes to retain for organizations.

4. Data matters.

Finally, what we learn from these constructs, is that data is incredibly important for strategies pursued over the long-run. Because these engagements for organizations are not decisive, because improvements are made over the long-run, these improvements may not be abundantly evident to the common observer. Thus, data is required to measure improvements over the long-run, to validate that the strategy is either working or, if it's not working, that corrections need to be made.

Without data that measure the goals of a strategy, an organization is flying blind without instruments to tell itself how far it has come. Organizations must always have a passion for data in order to be disciplined about measuring itself and benchmarking itself against the competition. How else could Ford have realized the effects of learning curves over the long-run and adjusted its prices appropriately? It is this data-drive approach that is critical to Minimum Viable Strategy and will be the focus of the construct as will be explained in later chapters.

In the opening chapters of this book, we have attempted to lay the groundwork before introducing exactly what Minimum Viable Strategy is. We have introduced a history of strategy and general strategic constructs across multiple disciplines that we will take with us as inspiration for building a new model for thinking about strategy. In the next chapter, we will describe exactly what Minimum Viable Strategy is, which we will then use later in the book as a framework for analyzing different cases in politics, war, and business where Minimum Viable Strategy was and was not used.

WHAT IS MINIMUM VIABLE STRATEGY?

In this chapter, we will seek to approach the definition of Minimum Viable Strategy in order to give the reader a clear understanding throughout the remainder of the book exactly what the concept is that is described, argued for, and expounded upon. Minimum Viable Strategy is as defined below:

> *the minimum required investment needed to be made to test a strategic hypothesis by collecting real-world operational and market data.*

I initially formulated this strategic thought process while studying international business strategy at the *UCLA Anderson School of Management* and read about the tremendous number of companies that failed while trying to grow their business abroad (Home Depot, Google, Best Buy to name a few that failed in a Chinese expansion).[95]   When thinking about how I would formulate and execute an international strategy for the company I was employed by at the time, The Honest Company, I considered what would be the ways I could reduce risk by testing market demand for our products abroad. After conducting some initial research, I came across a service called Bongo, which serves as somewhat of a broker for e-commerce companies for international shipments. In essence, Honest could ship its international shipments to this company from our domestic warehouses, they would apply necessary customs documents and pay the landing fees, and off the boxes went to their final destinations to places like the UK, Paris, Beijing, and others.

This process of international shipments can be tremendously expensive for both the company and the customer and isn't necessarily a sustainable strategy over the long-run for your highest volume geographies. But the alternative to this strategy is for the company to invest in millions of dollars of inventory to stock in a regional distribution somewhere in Eastern Europe or Shanghai before we have any real data on where the demand is. Thus, we could subsidize the price of shipping for a little while in order to collect market data before making large, "all-in" commitments to regional distribution operations.

This method of international direct shipments to customers globally also allows companies to test price elasticities of demand before setting hard prices in retail stores in such countries abroad. This can be a powerful research tool to help figure out what the right price point is for your product in the market over the long-run.

Some people might proclaim that the high shipping costs for this particular strategy are too high and, thus, makes this alternative an unrealistic method of creating sustainable value. The argument against this is that this is not the permanent, long-term solution. Permanent, long-term, competitive solutions often require a larger initial upfront investment that, remember, we do not want to make at this point because we don't know if our strategy will actually work. The Minimum Viable Strategy, therefore, helps companies avoid "all-in" scenarios too early in the decision-making cycle and gives organizations time to pivot to other strategies if required in the short-term in order to find the means to create a long-term, sustainable competitive advantage.

In the current startup vernacular, the word Minimum Viable Product is often used to describe what is the minimum product required to test market demand in order to reduce risk and resources invested. Minimum Viable Strategy is a similar approach with similar principles but applied to different decision-making processes.

In many ways, utilizing a Minimum Viable Strategy approach is a means of hedging risk when companies try to do things they've never done before. In a startup like the Honest Company, we were constantly doing things we've never done before, and we were constantly messing them up the first few attempts at them. Thus, in addition to learning how much companies failed at expanding into new markets from my academic studies at UCLA, I also learned how much companies just aren't that good at doing new things for the first time in my own business experience.

I began to see this pattern again and again the more I read and studied strategy and the history of war and business. Some of these patterns are reflected in the case studies described in later chapters, but between my academic experience, my business experience of constant failure of trying new things, and seeing the repeating patterns of these failures throughout the world of organizations trying new things, the strategic construct of Minimum Viable Strategy began to form.

Minimum Viable Strategy is, simply, a means of building strategy with the recognition that failure at something new is more likely than not likely and that, to be successful, one must build a strategy that takes that into account. Learning curves are inevitable, and by building a strategy around recognizing those learning curves, one ensures that the house isn't gambled on a venture that requires initial success without those curves.

This is more eloquently put by Julian Birkshaw and Martine Haas in their article "Increase Your Return on Failure" printed in May of 2016 in the Harvard

Complementing Traditional Strategy

ad Business Review, and it is worth quoting at length in this book for the sake of crystalizing the idea of Minimum Viable Strategy even further for the reader:

te*"In a return on failure ratio, the denominator is the resources you've invested in the activity. One way to raise your return is by reducing this number - by keeping your investments low. Or you can deliberately sequence them, starting with small amounts, until major uncertainties have been resolved. The numerator is the 'asset' you gain from the experience, including information you gather about customers and markets, yourself and your team, and your operation. Increasing these is the only way to boost your return."[96]*

usThe premise of Birhshaw and Haas's argument is that, by minimizing the consequences of failure, you maximize your return and minimize the downsides of projects.[97] Many of these failures offer instant feedback into market information and product fit in particular markets, which can be huge wins for the organization in the long-run.[98]

fieThis is the essence of Minimum Viable Strategy, which is to set strategic hypothesis about the organization and test those hypotheses by gathering information and, in the process, build the capabilities to execute new business ventures in a way that is efficient and competitive. This mode of thinking makes organization competitive in the long-run, which is the time frame in which we want to consider competitiveness.

Complementing Traditional Strategy

reTraditional corporate strategy is typically a methodical, slow process in order to set the direction for large organizations. This is probably a great approach as it is expensive and confusing to change strategies frequently, and companies that do so will likely not accomplish very much in terms of end results. In addition, employees will be confused as to what the latest strategy of the day is. This lack of speed in decision making, of agonizing over the details of market data, and of making small adjustments to strategy can be fatal, however, in a fast-paced world of market booms and busts.

This thinking of fasted paced strategy setting can be fatal, however, if not executed properly or if the description of what Minimum Viable Strategy *is* has been misinterpreted. Let us clarify: Minimum Viable Strategy does not propose strategy through "trial and error". As Todd Zenger in "Trial and Error is No Way to Make a Strategy" said:

> It's here that I take issue with the agility school of thought. The prescription boils down to this: In a world where sustainable competitive advantage is harder to come by, you need to experiment more in order to find it - rapid experimentation, therefore is the cure. Moreover, their advice to move, rather than to think, seems to accelerate as the complexity of the strategic landscape intensifies. Essentially, the philosophy seems to be, 'If you don't know where you're going, any path will do." [99]

I believe that this understanding of what Minimum Viable Strategy is and how it should be applied is a bit off base. To illustrate this, let's first look at the traditional strategic formulation processes as used by Proctor and Gamble and described wonderfully in the book *Playing to Win*. Strategy is described as being formulated by answering the following questions in order:[100]

1) What is our winning aspiration?
2) Where will we play?
3) How will we win?
4) What capabilities must be in place?
5) What management systems are required?

These are great questions to be asked while formulating strategy, and this process may work great for Proctor and Gamble, but for companies without unlimited resources to relentlessly pursue a strategy either until it fails or succeeds it is often unrealistic and can be potentially fatal to the company.

This methodology is, at worst, an all-in way of thinking and assumes, to a large degree, that through the rigorous process of strategic formulation that the company will be correct in its course heading and is therefore willing to bet the house on a strategy it formulated, sometimes without data.

This is where the Minimum Viable Strategy comes into play. It allows organizations to test strategic hypothesis without betting the house on a strategy that may or may not work. It is the relentless pursuit of two-way door decisions with the benefit of staving off one-way door, all-in decisions as long as possible until the fog of forecasting has cleared enough to make a substantial investment in a particular direction based on real-world experience, feedback, and data. This avoids strategy formulation in an Ivory Tower and brings it closer to the real-world operations of day-to-day business.

The Minimum Viable Strategy approach, therefore, is complementary to traditional strategic ways of thinking. While strategy should be seen as the end goal (questions I and 2) with supporting goals set to get the company or organization there (questions 3-5), the *Playing to Win* framework does little to tell of the specific actions required to make the answers to those supporting questions actually happen. And what if setting up management systems, capabilities, and the strategy that answers the question "How Will We Win?" takes a substantial time to test? What have you lost in the process? How much resources have you lost in going "all-in" on a strategy? What were the opportunity costs? Minimum Viable strategy attempts to either answer or stave-off some of these questions that traditional strategic ways of thinking fails to address.

Above all, what Minimum Viable Strategy attempts to detract from is the notion that there is still large room for swift, decisive victories. In war, the Germans called this approach the Blitzkrieg in World War II and the Schlieffen Plan in World War I. In the business cases discussed in this book, you will learn how Target approached swift, decisive business wins in Canada. However, as we have learned throughout history, whether "it is Napoleon's victory at

Wagram, the early success of the Schlieffen Plan in 1914, Hitler's blitzkrieg in 1940 or the rapid defeat of Iraqi forces in 2003, all turned into long wars of attrition because the other side refused to realize it had been beaten."[101] The same general concept is true in the world of politics and business: that "initial success is hardly ever decisive."102

It is with this knowledge that we take on the subject of Minimum Viable Strategy. The details of how to win past this initial success are often overlooked as the delusions of early success or the possibilities of early success often cloud the clarity of thought beyond those moments of grandeur or possible perceived victory. The strategist, therefore, must realize and understand that strategy is about how to win *over the long-run*. This is encompassing from early stages of success and beyond.

What Minimum Viable Strategy does is allow for the breathing room for strategies to stay grounded in reality, to separate themselves from delusions of decisive battles, and to approach strategy for the long-term. Minimum Viable Strategists realize that victory requires grit, determination, and the will to achieve victory through the execution of strategy over a very long period of time, not through a decisive battle. This is a difficult proposition to instill and expect strategies to uphold as it requires the ability of the human mind to see into the distant future as well as it can see into the present and to not allow themselves to succumb to the false promises of decisive victories that some strategies will sell.

As a West Point graduate, I cannot help but write this chapter without thinking about General George Patton, Old Blood and Guts. Patton is arguably one of the most skilled, decisive, and offensive minded generals in American history who pulled off stunning defeats over the Germans in North Africa and Europe. His maxims for war, grained into the minds of cadets early on at the Academy, involve such phrases as "The more you sweat in peace, the less you bleed in war." But one of the most important phrases used by Patton that is so difficult to reconcile with my own thinking of strategy is that of his belief in the constant offensive, to never dig in, to never stay still, to always be moving forward.

How can we believe in two seemingly conflicting beliefs in our mind simultaneously: that the Patton approach to war of always being on the offensive is critical to maintaining momentum and the advantage against the enemy and, on the other hand, the belief that, from a minimalist style of strategy, a more measured approach is required to win over the long-run.

What I want to crystalize to the reader is that Minimum Viable Strategy is not paralysis by analysis. It is not hesitancy to act decisively in a meaningful way. Paralysis has often been seen as a speed bump to swift action. "Indeed, in a 2015 Boston Consulting Group survey, 31% of respondents identified a risk-averse culture as a key obstacle to innovation."103 A Minimum Viable Strategy, as we will explain in later chapters detailing its methods of execution, is a focused approach that takes the organization as quickly and aggressively as possible to approaching strategy while minimizing the risk to the highest degree allowed for by the situation.

With Minimum Viable Strategy, the ball is always moving forward, not through irresponsible frontal assaults, but through measured approaches to achieving advancement. It is this continuous, measured advancement through a structured means of strategy and execution that Minimum Viable Strategy argues for.

Summarizing the Theory

We have covered a lot of ground in this chapter regarding what exactly is Minimum Viable Strategy. Thus, before moving forward in the book, it is helpful if the reader had a short guide to reference back to in order to summarize what exactly is Minimum Viable Strategy, what it entails, what it considers, and what it does for organizations. Thus, we will attempt to do that here.

What It Is

> Minimum Viable Strategy is, as defined:
> *The minimum required investment needed to be made to test a strategic hypothesis by collecting real-world operational and market data.*

In essence, Minimum Viable Strategy is an incremental approach to strategy, focused on executing with focus with the goal of winning in the long-run. It is also a measured but decisive approach to execution.

What It Considers

Minimum Viable Strategy is data-driven, with strategic hypothesis resolved through real-world feedback from opponents, markets, or customers.

What it Does

Minimum Viable Strategy allows for a number of things for strategists. It helps to:

- Narrows the field of strategic choices

- Allows for two-way door decisions to be made over one-way door decisions

- Enable organizations to overcome learning curves before reaching a point of irrecoverable organizational failure through minimizing "all-in" bets

How these principles are executed or not will be crystalized in the case studies in this book, which outline times in history when organizations have or have not taken such a strategic view and what the consequences were.

Minimum Viable Strategy is not strictly business theory. It can be applied to multiple disciplines, but we emphasize business as it is our most common playing ground in our day-to-day lives for many readers. Theoretical thinking, and the methods of considering how to win are, however, universal and can be universally applied.

 In this book, the reader will be exposed to one example of a Minimum Viable Strategy approach taken by Franklin Delano Roosevelt during the Second World War when, after the attack on Pearl Harbor in December 1941, it was still very much unclear as to what the right approach was for the United States when taking on its adversaries during the conflict. Roosevelt's advocacy of a Minimum Viable Strategy approach here was at great odds with the nation's top generals at the time, and you will see how conflict over strategy at the top echelons of power during the war could have led to very different outcomes for the Allies.

The reader will then be exposed to a political example, where we will follow the decisions made by the group of advisors to Kennedy called the Executive Committee of the National Security Council (EXCOM) during the Cuban Missile Crisis to advise the president on matters of security. Readers will also learn about the approach that was taken during the crisis to avoid global thermos-nuclear war. The committee appointed to handle the crisis (EXCOM) had an evolving view as to what the right approach was over the course of the "Thirteen Days", detailed in both Robert F. Kennedy's book Thirteen Days and the now released EXCOM tapes that captured the heightened sense of urgency, frustration, and conflict over strategy during the crisis. For this group, formulating the right strategy was, inevitably, a choice between peace or possible nuclear war, and this book will outline the alternatives, the Minimum Viable Strategy approach, and the benefits the group achieved by choosing a Minimalistic Viable Strategy over an "all-in" strategy.

Finally, the reader will be exposed to two business case studies of companies that did not taken a Minimum Viable Strategy approach and what the consequences were. Additionally, we will pontificate, just for a short time, what the companies could have done better and how things would have turned out differently had they used a Minimum Viable Strategy approach.

The first business case discusses Target's failed attempt to launch into Canada. We will explore the choices made, the mistakes that caused the failure of Target's expansion, and how a better approach could have possibly lead to more favorable outcomes.

The second business case will detail Lego's rise to success in the early 2000's and rapid decline, brought on by a combination of its own hubris and overreach. The case will detail how the group recovered using a more measured approach similar to the principles defined by this book and what could be classified as a Minimum Viable Strategy.

After the business cases have been outlined, this book will then provide to the reader steps for building a Minimum Viable Strategy as well as lessons for leaders on how to formulate and execute a Minimum Viable Strategy. Now, with that road map in front of us, let us move forward on our journey.

OPERATION TORCH

In early 1942, at the outbreak of World War II, America suffered the devastating naval and air losses of equipment and human life at the hands of the Japanese at Pearl Harbor. At the time, Franklin D. Roosevelt, then President of the United States and Commander in Chief of the Armed Forces, and his military chiefs contemplated on where to employ American forces over the coming years. These options would be formulated from the strategic *where to play* and *how to win* questions that these leaders would attempt to answer over the course of the war.

Almost immediately after Pearl Harbor, however, there was conflict and disagreement over what the proper U.S. strategy should be in the short-term, and disagreements arose between the President and his military chiefs on *where to play* and *how to win* in 1942. While they agreed on the overall winning aspiration of unconditional victory over German, Japanese, and Italian forces, the President and his military chiefs disagreed deeply on the strategy to achieve that victory.

The President, with mounting pressures from the public, favored action in 1942 in a territory of America's choosing where the untested American soldiers stood a "reasonable chance of success." General George Marshall,

US Army Chief of Staff and architect of much of the strategy used to build the US military to a world-class power by the end of the war in 1945, favored a cross-Channel invasion of Europe in 1942, which was the equivalent, in the President's view, of an "all-in", one-way door decision that the American military was not prepared to take on with their current level of experience.

Disagreements flared over the choices that needed to be made. One can see clarity in FDR's proposed strategy, writing:

> "Americans might scoff at the British failure to fight the Germans effectively, despite two years' experience of German tactics and inter-service skills in action. *Would Americans fare better in battle, though, straight off the mound?*"[104]

FDR was justified to doubt the American military's capabilities in 1942. The Army was comprised primarily of citizen soldiers, not "professionals" with the "self-sacrificing discipline that seemed natural to German and Japanese troops."[105] The Germans at this time in 1942 had years of combat experience under their belts against an array or forces while the Americans, who would eventually go on to fight the Germans, lacked any such experience and would be on the offensive in a territory that had been occupied by the enemy force for years. It is unclear, therefore, in retrospect how Marshall or the other chiefs thought that this operation they proposed in Europe could be successful at the outset given these circumstances.

The military chiefs accused FDR of pandering to political pressure, where there was mounting pressure at home to open a second front and put American soldiers into action somewhere in the European hemisphere in 1942. "Far from responding to political, and popular pressure, the President was, however, doing the opposite: patiently preferring, as U.S. commander in chief, a military operation that had a reasonable chance of success. Moreover, one that might change the course of World War II if it succeeded."[106] Indeed, much of the pressure of the day was centered around putting men into action in Europe, Marshall's preferred plan, while FDR drove hard for an approach that targeted the "underbelly" of the crocodile of Europe in Africa versus targeting the "hard snout" through a landing in Europe.[107]

In this historical example of strategy formulation at a cross-roads between the President and his generals, one can see the weaknesses of the framework outlined by *Playing to Win* for strategy formulation. While it is clear that the framework, although not explicitly defined at the time but generally understood organically to the generals of the age, has allowed these decision makers in World War II to see clearly *what choices need to be made*, it is unclear that it has provided a framework to guide leaders in choosing appropriate strategy. The *Playing to Win* framework tells us that "tough choices" need to be made, but Minimum Viable Strategy provides a framework on how to actually make those tough choices in the face of multiple, seemingly fair choices to decision makers.

In this case, both *where to play* and *how to win* were choices that the American military heads were facing in 1942. Marshall favored Europe through direct contact in a cross-channel invasion while FDR favored a more indirect approach through North Africa and envelopment followed by direct assault in Europe sometime in 1944. Both had their respective camps of people who strongly believed in the other cause as well.

The Secretary of War Henry Stimson, all of the military chiefs and virtually the entire War Department sat in the Marshall camp while Winston Churchill, the British cabinet, and the Soviet Leader Joseph Stalin sat in the FDR camp for North Africa.[108] Thus, it is clear that there are frequent cases when highly capable, highly intelligent individuals will often have vastly different opinions about the tough choices that are required to be made in strategy formulation, and a better guide is required to help make those choices.

FDR's thinking leads one to see the strengths of Minimum Viable Strategy and how one can go about formulating such strategies. The terms "reasonable chance of success" that FDR says of his preferred plan reveals a shade of minimalistic viability in his strategic thinking. Minimum Viable Strategy leads us to ask:

> *What is the minimum required investment needed to be made to test strategic hypothesis by collecting real world operational and market data.*

In FDR's mind, the minimum required investment consists of an invasion of North Africa with the strategic hypothesis of "If Americans are given opportunity to fight the Germans on grounds of their own choosing where Germany is not strong, they can win." The data he was seeking to collect, in this case, was twofold. The first set of data, as indicated by the hypothesis, was proof that Americans could indeed win in such a conflict against German forces in North Africa.

The second data set he sought to collect was whether American fighting forces would *learn* from fighting the Germans and iterate their tactics and battle strategies to fare better against German forces should America mount a European Invasion at a later time. Roosevelt, thus, in 1942 had a "profound shift in his thinking as his nation's commander in chief. Millions of American troops were being called to serve their country. They would do fine, he was sure, if they could be given the chance to learn the arts of modern warfare against German or Japanese troops, on ground of their choosing, *not the enemy's.*"[109]

Indeed, later in 1942, the Canadians would attempt a less-than-well executed raid into Europe, which would prove disastrous[110] It is clear, therefore, that if the Americans had mounted an invasion force at this time, untested on any battle grounds comparable to Europe and unproven against any enemies, the results of such a premature invasion could have spelled disaster, not only for the cause of victory, but for all of world history as we know it today.

In the end, Americans did, indeed, falter at the hands of the Germans early on in their experiences in Northern Africa, such as at the Battle of Kasserine Pass. The Germans, led by experienced commander Erwin Rommel, would inflict severe casualties on the untested American troops who were, in almost all cases, facing a real enemy for the first time. But learn they did, as Roosevelt expected they would, and American field commanders were quick to adapt their way of fighting to match and eventually turn back the German forces.

While America did, in time, invade Europe in a cross-Channel invasion, it would not be until much later in June, 1944, years after troops spent time fighting Germans in North Africa and Italy. But the beauty of North Africa, in Roosevelt's mind, was that it "could not fail". [111] At the time of the North African invasion during the war, there was much concentration of Nazi forces then focused on the Eastern Front in the Soviet Union, so there was little chance that the German Army would be able to reinforce their North African forces in order to deflect Operation Torch, the code-named operation for the North African Invasion.

Even though Roosevelt believed that the operation, in itself, could not fail, if it did such a failure would not spell ruin for all hope of an American success against German forces. Roosevelt, having been Assistant Secretary of the Navy during the First World War, undoubtedly wanted to avoid the mistakes made during that conflict by military commanders who needlessly put soldiers against the enemy with little hope of gaining much ground. A cross-channel attack early in 1942 would have resulted in needless casualties and would have resulted in little gain of ground, which Roosevelt predicted would be given up regardless in time if it were a weakened position attempted to be held against a reinforced German army.

While many business strategists will often take the strategies of war and attempt to apply them to business principles in order to draw conclusions about their own business strategies, it is clear to me that, after my having experienced strategic formulation in both the business world and the world of war, the process to develop military strategy can and should take lessons from business strategy formulation and apply them to military strategic thinking. For example, the principles of war are depicted in Chart 9 below:[112]

Chart 9: From the Worcester Polytechnic Institute

Mass	Concentrate combat power at the decisive place and time
Objective	Direct every military operation towards a clearly defined, decisive, and attainable objective
Offensive	Seize, retain, and exploit the initiative
Surprise	Strike the enemy at a time, at a place, or in a manner for which he is unprepared
Economy of Force	Allocate minimum essential combat power to secondary efforts
Maneuver	Place the enemy in a position of disadvantage through the flexible application of combat power
Unity of command	For every objective, ensure unity of effort under one responsible commander
Security	Never permit the enemy to acquire an unexpected advantage
Simplicity	Prepare clear, uncomplicated plans and clear, concise orders to ensure thorough understanding

These principles are taught at West Point in conjunction with the course *Military Art* and *Science* in order to offer a clear understanding of what operational effectiveness means in war. These principles, while helpful in framing choices, are not necessarily the most effective means of thinking through strategy in war. They do not provide a framework for logical thought processes and decision making but are merely nine suggestions on how to structure that thinking.

There are yet other strategies often quoted in business circles from texts of military strategies. "Know thy enemy better than you know yourself" is a quote I've seen on many business strategy papers that have attempted to port military strategies like Sun Tzu over to the business world to assist with strategy formulation. While these are helpful, neither the Principles of War for war strategists nor Sun Tzu for business leaders offer a useful, step-by-step framework for thinking about formulating a clear strategy that can be executed upon to completion. The *Playing to Win* strategy framework is a start, and I've show here that it can be applied to strategies for war as well, but it needs an additional layer to help decision makers complete their task of strategy formulation, which the Minimum Viable Strategy framework provides.

Therefore, military leaders, when combining the *Playing to Win* framework with Minimum Viable Strategy choice formulation and selection framework, should walk away with a clear understanding of, not only what the tough choices are that need to be made, but what the *right* choices are, which is what was lacking in the Roosevelt administration: clarity of what choices should be made. Military leaders, therefore, can and should ask, in the spirit of *Playing to Win*:

What is our winning aspiration?
- Where do we want to play?
- How do we want to win?
- What are our strategic hypothesis based on different *where to play* and *how to win* strategic options?

It is the final piece regarding the strategic hypothesis formulation that differentiates Minimum Viable Strategy from the *Playing to Win* framework, which will be explored in greater detail in chapters later that cover how to formulate a Minimum Viable Strategy precisely. In general, this exercise should derive a set of strategic hypotheses that should be analyzed and decided upon as to which offers the most value at the least systemic risk to the organization. In FDR's cabinet, the military leaders are left, therefore, with a set of strategic choices to be made that involve tough tradeoffs from one another. These tradeoffs, in this example, include:

If the US military chose to invade North Africa, this would only put off the inevitable of needing to invade mainland Europe, giving Hitler enough time to reposition and strengthen his position in order to better repel an attack.

If the US military chose to invade Europe, it could potentially experience a devastating loss at the hands of the Germans, thus putting its chances for success back even further in the long-run than if it had chosen to invade North Africa in the first place. It would impair American moral and weaken the overall US position globally.

If the US military chose to double-down on the Pacific theatre of war, which was also proposed by Marshall and the rest of the chiefs, then, not only would Hitler have time to reposition his forces for greater defense, but this would put Britain at severe risk of being completely defeated by the German Army. A double-down in the Pacific theatre, however, would have allowed for a sense of focus and concentration of forces against a single enemy at the time, which appeared to be in line with traditional military thinking and the principles of war, specifically economy of force and mass principles.

The FDR strategy of invasion was a first step. It would not be the last, of course, and it was not the end solution but only an initial phase of a greater plan to get the United States into the war, at last, against the Germans. Nor was this a strategy by trial and error as some might argue. The plan was not to merely attack the German Army in North Africa simply to "try something" or to "throw an idea at the wall" to see what sticks. Not in the least.

This was a fractional, incremental step that the President was taking as part of a larger strategy for American victory against the Germans and all of the might of the US Army was put into making it a success. Indeed, at the time the invasion was executed, it was the largest amphibious assault force that had yet been assembled in human history to that time.[113]

In the final analysis, FDR hit the nail on the head with his North African campaign and, for Marshall, he never did "concede that the President, in his role as U.S. commander in chief, was demonstrating a greater military realism in devising Allied strategy in 1942 than his U.S. Army Chief of Staff."[114] Hindsight is, as we will learn later, always 20/20. Yes, the strategy worked, but would we be lauding such a strategy if things had not gone as planned? What if Rommel had been able to prevent and subvert the invasion?

Such questions are difficult to ask, but, as said before, the glory of this strategy in 1942 is that it could fail, not necessarily that it did succeed. And by having such a strategy, the Americans gave themselves the ability to learn from their mistakes and from their failures, which, due to their lack of experience in fighting the Germans, they expected to and did have. This is the beauty of Operation Torch and of thinking in minimally viable terms for strategy.

Attack, Not Envelopment

Some might argue that this means of executing strategy is one of paralysis, that it does not directly engage with the enemy in a means to bring about decisive battle to end war in a Clausewitzian fashion. To address this issue, I would first highlight a counter example in history, that of the strategy initially proposed by General Winfield Scott at the outbreak of the Civil War. At the time, Scott was the most highly regarded General in the American military, having served as a commanding general in the Mexican American conflict and having had high-level leadership roles in other American military endeavors of the age.

Scott's plan was to envelop the South, referred to as Scott's Great Snake strategy.[115] Scott wanted to obtain victory through the least amount of violence and, hence, death as possible. But, as was said at the time of the strategy, it was not thought this would be successful because the North could not "win the war without beating the Rebels."[116] Thus, the strategy, conceived by a highly regarded general, was not executed because it did not make the South feel the pain of the war, nor did it put men into action that could actually result in any type of victory, only protracted resistance, thus legitimizing the South the longer they hung on.

Scott's approach is not a Minimum Viable Strategy because it does nothing to advance the organizational goal of achieving victory nor does it obtain organizational learning to climb the learning curve and set it on a course toward achieving operational excellence. Roosevelt's strategy of employing troops into North Africa was a first step of, not envelopment or avoiding conflict, but a means of allowing for the scaling of the learning curves before the stakes were higher during an inevitable cross-Channel European invasion. It is this process of incrementally climbing the learning curves during new ventures and enterprises that FDR sought to undertake through the North African campaign without "putting all their eggs in one basket" as "Marshall's preferred strategy" would have had the country do.[117]

It is this chapter, in conclusion, that has introduced us to two concepts regarding Minimum Viable Strategy: the importance of formulating strategic hypothesis and thinking about strategic choices in terms of how they assist to scale the learning curve. These lessons derived from the case will allow for us to build a greater sense for how to think about Minimum Viable Strategic formulation in other scenarios in a thoughtful, disciplined way.

In the next chapter, we will explore the Cuban Missile Crisis. It is during this crisis that the Kennedy administration took lessons learned from the Bay of Pigs disaster and implemented organizational changes that allowed for them to formulate what can be regarded as a Minimum Viable Strategy for bringing the crises to a peaceful resolution.

THE CUBAN MISSILE CRISIS

In October 1962, the world came closer to nuclear destruction than it ever has in its short time with nations that have had the powerful weapons and the ability to use them. The Soviet Union began placing nuclear weapons in Cuba capable of reaching all major American cities except Seattle early in the month. The US became aware of the existence of these weapons when American spy planes caught a glimpse of the activity. The discovery of these weapons set off one of the most historic and gut-wrenching set of White House Executive Committee meetings ever to take place, and most importantly a large part of the deliberations was captured on a White House tape recorder, providing invaluable insight into what was actually said by whom and how opinions and ideas evolved over time in the discussions over what to do about the missiles in Cuba.

The prospects at the initial outset of the meetings were grim and the options on the table were almost unanimously decided upon when the initial EXCOMM (the Executive Committee of the National Security Council; or the President's advisors during the crisis) meetings took place. At the end of the first meeting, "President Kennedy summed up the options on the table: attacking the missile sites; air strikes against the missiles, the SAMs, the MiG's, the airfields; the first two choices plus a naval blockade; and consulting with the allies before the strikes."[118]

Reality, however, began to set in early on as some members of the committee began to question the results of such an attack on Cuba. "I don't know quite what kind of a world we live in after we've struck Cuba and we've started it," said Secretary of Defense Robert McNamara.[119] The major concern and, thus, the biggest obstacle against airstrikes at the time was what the reaction from the Soviet Union would be should the United States attack Cuba to take out the missiles.

The EXCOMM team, however, faced a major obstacle at the time of the deliberations, that being the element of time. The window of opportunity for such an attack was narrowing as the missiles were only days from becoming operational, opening up American vulnerability to a retaliatory attack from such sites should the United States attack in an effort to destroy the Soviet missile sites.

The element of time put an additional layer of pressure on EXCOMM as they balanced speed with thoughtful deliberation, inclusion, and vetting of their strategy for dealing with the crisis. As made clear by President Kennedy's initial summary of the options on the table at the conclusion of the first day, because the element of time was so critical at the moment, the expedience of an attack and the immediate results it would produce were, to the EXCOMM, the logical solution to the problem at hand to guarantee the safest outcomes, that being the elimination of the offensive missiles from the Western hemisphere.

But there were major costs to such a choice, and, yet, still large risks with dire, unpredictable consequences. If the United States were to attack the missile sites, large questions loomed over the EXCOMM as they further contemplated the action. Would the Russians take Berlin? Would they retaliate with another missile located in Russia capable of reaching the United States? If all of the missiles were not destroyed, would they attack the United States with the remaining missiles left on Cuba?

All of these were possibilities discussed during the deliberations and no one, not the President, the Secretary of Defense, the Head of the CIA; no one knew the true probability of what was to happen should the US attack and subsequently invade Cuba. Thus, there were major drawbacks to such a plan with large, unknown consequences that loomed over the horizon of time should the group choose to "cross the Rubicon" and take the island. Whatever action they were to take was a "hell of a gamble."[120]

One-Way vs Two-Way Door Decisions

To characterize it in terms of strategy, an attack on Cuba was, in essence, a one-way door decision. To attack the sites, which at the time were manned by Russian technicians and soldiers, and to then follow on with an invasion almost certainly meant that the United States would be travelling down a path that it could not reverse. Attacking the sites meant that there was a high likelihood of killing many Russian soldiers, the consequences of which almost certainly would mean a reprisal from the Soviet Union in some military fashion.

The entire episode began to resound of all the things Kennedy learned not to do as President. During this time, Kennedy was reading The Guns of August, a novel that followed the outset of the First World War.[121] The thesis of the book is that the Great War started from a series of choices made by German leaders that, once made, became irreversible. Because the Germans had mastered the execution of the Schlieffen Plan, the plan designed to invade France that had been rehearsed for years leading up to the war, they became so well attuned to its execution that once the order was given to invade, it could not be redacted. Even in an attempt to do so after the order was given to execute the plan by the Kaiser met with resistance by his military leaders, claiming it was too late to turn back.[122]

The result of this issuance of orders to invade France was the deadliest war the world had ever seen up to that point, and many leaders, both in Germany and other aggressor nations after the war, struggled to understand how the war, whose beginnings seemed unclear at the end, had all started.[123] Kennedy feared the possibility of starting a destructive war that the leaders of nations on both sides would be unclear as to the events that started such a conflict at the end and, thus, sought ways to remain flexible to prevent such a catastrophe.

One can see Kennedy's writing in 1960, quoting the advice of the military theorist Basil Hart: "Keep strong, if possible. In any case, keep cool. Have unlimited patience. Never corner an opponent, and always assist to save face. Put yourself in his shoes - so as to see things through his eyes. Avoid self-righteousness like the devil - nothing is so self-blinding."[124] Throughout the decision-making process, it is clear that Kennedy sought to remain flexible by never cornering the Soviets or subsequently force them to take aggressive action to "save face".

Indeed, the reality of invasion being a one-way door decision soon began to materialize as the crisis persisted and opponents of the invasion in EXCOMM began to offer the option of blockade of the island of Cuba as a means of reducing risk with the possibility of achieving the same outcomes as the attack and invasion option. Opponents of this option, primarily the military chiefs, argued that it did not exactly eliminate the missiles from the island, the actual and primary threat to the United States, and that the quarantine will take time to be effective, during which time the missiles will have become operational. These considerations, in their mind, made the blockade more dangerous to the United States because it allowed the time required for the weapons to become functional.

In fact, General LeMay, Chief of Staff of the Air Force at the time, would say that such a plan, which included subsequent removal of US missiles from Turkey in exchange for Russian missile removal in Cuba, was "almost as bad as the appeasement at Munich."[125] There is no doubt that this comment struck deep with Kennedy, whose father, whom Kennedy had a strong personal bond with, was a proponent of the disastrous agreement at Munich where the United Kingdom and other European powers gave in to Adolf Hitler's demands to take parts of Czechoslovakia without reprisal. This is significant because the appeasement at Munich, many claim, accelerated aggression between the UK and Germany because it displayed signs of weakness by the UK, which Hitler and Germany later exploited.

The military chiefs, adamant about the need to strike, and guaranteeing that an attack plus an invasion would be the best option for the United States, struck a chord with Kennedy as he remembered the Bay of Pigs disaster where the chiefs and the CIA guaranteed a successful overthrow of Castro with limited action on behalf of the United States. During the Bay of Pigs invasion, experts claimed that the Cuban people would rise up against Castro the minute the invasion began, but this turned out not to be true (a false assumption), and the invasion by CIA trained Cuban revolutionaries was a complete failure.

The Bay of Pigs hung in the back of Kennedy's mind throughout the crisis as he contemplated the way forward. During the Bay of Pigs, probabilities took part in the decision-making process. "The Joint Chiefs of Staff concluded that the plan had a 'fair chance' of success. The man who wrote the words "fair chance" later said he had in mind odds of 3 to 1 against success. But Kennedy was never told precisely what "fair chance" meant and, not unreasonably, he took it to be a much more positive assessment."[126]

There were plenty of "if's" on the table with the Bay of Pigs, as there were with Market Garden described in an early chapter, that were never fully explored, and the dependency probability of the entire situation never fully assessed or vetted. So, intuitively, Kennedy, seeing how much *needed* to go right with an airstrike and the succeeding circumstances to avoid a complete global catastrophe, was skeptical about the airstrike option as a first choice.

Conclusively, after all deliberations were complete, there were two options, in all reality, on the table: blockade or attack with invasion. One offered expediency at the risk of incalculable consequences and backlash from the Soviet Union. The other offered a safer proposition, a two-way door decision, at the expense of immediate results and, thus, possibly putting the US at risk by allowing the missiles to become operational. The decision, then, came down to the President to make. In either choice, the administration would be "throwing down a card on the table in a game" which they didn't know the outcome.[127]

The Decision

At the final conclusion, the President chose to execute the blockade, at the time dubbed a quarantine because the term quarantine had fewer military connotations than the term blockade. The EXCOMM would succumb to the grim fact that it did, indeed, lack control over the events that would follow if the United States attacked Cuba. This, however, did not alleviate the stress felt by the committee upon execution of the blockade.

There were, at the time, still risks to be faced. Would the Soviet Union execute first strike capabilities, knowing that the crisis may well escalate to that point anyhow? Would they take Berlin in exchange, which would crumble the NATO alliance? Would the Soviets run the blockade? If they did, would the American Navy execute their blockade procedures and disable the Russians ships? If the Americans did that, what was the path of escalation from there?

The road ahead at the time the decision to execute a blockade was made was still very much unclear. But what was clear was that no military action was taken by the United States that required a prompt Soviet retaliatory response. This, in effect, left the United States with a wider range of options to employ in response to the blockade in order to find its way out of the predicament, in much off the spirit that the military theorist Hart had recommended as Kennedy wrote in 1960.

Why, then, is the decision to execute a blockade over an attack plus invasion considered a Minimum Viable Strategy? The first question we must answer is, "what exactly is strategy" again in order to determine whether the Kennedy administration was actually formulating "strategy" or where they simply planning tactical maneuvers or "setting a vision"? Let's first revisit the definition of strategy from *Playing to Win*:

> *Strategy is an integrated set of choices that uniquely position the firm in its industry to create sustainable advantage and superior value relative to the competition.*

This definition may sound like it only applies to the business world, but let's consider the Cuban Missile Crisis in the context of history. The essence of the Cuban Missile Crisis was to ensure that the United States maintained an unequal balance of power in its favor against the Communist Soviet Union by removing the nuclear weapons poised to become operational from Cuba. This was, in essence, a set of *how to win choices* made by the administration because of its set of *where to play choices*.

To explain further, the United States chose in the 1940s forward to pursue a strategy of Containment in areas thought to be susceptible to the influence of Communism around the world, looking to stop the aggressive or non-aggressive spread of Communism globally. This grand strategy of Containment, followed across multiple politically diverse presidential administrations and through four decades of policy making, is likely one of the most successful grand strategies in world history taken on by a country. The success of this grand strategy culminated with the fall of the Berlin wall in 1990.

Containment was, in essence, a *where to play* choice and multiple *how to win* choices were made by multiple presidents. Some of those choices include the Marshall Plan and the Berlin Airlift. Other hard choices made by presidents include deploying American soldiers to fight the invasion of South Korea from northern aggression as well as deploying soldiers to Vietnam in the 1950's and late 1960's to act as advisors to South Vietnam against North Vietnam's aggressive communist regime, later escalating into a full-scale war that the United States would engage in in the late 1960's and 1970's. And yet still was the space race, a strategic *where to play* and *how to win* choice where, in response to the launch of Sputnik by the Soviet Union, the United States chose to execute its Containment strategy by choosing to compete in space and winning in space by aggressively ramping up its space program through NASA and funding math and science education nationally.

The Cuban Missile Crisis was, therefore, yet another *how to win* choice required to be made based on the greater winning aspiration and *where to play* choices that were already made by the United States and Kennedy administration. It was a supporting part of the nation's Containment grand strategy, and tough choices needed to be made to ensure that the nation upheld its values of defending the free world from the spread of Communism.

What the *Playing to Win* framework does not provide when making these tough choices is a way of thinking about the different choices to be made and how to make the best choice to execute, in this case the how to win choice. There were multiple choices that the EXCOM considered seriously and were close to executing, and it was not entirely clear to the group as a whole, even when the decision was made to move forward, that the blockade was the best choice to be made at the time. Only in hindsight can we see, with the clarity of time, that this choice was the obvious and superior one. Hindsight is always and forever will be 20/20.

To revisit the definition of a Minimal Viable Strategy, I'll provide it below. Minimum Viable Strategy is defined by this book as:

the minimum required investment needed to be made to test strategic hypothesis by collecting real world operational and market data.

The blockade was, therefore, the minimum investment EXCOMM could make in terms of risk to the nation and to the world in order to test if Russia would give in to political pressure and, hence, remove the missiles from Cuba without subsequently attacking other areas of the globe, namely Berlin. Other investments considered required different hypothesis and different levels of risk for the same outcome. For example, the option to invade involved testing if Russia would retaliate with missiles on U.S. soil if American soldiers invaded Cuba after an extensive bombing campaign.

Both hypotheses were formulated to achieve the same outcome, the removal of the missiles from Cuba, but involved different levels of investment and different probabilities for potential outcomes. The first allowed for failure to a larger degree that the second option of invasion did not. The invasion strategy was an "all-in" option with no turning back, while the blockade allowed for some measure of failure on both the U.S. and Russian sides.

Thus, the blockade was executed and the missiles subsequently removed. By not invading, the U.S. allowed for the Soviets to extract the missiles while still allowing the Soviets to save "face" and not humiliate themselves in the process. Perhaps victory with a degree of respect for your adversary in politics and war is just as important as is the outcome of victory itself.

We will now transition away from the cases of war to the cases of business, where two world-class organizations prove how dramatically poor decision making can be in world-class organizations. We will explore the faults of the Target Canadian launch as well as the Lego experience with near-bankruptcy in the early 2000's.

TARGET CANADA

Target is a discount retailer founded in in 1902 by George D. Dayton in Minneapolis, Minnesota.[128] With almost 1800 stores as of 2017, the large retailer is known for its iconic red bull's eye logo. Target has sought to position itself against its competitors as a marketplace where consumers can find quality products at a discount price versus its direct competitor Wal-Mart, which is typically seen as a bit lower quality than Target. In 2014, the company operated, in addition to its stores, 40 distribution centers and employed 347,000 employees.[129]

The Target Corporation at the turn of the new millennium began to consider its options for expanding internationally. What seemed like a natural extension of its current competitive offering in the United States, Target made the decision to launch into Canada in January of 2011, where it "paid $1.8 billion to purchase the store leases of Canadian discount retail chain Zellers Inc. from the US investor who owned the Hudson Bay Co. assets."[130]

The expansion seemed like it could not fail. Canadians, in general, were already familiar with the Target brand and many Canadians surveyed had visited a Target store in the United States recently in a cross-border trip.131

It became clear how Target was assessing its strategy by answering its *where to play* and *how to win* choices. In January 2011, it made a deliberate choice on *where to play* by making a significant investment in leases that would eventually be its storefronts in Canada. In its successive *where to play* choices, Target would maintain its positioning as a retailer with quality brands at a discount price, however, despite some market trends amongst Canadian shoppers that indicated that this positioning might not give Target the most strength in that particular market.

With its subsequent *how to win* choices, however, Target would eventually make decisions that would ultimately lead to the demise of its Canadian strategy. Upon initiating the decision to launch to Canada, Target began to place its chips on the table in what amounted to an "all-in" strategy for its Canadian operation. It hired "27,000 new employees across Canada", a massive hiring phase for any major retailer.[132] In addition to the rapid employee expansion into Canada, Target would also unveil approximately 125 stores that would all open in less than one year, opening in "cycle openings of 24 stores every two months, as well as three distribution centers."[133]

Target Canada's Distribution Infrastructure

These new staff members and stores would all be supported by a distribution network in Canada that "differed significantly" from Target's distribution structure in the United States.[134] In the United States, Target operates "a total of 40 distribution centers scattered across the United States, including 26 regional DCs, four import warehouses, four food DCs and three dedicated Target.com DCs." [135] In addition, other steps in the distribution network, called import warehouses, helped to alleviate the DCs that played regional distribution roles from being overloaded with inventory that was not needed in the near term. [136]

Instead of operating its own distribution network, as it did in the United States, Target chose to outsource this portion of its supply chain network. The

DCs it outsourced operations to "employed around 1,500 people and were outsourced to a new third-party logistics partner, Eleven Points Logistics."[137] These three DCs operated across the country and served between 40-50 stores across Canada on a software system that differed from the system used by Target DCs in the United States.[138]

The different operating structure setup for Target Canada and the operational complexities it introduced to such a massive launch were major reasons why Target Canada inevitably failed to materialize into a successful venture for the conglomerate. The issues plaguing the distribution centers centered around inbound inventory flows, caused by higher than expected purchasing volume. This subsequently meant that inbound flows exceeded outbound flows due to constraints at the distribution centers because of data discrepancies.[139] The data discrepancies, the sources of which could not be identified, caused the processing of inventory upon arrival at the distribution centers to become the source of the bottleneck for inventory flows.

The fact that Target Canada operated on non-Target, unique operating systems was a core reason behind such data flow issues. These types of data discrepancies are not uncommon among distribution or warehousing launches, and are to be expected and worked through during any facility launch. However, because of the sheer scale of the Target Canada launch, the Target CEO at the time "admitted that Target's aggressive entry into Canada resulted in poor systems implementation and hastily made decisions.[140] These inventory flow issues in Target Canada's distribution network ultimately led to empty store shelves, which left a poor initial impression on the Target Customer during the early lifetime of Target Canada's retail experience, a vital time to satisfy customer needs during their first impression with the brand.

Target Value Proposition in Canada vs. US

Questions also arose if Target was the right fit for the Canadian consumer and if its positioning in the United States actually fit the mold for what worked for retailers in Canada. Because the U.S. and Canada share one of the most open borders in the world, and because Canadians and U.S. consumers share so many qualities, it is likely that many assumptions were made by Target going into the Canadian launch that, inevitably, turned out to not be true.

The first critical data point that would separate Canadians from Americans was the average amount each household spent on discretionary spending. "Americans spent an average of $17,900 per year in retail outlets compared to the average Canadian consumer who spent $17,000."[141] This difference did not position higher-than-average priced retailers in Canada to typically perform well.

Additionally, many of the prices in Target Canada were higher than what the cross-border shoppers saw for comparable products in the United States. "The company claimed the higher prices were due to higher duties, higher costs for transportation, and higher labor costs."[142]

The combination of all of these factors and others caused newly minted Target Corp. CEO Brian Cornell to announce the plan for Target to pull out of Canada in January of 2015, stating that he was "unable to find a realistic scenario in which the 133 store Target Canada would become profitable before at least 2021."[143] In the end, he said that the failure of the venture was due to the fact that Target had "missed the mark from the beginning by taking on too much too fast."[144]

What Could They Have Done Differently

When analyzing the failure of Target Canada, one must inevitably ask a series of questions when reviewing the strategy that Target used to employ in their Target Canada launch. Those questions could be:

• Was their demise inevitable?

- Could any strategy have worked for Target, or was the market for Canadian retail shoppers simply not prepared for the value proposition that Target had to offer?

- When asking the where to play questions, were they answering these correctly in a meaningful way?

- Was their how to win choices to blame?

It is clear that, indeed, better choices could have been made, but the Target executive team did clearly make what are considered, in a broader sense, tough, decisive, clear choices during their Canadian strategy formulation. They chose to play decisively in the Canadian retail market using a similar value proposition that had successfully worked for them in the United States in multiple markets that should have produced a comparable customer base to support a Canadian retail operation. Tough choices are, indeed, the prescription of the *Playing to Win* strategy doctrine and, in this case, it is clear that something more is needed in terms of strategy development to guide organizations, not just to make tough choices but to make wise choices.

What is unclear, however, is what exactly could have been done differently. A Minimum Viable Strategy approach asks for:

the minimum required investment needed to be made to test strategic hypothesis by collecting real world operational and market data.

Was, indeed, the Target Canada strategy approach the "minimum required investment" needed to test strategic hypothesis for international expansion to Canada? Some questions that clearly needed to be tested through strategic hypothesis establishment were:

- Does our value proposition work in the Canadian marketplace?

- Do the store locations we have chosen make sense from a market penetration standpoint?

- Will outsourcing our distribution work in the overall context of our operations network?

- Does signing with Starbucks over Tim Hortons to provide coffee work from a customer experience and strategic partnership standpoint?

These were critical questions that needed to be addressed, tested, and refined through real data collected with actual store launches. Certainly, models could have been built and assumptions could have been made, but, as Cadets at West Point are taught about military planning: *the plan is only as good until the first bullet is fired.*

This principle is a key part of the Minimum Viable Strategy approach. While Target, with its seemingly endless supply of resources and retail experience, thought the Canadian launch was a homerun, the Canadian consumer, on the other hand, did not think so. And unpredictable circumstances happened, as they do in almost all international expansions. However, because of the massive scale and speed of the "all-in" Target Canada launch, it was difficult to stop the freight train of the launch while it was already in motion.

The unstoppable freight train heading toward disaster is reminiscent of Kennedy during the Cuban Missile Crisis whom, during the crisis, feared unleashing a similar unstoppable train by approving the invasion of Cuba. His readings of the *Guns of August* influenced this "unstoppable train" thinking where the book argued that Germany, once the decision was made to invade France, could not reverse the decision during the First World War. The German Army literally transported their soldiers in trains that were set to rigorous departure schedules that had been rehearses time and again, waiting for the opportunity to execute it in the actual eventuality of war with France. Once the decision to invade had been given, the soldiers, whom had rehearsed the train departures so much, had executed the invasion strategy so quickly and efficiently that the invasion order could not be reversed by the Kaiser.

The decision to go into Canada at scale by Target, which began with the massive purchases of leases, enflamed a massive effort to support the "all-in" strategy that was conceived in a fixed position from the outset given the purchases of the leases. Thus, from the get-go, there was no flexibility baked into the Target Canada model. The purchases of leases created fixed positions that the company could not escape from. This ability to maneuver and change over time is key as learnings when operating in a new country develop, which, when doing so, will lead companies operating in these new spaces to have different ways of thought that drive rapid changes in company operations and expansion plans early on in the life-cycle of international expansion strategies.

Target Canada, therefore, did not have the room to fail tactically in this expansion plan. Once the leases were purchased and the decision had been made, and such a large capital investment had been exercised in pursuit of a massive launch into Canada, Target gave itself no room to change course in light of new developments during its Canadian experience. Franklin Roosevelt knew that the American Army needed this room to fail, which is why he avoided an invasion of Europe in 1942 and, instead, chose a less fortified position to gain data, gather learning, and build-up toward an eventual invasion in 1944. Target had no such room to fail in order to overcome learning curves in its Canadian launch.

This is not to say that the American Army short stepped its invasion of North Africa in 1942. This is not the case. Operation Torch and the invasion of North Africa in 1942 was at the time one of the largest invasion forces in human history. It was executed at a scale that the American Army knew would succeed given the presumable light resistance they faced during the invasion. However, the point is that they chose a strategy that was not a one-way door decision where, if they failed, they would be forced to retreat and perhaps lose their hopes of victory in Europe altogether.

Target, alternatively, took the "invasion of Europe" approach instead of looking toward executing on a few stores flawlessly. Had Target taken a more phased approach, it would have, after the learning had been collected on how to succeed in a few stores, been able to perhaps open additional stores in a more rapid cadence. Acceleration, in this case, was as, if not more important, than velocity.

Faults of "All-in" Strategies

What we have learned, therefore, is that there is a seemingly illogical thought that the Target Canada launch needed to be "all-in", and the critical question is why and was this necessary? Certainly, the opportunity to purchase leases for existing retail stores and remodel them offered Target the opportunity to launch stores at half-price compared to original construction. But at what cost did this come to the launch and the brand in the long-run?

What we learn from these examples is that often when jumping "all-in" too early, there are often too many problems that plague an organization to surmount and, thus, a choice to retreat is favorable than pushing forward, whereas a more gradual approach would allow for the tackling of one problem at a time and, thus, present a more clear picture of the road ahead.

LEGO: MVS IN REVERSE

Lego, a toy company founded in the throes of the great global economic depression in 1932 in Denmark by Ole Kirk Christiansen began producing brick building toys in the late 40's and specialized itself in creating toys for children who like the experience of building things themselves using the now famous Lego brick. The toy company, over the decades of refining its brand and product offering, quickly became a household favorite amongst both parents and children. For children, the pursuit of creation through the use of the Lego brick is an adventure, and for parents the educational qualities of construction are appealing versus other mind-numbing entertainment alternatives.

Lego, however, in the 1990's, after building up its trust and core brand amongst consumers, began to feel the onslaught of the coming wave of computers and video games into the lives of children, and the Lego executive team feared that computers and electronics would one day supplant the analog experiences of play that Lego provided. This feeling was not entirely unique to Lego in the toy industry nor was it unfounded as the percent of total play time from children began to increasingly turn to digital experiences versus the Lego style of analog systems of play.

Thus, Lego turned to the what the latest business consultants of the era were saying about how to achieve new levels of growth. They explored what David Robertson, the author of Brick by Brick, calls the "Seven Truths of Innovation". Lego's pursued a growth strategy with Blue Ocean Strategy constructs of thinking, implementing what was thought to be disruptive innovations, and opened up to the wisdom of the crowd.[145] However, this way of devising company strategy almost destroyed the company, leading it to near bankruptcy in 2003.

Today, Lego, under the leadership of CEO Jørgen Vig Knudstorp, has become one of the most successful, innovative, and largest toy companies in the world after promising in its post-bankruptcy scare that it would focus on niche opportunities to limit its risk exposure. In this chapter, we will explore how Lego was led astray by conventional and "modern" business consultant thinking, how it violated the principles of Minimum Viable Strategic thinking while executing its growth strategy using the "Seven Truths of Innovation", and how Knudstorp was able to bring Lego back from the brink.

Lego, during the time it feared that its time-honored brick would be supplanted by digital play experiences in the 1990s and early 2000s, began chasing the latest management fads that appeared in business consultant vernacular. Core to its approach, and its near downfall, was the thought that Lego needed to free the inspirational and creative power of its people by decentralizing new product decisions to lower levels of its management structure. It sought to allow its people more time to think creatively in the hopes they would achieve better product results. It looked to companies like Google, who at the time allowed for developers to spend 20% of their day working on self-directed projects, and companies like W.L. Gore, maker of Gore-Tex, which has a boss-free workplace.[146] These companies saw industry exceeding profit margins and growth comparative to their peers, so why couldn't a similar creative approach work for Lego the executives asked?

This creative energy that Lego sought to unlock by allowing more freedom for their designers to design creative things also played into another "truth" that Lego sought to aspire to execute and that was being sold by business consultants then and is still being peddled by folks looking to sell a seemingly novel idea. That "truth", one of Seven Truths that turned out to be deadly sins rather than truths, was that "relentless experimentation begets breakthrough innovation."[147] The business strategist Gary Hamel underlines this notion in The Future of Management where he asserts "Innovation is always a numbers game, the more of it you do, the better your chances of reaping a fat payoff."[148]

While the adage by Linus Pauling, or, rather, called the Pauling Principle, which implies that to have a good idea one needs to have a lot of ideas, certainly resonated with Lego, the problem was with the execution of that adage and the pursuit of multiple experiments is that it gradually destroyed the Lego operational discipline. When sales growth stopped, Lego sought to boost sales by increasing the number of products in its portfolio. After all, experimentation is the "prelude to progress."[149] This thinking, however, would almost kill the brand.

The number of toys Lego made from 1994 to 1998 tripled, despite being in business since the 30s. The end "result was a lot of business but very little good business."[150] The costs to produce these products rapidly increased with each new product offering, but the sales on those products flatlined.[151]

In addition to having a large increase in the number of products sold in a short period of time, Lego was also undisciplined in the execution of its production, which was a rooted in its increasing production costs. Lego executives, when researching why the company had gone astray, "discovered that over the years, as new products represented a larger amount of annual revenues, newer-generation Lego sets had become more elaborate while providing little profit in return."[152]

The designers responsible for the rapid increase in new products were creating these new products without regard for operating costs, and the increase in the number of unique bricks needed to create these products rose. The production costs rose because these unique bricks often required new molds to build, which costs upwards of $50,000 per brick, and the increase in suppliers required to manage the corresponding increase in the brick portfolio made the Lego supply chain increasingly complex and difficult to manage, increasing costs.[153]

But Lego was innovating and pursuing Blue Ocean markets, as the consultants and the latest business trends led them to do. The problem, however, was that Lego's execution of a large number of experiments and Blue Ocean markets was not coupled with the discipline required by a business to do it well. Indeed, Blue Ocean strategy went "against making incremental improvements to existing products and, instead, pushed businesses to swim for the open water in untapped market spaces. Blue oceans are vast markets unsullied by cut-throat competition."[154]

What Lego ultimately realized in the execution of its Blue Ocean strategy and its attempts to allow for the creative energy to be released from its designers is that the experiences and management practices of companies like Google and W.L. Gore that do allow for so-called 20% time are not easily replicable. In fact, for many companies, including Lego, "building a newfangled innovation model from the ground up - while struggling to nail quarterly performance targets and fend off competitors - is not a viable option."[155]

In addition to trying to replicate the management practices and strategic approaches to design and innovation, Lego attempted to aggressively scale out new technology capabilities in order to compete in the new digital world. The new project, dubbed the "Darwin Project", was an ambitious effort to replicate the Lego style of play in the digital world in minute and precise detail while also cataloguing the entire suite of Lego bricks in this so-called digital platform of Darwin.

This projected was a huge "all-in" investment made by Lego and required enormous amounts of capital to recruit and staff the project. It also required large sums of investment to purchase the Silicon Graphics computers needed to create the 3D Lego models in the precise detail required by Lego.[156] In fact, this installation of Silicon Graphics computers was one of the largest made in Northern Europe at the time, which to many observers and perhaps to Lego itself should have been a warning that it was venturing dangerously outside of its core capabilities as a business and sailing in waters it had no experience in before.

Lego, in a more aggressive move to push into new business categories and Blue Oceans, began to open theme parks and retail stores at the same time it was also building out its Darwin Project and unleashing its designers to "make stuff happen" by designing at the speed that rapid innovation would allow. Lego made a number of "big bets" in just a short amount of time, only a couple of years, in multiple new business ventures and, ultimately, it "lost its focus and discipline and if only a couple of those bets went bad, everything would come crashing down."[157]

The rapid opening of theme parks and retail stores were cash drains on the business due to the high capital requirement of operating such physical customer experience platforms, and the unprofitable theme parks and attention-requiring retail stores only compounded the lack-luster performance of the other major projects Lego sought to pursue. These projects, bold, aggressive, and everything that consultants of the times said Lego should do, ultimately starved it of the capital required to innovate with products that it historically succeeded at selling as well as caused Lego to lose focus. Had they launched just theme parks, or just retail stores, or focused on rapid product experimentation in tandem with controlling its supply chain, perhaps it would have not only had the managerial focus required to succeed, but also the capital necessary to climb the steep hill of learning curves.

Lego also, as previously mentioned, not only lacked the focus to manage any one of these, but also lacked the managerial system. When one of these "big bets" went south, it didn't realize it until it was too late.

As David Robertson puts the problem faced with such rapid innovation in multiple, untested waters by both Lego and other companies in general: "Big, bold moves often come with the risk of a long-term slide, even when the early results are positive."[158] Although more sales did, indeed, come with a pursuit of the "Seven Truths" of innovation, the costs simply took off exponentially in comparison to those sales. These costs not only consisted of hard capital expenditures, but also talent acquisitions in order to pursue these growth efforts, an expense often under-forecasted by companies looking to expand to new markets or new business categories.

In many ways, the euphoria and push to move into Blue Ocean markets was not only fear-based motivation from the coming of video games and computers into children's play experiences, but also brought on by the success of Lego Star Wars, a licensing deal between the Toy Maker and the mega-blockbuster sci-fi film series. The Lego Star Wars themed sets, which almost were not approved due to the conservative nature of the Lego executives at the time, outstripped sales forecasts enormously. This success caused Lego to beholden itself to Chancellorsville syndrome, a concept described by Civil War Author James McPherson as the tendency for people and organizations to base future success on recent past performance as experienced by General Robert E. Lee at the Battle of Gettysburg.

As *Brick by Brick* describes the mood of the time: the success of Star Wars told Lego executives to keep expanding into new areas instead of "researching and tackling them one at a time."[159] Perhaps the initial reluctance to do the deal with Star Wars to begin with should have been a warning to the executives that Lego wasn't structured at the time to innovative rapidly and to expand into multiple Blue Oceans simultaneously.

The Lego team did not see, or chose not to see, the coming storm. There was no major Star Wars movie on the horizon in the early 2000's, yet the euphoria of growth by Star Wars amongst executives remained a fundamental false assumption that the executive team and clearly many other members of the organization made: that past performance was indicative of future success.

Once sales did slow, cash became constricted and problems surfaced after a few years of losses. One member of the Lego's strategic planning team, Jørgen Vig Knudstorp, not yet CEO at the time, sought to find out how did it all happen and, more importantly, how to fix it all.

Knudstorp, during his research, found a number of areas with severe lack of discipline in key areas of the business, especially those having to do with cost control. He found that its supply chain was "dysfunctional" and that, because designers did not "grasp the business implications" of their new-found creativity, the costs of goods sold were continually increasing.[160]

Had Lego maintained a solid financial management toolkit to track these trends, it might have been able to nip it in the bud before it got out of hand, but because the profit and loss statements were "fractured", there was no clear financial accountability across the organization. [161] In essence, Lego did not truly know where it's money came from specifically, and they couldn't identify why the theme parks were such a cash drain on the business.[162]

Looking back, it is clear in retrospect that Lego's near decline, according to Knudstorp, was caused by three basic problems:[163]

- A belief that Lego could sell more than it actually could
- A complex supply chain and product portfolio caused by overly creative design teams
- A movement away from brick based products

One assessment of the failure also proclaimed that Lego did not "pace its innovations" enough to let them succeed or fail. By doing everything at once, it bled its balance sheet, especially when attempting to do stores and theme parks at the same time. Despite the losses, however, the euphoria continued.

The theme parks kept losing money, but executives wanted to continue to build more.[164] In the end, the company did not realize that it was "delusional to think it could tackle retail and theme parks at the same time."[165] They didn't realize that a measured approach allowed for risk reduction versus the all-in strategy they were taking at the time, and even after they did go "all-in", they were too content with business-unit failure and too reluctant to cut off the units after they bled the company dry.[166]

Knudstorp was, in essence, attempting to "stop the bleeding" of cash so Lego could survive another day.[167] The dramatic pullback on these "innovation projections", supply chain reorganization, and organizational realignment helped to focus the company.

The Turnaround

Lego's turnaround is a true testament to the effects of good business management. After pulling back from the brink of bankruptcy, "between 2004 and 2010, revenue grew by 139%"[168] The start of the turnaround began when Knudstorp assembled his team of executives to begin looking at all aspects of LEGO supply chain operations.[169]

When he discovered that new Lego sets had too many unique parts, he set limits as to how many new parts each set could contain, thus constraining the design team from creating incredibly complex supply chain operations inadvertently through "good ideas." This practice also helped increase inventory turns as well as improve profitability for each new product launch as new custom piece molds did not need to be built as often as they were in the past, a huge part of previous set costs. This "framework" for innovation set boundaries on designers and grounded their thought processes in the realities of business, which, as I've also seen at the Honest Company, can be a challenging thing to do.

Assessing Asia: MVS in Practice

After CEO Knudstorp turned around the Lego brand and built its profitability and growth to a healthy base, Lego began looking at additional global market opportunities to expand its base market of Western Europe and the United States. The executive team began looking at the growing opportunity in Asia and how to hedge against the vast uncertainties of growth in the market for the brand while still looking to take advantage of the market opportunity. While the marketing research "forecasted that Asian toy markets were set to grow rapidly in the next five years," there has always been an air of skepticism about Asian forecasts, especially given Lego's irrational exuberance and near-bankruptcy experiences of the early 2000s.[170]

The crux of the question for Lego in how to approach the market came from how to enter it from an investment perspective. In 2012, when making the assessment, Lego was operating with a distributor model, which reduced the investment Lego needed to make in order to sell goods to these markets (essentially they sent goods to a distributor, who later sold them to stores).[171] Lego's benchmark for making a capital investment to switch to a "direct sales model" was $5M US in sales, operating under the assumption that Lego employees could operate better and more efficiently than the companies it outsourced its distribution to.[172]

To approach the question of an Asian strategy, Lego devised a "three-stage strategy", which was composed of the following steps:

1. The company would first set up its own distribution centers, outsourced to third-party logistics providers. The goal of this step was to build up its inventory levels in the regions it projected sales growth while also shortening "lead times to local customers."[173]

2. Second, Lego would set up its own "packing facility" in Asia in order to stage more unfinished goods and, hence, be more flexible when it

produced finished goods and when it delivered them to market. This strategy allowed for them to carry less inventory in the region.

3. Third, the Lego group would, "depending on the successes" of the Asia market, consider "building a factory in the region."[174]

The crux of the strategy was centered around forecast uncertainty, a classic Fog of Forecast problem we discussed earlier in the book. According to the Lego executives, "In order to supply the most optimistic sales forecasts in Asia," Lego would need "to build costly new capacity for warehousing, packaging, and - possibly - molding. However, what if the Asian market stagnated and Lego products didn't sell as much as expected?"[175] This outcome would be, according to Lego senior executives, "catastrophic".[176] Or, as one executive put it:

We're about to invest billions of Danish kroners in infrastructure over there. And we want to keep all our manufacturing in-house. What if we're to invest in all this and then just have the same market that we have today? It just wouldn't pay off for us. As a company, I would say we're much better at scaling up than down.[177]

Indeed, the problem is magnified greatly when looking at the Asian near-term forecast "uncertainty", for there, which a Lego executive at the time put it, was at least a 30% variance from the projected forecast in either direction.[178] When assessing the situation, it is clear that this variation in forecast, should it play out against Lego's favor, would further exacerbate the inherent problems associated with pouring large amounts of capital into building out an in-house distribution and manufacturing operation in Asia to meet these uncertain forecasts.[179]

It is clear that Lego learned lessons from the early 2000's and were taking a phased, measured approach to entering a new, untested, and uncertain market. They were, in short, using Minimum Viable Strategy techniques toward entering a new market by making a minimum investment through setting up third-party distribution channels, testing hypotheses regarding market demand, and then leveraging up when the hypothesis proved true or having the operation leverage down if the hypothesis did not prove out.

The three-phased approach baked in maximum flexibility and avoided an "all-in" strategy, which would have alternatively been to make the assumption that demand forecasts for Lego were accurate and, therefore, the first step should be to produce the manufacturing capacity right from the start to reduce costs of the venture in order for it to be more financially viable in the short run. The risks, however, of the investment outweighed the potential rewards of the savings, and Lego was willing to incur higher variable supply chain costs in early phases to allow for the flexibility of pulling back if necessary at reduced expense as to not materially affect the business.

As it turned out, Lego did see the growth it forecasted in Asia, with near "double-digit growth in 2013."[180] A new manufacturing and distribution facility in China were in planning stages in early 2015 in order to meet the growing demand.[181] This facility is scheduled to open in 2017, complementing similar facilities in Denmark, the Czech Republic, Mexico, and Hungary.

This factory that the team committed to would be a $600M investment that would service and be located in Asia, specifically Jiaxing, China and will be completed in 2017. It is designed to be 800,000 sq. feet, with the capability of scaling up to 1.3M sq. ft. In order to mitigate against demand risk, the team also put in place plans to scale-down construction and withdraw from the site if necessary.[182]

In summary, as we can see in the Lego case study, the company made a number of "big bets" in the early 2000's under false assumptions that aggressive growth would continue into the near term, only to find those assumptions not prove to be an accurate, realistic world view. After pulling back from the brink, Lego began to take a more measured approach to strategy, specifically with Asia, where it made minimum investments to test market hypothesis regarding demand before putting large amounts of capital into the Asia project. Their actions are in line with Minimum Viable Strategy, and both their departure from sound business practices and turnaround are clear lessons for leaders looking on how to make solid *where to play* and *how to win* choices in today's business environment.

DEVELOPING AN MVS

Now that we have developed strategies to identify opportunities to implement a Minimum Viable Strategy approach through studying cases where its implementation either was used unknowingly or should have been used deliberately, we will now approach the process of developing a Minimum Viable Strategy. We will explore what the process is like and what questions need to be asked.

The first and most obvious question is, "How do you know when the situation calls for a Minimum Viable Strategy approach? When do I use Minimum Viable Strategy and when should it not be used?" To answer these questions, let's review the cases described in previous chapters to come to some conclusions.

For a military and political perspectives, both the Cuban Missile Crisis case study and the Franklin Roosevelt case study involved leaders who were confronted with a single, major decision point in regards to how to employ force to affect change in the current world situation. For both, it was not a matter of "if" but "how" and "to what extent" should they do it. There was no "GO / NO GO" decision for these leaders, but, rather, how to go. A decision needed to be made.

It is this single decision point characteristic that continues to repeat itself and, while this is a general indicator of a situation where Minimum Viable Strategy can be employed, it is not required. The reason that these specific cases involve instances when Minimum Viable Strategy is appropriate is because in the instances when their decisions came down to a single inflection point the decision makers were faced with a number of options, mainly "all-in" types of options along with other less risky alternatives.

These "all-in" options for these leaders were points of no return for the situation and, in a deeper way, for the world. Kennedy's "all-in" option was an attack on the missiles in Cuba followed by invasion, which was a serious consideration at the time of the crisis and had significant merits as an alternative to the eventually chosen path of a blockade. But the drawbacks of irreversible consequences were too much for the Kennedy cabinet to justify, and a different approach was chosen. But invasion was, as some would argue, expedient and the only sure guarantee for missile removal, making it an attractive option for many of the leaders in the initial cabinet sessions of the crisis.

For Roosevelt, his "all-in" alternative was the invasion of Europe in 1942, a choice that his military chiefs, mainly his Secretary of War and General Marshall, were strong advocates of. This choice, however, was an "all-in" choice as it would require all military resources the Allies could muster to that point to make a European beachhead landing successful and, if it failed due to high German resistance, the failure could have spelt significant setbacks and peril for the Allies and would have hindered greatly their chances at winning the war in a few years, if at all.

For military situations and instances when a Minimum Viable Strategy approach could be used, the scenarios are clear but more needs to be done to explain further when a Minimum Viable Strategy approach is appropriate. For example, some may ask if a Minimum Viable Strategy approach would have been appropriate in June 1944 on D-Day, where the Allies landed millions of men on the beaches of Normandy during the largest invasion in human history. This thinking is false, and this book will explore in greater detail why this is so, when a Minimum Viable Strategy approach is and is not useful, and further when to identify those instances and how to execute a Minimum Viable Strategy as expected.

For business situations, however, where the weight of the world does not hinge on a single battle, or a series of beachhead landings, or a confrontation with a formidable nuclear superpower, the choices and options to pursue a Minimum Viable Strategy are typically much clearer. Jim Collins calls this approach of collecting data his "Fire Bullets Then Cannonballs" approach, but he does not tie this approach back to a broader framework of strategy, which we do here in this book.[183]

These business situations are typically those in which the business wants to expand into new markets, new channels, or new product categories. The Minimum Viable Strategy approach should not be confused with the Minimum Viable Product approach, where empirical data is collected by a startup on a new product, quick feedback is obtained, and changes are made in an agile way in order to reduce risk by reducing the time invested in developing a product early that may or may not have market opportunity.

A Minimum Viable Strategy approach, on the other hand, focuses on getting feedback on specific activities. While an MVP (Minimum Viable Product) is product focused, MVS (Minimum Viable Strategy), is activity focused. For example, such activities that should have been analyzed by the Target Canada team would be key performance indicators of their outsourced third-party logistics providers in comparison to their own proprietary distribution channels. By taking a softer approach and only launching a very limited line of stores first to gain empirical data on these activities would Target Canada have been able to understand and root cause the issues driving the poor performance of this particular activity.

Developing a Minimum Viable Strategy

Minimum Viable Strategy, as has been described earlier, is part of an overall framework of strategic formulation and, thus, should be viewed in the context of developing a broader business strategy. We draw this framework from *Playing to Win* as we believe it provides the best, most straightforward framework for key leaders to understand and execute upon. Minimum Viable Strategy acts as a means to supplement that thinking by assisting the managerial activities that *Playing to Win* does not provide thorough guidance on, as well as the decision-making process where managers need to make "tough choices" and "strategic tradeoffs" while pursuing business opportunities.

The *Playing to Win* framework can also be used in military and political settings as a process for setting strategy and grand strategy for armies and nations. It seeks to ask questions first about the current situation and, to a large degree, focuses leaders into a particular set of directions and choices. It was clear to me as a soldier in Afghanistan in 2009, serving on behalf of the American Army, that a similar framework could and should have been used by our national leaders at the time to formulate and distribute a winning strategy that made sense to ground-level soldiers and could be executed upon and extrapolated from.

Instead, military leaders study Clausewitz, Liddell Hart, Sun Tzu, and use their principles of war to guide their strategic thinking. The problem with studying these strategic philosophers is that they provide silos of thought about war, pitfalls to avoid, and specific, often tactical ways to win against an enemy. What they do not provide is a framework on how to formulate military and political strategy that can be executed against by large organizations. They are, instead, subsets of answers to questions on *how to win*, not complete strategic frameworks in their own right. The framework we attempt to provide in this book seeks to provide that framework.

Thus, we will recap the questions that need to be asked from a broader strategic standpoint. Those are:[184]

1. What is a business's winning aspiration?
2. Where does the business want to play?
3. How does the business want to win?
4. What capabilities and management systems are required to win?

It is typically in questions 2 and 3 that businesses begin to face tough choices. For example, Target, when considering its Canadian market approach, would have answered that it wants to play in Canada and its winning aspiration is to have a dominant market share of the Canadian retail space in a similar light that it does in the United States. These are fine winning aspirations and answers to *where to play*.

However, it appears that Target, as mentioned earlier, failed to properly answer the *how to win choice* by making an "all-in", "one-way" door decision when it should have taken a more phased approach to its how to win strategy. But *Playing to Win* encourages us to make tough choices. Target did this, but *Playing to Win* and other strategic books do not discourage companies from making fatal tough choices when other approaches could have been used instead.

How do we, then, ensure that when making tough choices that those choices do not, as in the case of Target Canada, put the company at significant, existential risk? We must first look at how we can define "winning" at a more tactical level in terms of business activities to know how not to put the organization at significant risk. Only by knowing why it is that the organization can win when answering *how to win* at a tactical level can it know if it can realistically make a choice that can move it in the direction of its winning aspiration while not betting the house on an untested strategy.

When answering the *how to win* question, companies need to know what key performance indicators actually drive winning. What, then, do they want to measure? What is winning for a country in battle against a rival? What is winning for Kennedy in the Cuban Missile Crisis? Not at a macro-level as is defined by the winning aspiration of the business strategy, but at a micro-level. Each activity the business undergoes must have a means of measuring overall success that then builds toward the overall success of the winning aspiration for, if strategy is a sum of a business's unique activities that deliver unique and long-term sustainable strategy to customers, then they must have a means of measuring those particular activities for the long-term to ensure enduring success.

For military strategists and political leaders formulating a Minimum Viable Strategy, the questions are similar. How does each activity (each battle, engagement, beach landing) measure against our idea of what winning looks like for that particular activity? Did we improve from one battle to the next? How did we improve? What did we learn from the last battle? These are questions that a *how to win* approach using Minimum Viable Strategy must ask.

Thus, knowing these things, we are proposing the following framework that builds on the *Playing to Win Strategy* for strategic formulation for business leaders. The following questions must, therefore, be asked:

1. What is a business's winning aspiration?

2. Where does the business want to play?

    a. How is this *where to play* answer different than where the business is currently playing?

    b. What factors are driving the differences, if any, for the change in course for where to play choices?

3. How does the business want to win?

a. What are our *strategic hypothesis* based on our where to play and how to win choices?

b. What are the specific activities the business performs today that make it successful?

i. What are the key performance indicators of success for those activities?

ii. How do we know those key performance indicators are measuring the right level of success?

iii. Are these key performance indicators for each activity right level of success for our winning aspirational goal?

c. What are the specific activities the business must perform in the future in order to be successful against its currently formulated winning aspirational goal and where to play questions?

i. What are the key performance indicators for these activities that we must meet to win?

ii. How do we measure these key performance indicators regularly and accurately?

iii. Why do these key performance indicators tie back to winning for the business?

d. What are the minimum number of data points I need to validate in order to provide feedback to my where to play and how to win choices?

i. What are the minimum resources required to collect these data points for the business in order to drive better decision making with further capital investments?

This last question is perhaps the most critical. Did Target need to launch so aggressively into Canada? Would only a few stores have helped it shape a better approach over the long-term in Canada versus trying to strive for a short-term, sloppy victory at such great cost?

These are the questions that must be asked to both select a Minimal Viable Strategy approach and to make the proper selection during strategy formulation. Both are difficult processes to consider, but as we have discovered in this book, the consequences of selecting the wrong approach can be dire.

Strategy development, as we will learn later, however, is an iterative process that must be done regularly with doers who are the thinkers. As a plan is only as good until the first shot is fired in battle, so too is it for strategy. As we will discuss in the next chapter, leader selection to both formulate and execute our strategy, whether it is a Minimum Viable Strategy or not, is key to organizational success.

Sustaining Minimum Viable Strategy

While we now have an idea of what Minimum Viable Strategy looks like in terms of developing its core structure for your organization, we now must create a structure to iteratively learn, change, and execute on that strategy for the long-run. What must be understood before beginning this specific segment of our journey is that it is important for the strategist and the leader to understand that the question of how one will perform at the first go of this is not one where the answer should be guessed upon. The executor of a new strategy, especially when it pertains to performing new functions or entering new markets for an organization, will more than likely fail, or at least fail to meet initial high expectations. This should not cause an organization to recede from venturing out to try new things or to develop strategies to compete for the long-run, however. For, as William McKnight, former 3M chairman, once said "The best and hardest work is done in the spirit of adventure and challenge...Mistakes will be made."[185]

Here, then, are the specific executable activities that need to happen to develop and maintain a Minimum Viable Strategy, listed below:

Step 1: Formulate a Strategic Hypothesis

Organizations will need to form a strategic hypothesis that requires testing in order to develop an overarching how to win approach. If we dig deeper into the Target Canada case study, we can formulate what could have been a strategic hypothesis for the organization by saying:

> If Target opens a store in Canada, its performance will be financially comparable to that of an average Target store operated in the United States.

This If/Then statement allows for us as strategists to have a cause and effect scenario to measure against. We expect that if we operate a single store in Canada as Target, it can achieve financial success comparable to that of an American store. Financial success is important to us as it allows for us to commonly measure this store against other American stores, helping us to determine the Target project's financial viability.

Lastly, the organization needs to align on what the hurdle metric is for the experiment, or what it considers to be a "success" in a more specific way. This benchmark should ideally be set at the outset of the investment. For example, such questions to identify what this hurdle metrics is for the Target example could have been, "Does the store need to reach a certain operating margin?" Once all members of an organization are aligned on specifically what figure identifies success in the investment, next steps can be taken to identify how to capture the data required to measure the hypothesis.

Step 2: Identify the Data Needed to Be Collected

We require data in order to measure hypothesis. Feelings and emotions have no place in our analysis. As strategists, we must ward off against the use of hyperbole or anecdotes by others in our organization with "experience" or who have "spoke with a customer", where   qualitative metrics take precedence over quantitative.   While it is important to have qualitative metrics that validate data, generally, the reverse should not be true. Qualitative metrics should not be extrapolated by an organization to make broad assumptions in the place of data.

Instead, we must coldly look at data to inform decisions.   To make data-driven decisions, however, we must first identify what is important to collect.

The data in need of collection against our Target Canada strategic hypothesis are simple.   To measure the financial performance of the store, we require sales and operating expenses, which might also require some synthesizing as operating a single store in Canada might mean higher variable costs to some degree, but these assumptions should be made transparent to leaders making critical decisions.

Regardless of what the data is, it is important that the organization be aligned on what data needs to be collected and a clear owner, proper nouns are better in these cases, are identified for whom will collect and report on this data on a regularly scheduled cadence.   Ambiguities in execution always result in failure.

Step 3: Identify the Hurdle Metric

In finance, a hurdle metric is defined as:

> *"the minimum rate of return on a project or investment required by a manager or investor. The hurdle rate denotes appropriate compensation for the level of risk present; riskier projects generally have higher hurdle rates than those that are deemed to be less risky."*[186]

For our purposes, we define the hurdle metric as what the set of data needs to tell us, the organization, in order to validate or invalidate the hypothesis.

For example, FDR's hurdle metric would have been succeeding in battle against the Germans by 60 days of having been in North Africa for Operation Torch. For Target, it could have been a certain revenue metric in a single store launched in Target had they approached the Canada launch with a Minimum Viable Strategy approach.

The hurdle metric should be what is considered "success" given the data collected, which should inform the organization intuitively about how the new venture, project, business, or campaign is doing at a fundamental level. It is a "hurdle" because it is a bar set that must be met or overcome to be a considered "success" and a performance less than the hurdle is met with skepticism about a viable way forward for long-term success.

Step 4: Collect & Validate Data Needed for Hypothesis Validation

Organizations must ensure that they have the proper tools to collect data before embarking on measuring a strategic hypothesis. All too often, organizations lack these capabilities and fail to articulate in retrospect if an initiative failed or succeeded. Being clear about how exactly, at a minute tactical level, this will happen in real life in terms of data collection is critical for a successful strategic hypothesis testing.

For our Target example, it is assumed that a large organization has these financial reporting capabilities. It is the job of the leader, however, to ensure the right questions are asked so that false assumptions are not made and that proper noun individuals are assigned the task of making sure data collection happens on a regularly scheduled cadence.

Step 5: Routinize Data Review Sessions

The process of learning, and of testing hypothesis, is an iterative process that begins with a review of the data. Often, collecting the data is the easy part. Most organizations have more data than they know what to do with.

The difficult part of data collection is determining what is important and what is not. Organizations must make deliberate choices on what metrics to improve, how to measure those metrics, and what the appropriate amount of time is to review those metrics and whom is the specific, proper noun owner of that metric that will be held accountable for it.

Once example of this routinizing of data review sessions is at Best Buy branded stores in China, which, in 2009, were not performing well. Kal Patel, who was head of Best Buy's Asia Operations at the time, "pushed the store managers to make a lot of changes - new layouts, ways of working with suppliers, and pricing models, and instituted weekly unit meetings. 'On Friday mornings, we'd have a review: What did you set out to learn? What did you learn? What is it costing you?"[187]

These meetings with Patel were not long, 10 minutes or so, but they weren't intended to be. They were in the spirit of the Agile Management way of thinking, which this book will go into detail and argue that leaders should adopt, even in non-software environments, to manage Minimum Viable Strategic approaches to business.

This approach ensures that leaders don't wait for strategic review sessions every quarter, which can be damming to wait to make strategic choices so infrequently about the business. If things are going sound, that data is transparent and decisions can be made quickly to correct.

The point of this step is to, however, ensure leaders set a regularly scheduled timeframe (daily, weekly, bi-weekly) to review data collected and determine takeaways and next steps. Without this data collection review, those that are held accountable for collecting the data will inevitably not see the fruits of their labor and will lose the rigor required for its collection.

For the Target example, I would have expected executives to review costs and sales figures weekly to track the store's performance against its American peers. Questions such as, "Are these the right metrics, is the data accurate, and is this enough to validate or invalidate our hypothesis" should be asked in these regular reviews.

Step 6: Validate or Invalidate the Hypothesis

The data collection and review now being solidly in place, it is time to now measure the hypothesis. This data, ideally collected through either business experiments or small "bets", needs to validate or invalidate the hypothesis. This step should be relatively straightforward if A) everyone agreed to what the hurdle metrics for success was at the beginning of the hypothesis and B) everyone agrees on the validity of the data. Leaders need to ensure that at this point everyone agrees and is aligned around if the hypothesis was validated or invalidated given the data.

Step 7: Repeat as Necessary

At this point, a hypothesis is either validated and next steps can be taken to either A) add additional investment and, thus, expand the strategic hypothesis B) decide more time is needed to validate or invalidate the hypothesis or C) decide that enough data has been collected and that the hypothesis was invalidated, prompting a pull back of the investment

If the hypothesis is validated, new hypothesis are formed such as "Can Target operate multiple stores successfully in Canada that operate financially sustainable comparable to American stores?" We've thus expanded our hypothesis to include multiple stores instead of one, expanding the level of investment and the scope of the "bet". Such is the nature of Minimum Viable Strategy: a continually focused effort to prove or disprove hypothesis in a measured, controlled way that moves the ball forward continuously and aggressively toward achieving a larger vision of how to win through allowing for decisions to be made clearly using data-driven methodologies.

Routinize Forecast Review Sessions

A critical part of strategy sustainment is to not only reviewing data and testing hypothesis, but also the act of reviewing the forecasts for sales, revenues, expenses, or other metrics that were used to develop the strategy is equally critical as these serve as basic assumptions for strategy. In essence, many of these forecasts are a prediction of the direction of an organization or the macro-trends impacting the organization; thus, the organization should review how well its prediction capabilities are or if the confidence levels of those predictions have changed dramatically.

Many organizations never complete this task, despite putting a "great deal of energy into making predictions year after year." This book suggests, as the authors of *Your Strategy Needs a Strategy* write, to review regularly the "accuracy of your forecasts" with objection and rigor, but also for businesses to look at "to what extent companies in your industry change relative position in terms of revenue, profitability, and other performance measures." *Your Strategy Needs a Strategy* suggests measuring macro-trends in the industry, the rate at which companies are growing, how they are innovating, and how technology in the industry is changing the status quo of how businesses compete.[188]

Routinizing these forecast and competitor review activities takes mere discipline on behalf of the organization, as does the Minimum Viable Strategy approach. It requires the discipline and grit of leaders to set deadlines, identify information to be collected, assign and prioritize that information, and put a date on the calendar that, come hell or high water the organization will meet to discuss what has changed about the organization, its environment, and its competitors. Without leaders that have the discipline to sustain this regularized type of review, then this analysis will become outdated a couple of months after it is first complete.

How to Define the Minimum Resources Required

As you may have already come to understand, a big part of developing a Minimum Viable Strategy, after the data points that need to be collected have already been identified, is to answer the following question:

ii. What are the minimum resources required to collect these data points for the business in order to drive better decision making with further capital investments?

To help answer this question, we first must determine what our strategic options are for minimizing risk in order to determine what the "minimum resources" required are. This is an extremely critical part of successfully formulating a Minimum Viable Strategy because it is the root of where "all-in" strategy and Minimum Viable Strategy differentiate from one another.

While "all-in" strategies such as the Target Canada model rely on forecasting predictability, those believers in a form of Minimum Viable Strategy believe that "in times of rapid change, forecasts become obsolete almost as soon as the ink dries on them."[189] Thus, Minimum Viable Strategists rely on looking for the investments that their organizations are willing to consider failures the minute they are executed upon, which implies that their cost and effort will not ultimately affect the overall chances of success in the long-term for the organization.[190]

This approach is, therefore, a way for organizations to "test the waters, conserve capital and delay final decisions until the tea leaves become clearer."[191] These small bets help companies to hedge their risk, to test hypothesis in new areas of operations, and if, for example, if the new bet is an acquisition, to integrate the new company more quickly into the larger than an otherwise larger merger would have, reaping faster payoffs.[192]

These strategic options are, inevitably, a series of trade-offs that must be considered. These trade-offs are between a company's capital and its current internal capabilities to execute strategy, measured on a scale that looks at its risk potential to the organization. To make this comparison and to formulate strategic options for minimizing risk, we look at the Capability to Capital Investment Ratio.

Capability to Capital Investment Ratio (C2CIR)

Many of these small bets will require capabilities to execute that an organization simply doesn't have the ability to manage, which is something to consider when arranging strategic options on the table and weighing the costs and benefits of each. But this is the point. Reducing the size of such bets and, perhaps, capabilities is the most important aspect of investment consideration for organizations, sometimes more than cost.

If Ford decides it wants to build a large car factory in Kentucky, this is not an "all-in" bet as it has plenty of capability experience in car manufacturing and the Capability to Capital Investment Ratio is high. What this means is that Ford has a long history of manufacturing cars in the United States and that the experience it can expect in Kentucky is relatively close to that of its experiences in other parts of the United States. Therefore, it has a high capability score (on a scale of 1-10 it would be a 10).

Ford's capital investment rate on a scale of 1-10 would be a 5. Capital investment is relative to what level of risk the company can withstand given its current business operations and risk profile. Given this is a medium level of investment for the company versus its on-hand cash and cash flows, it is assigned a 5.

Thus, taking the capability rating of 10 over the capital investment rating of 5 gives the risk profile of this investment a 2. This means that, given the company's current capabilities, it has a reasonable chance of success given the risk of the investment.

Minimum Viable Strategy needs to be employed, therefore, in situations where this ratio gets closer or below 1. If Ford wanted to build and sell airplanes for commercial industry, its capabilities rating would be closer to a 3, perhaps, and, given a high level of investment versus the company's risk profile, the capital investment would probably be a 10 for airplane manufacturing infrastructure. This would place the investment's capability to capital investment ratio at 0.3.

This 0.3 can be seen as relative odds of success. Thus, a 1 would mean there is an equal chance of success as there is of failure, a 1:1 odds. A 0.3 would mean that the risk of failure is higher than that of success. A 2 would mean that a company is twice as likely to succeed as it is to fail.

In this scenario where for had a 0.3 risk level when going into plane manufacturing, we should pursue a Minimum Viable Strategy approach as our capabilities match or are less than the level of capital investment required. It is an indication that a phased approach is required given the relatively high level of risk involved.

This is not scientific nor is it meant to be. It is a tool for leaders to think about the world in non-scientific terms. Net Present Value calculations were surely used for the Target Canada launch, and surely, they showed a positive NPV over the long-term. Too often these numeric only analyses only focus on figures that contain deep-rooted assumptions about organizational capabilities and cannot account for what cannot be quantified: the ability for a leader to synthesize, given their experience, what an organization is and is not capable of doing well today versus what it can reasonably do well tomorrow.

There is no exact science for coming up with the capability score or the relative capital investment risk level score. This is not the point. The point is that this serves as a framework of a thought exercise for leaders to take a hard look at organizational capability to risk to determine if a particular venture should or should not take a minimally viable approach.

We can see in the chart below (Chart 10), that when plotting the case studies described earlier in the book, the Target Canada case is a clear use-case for a Minimum Viable Strategy approach given the relatively capability level to investment level for the venture. Alternatively, in the case of the Ford example mentioned before, it's clear from the graphic that a Minimum Viable Strategy approach is probably not the best approach.

The difficult part is the area occupied between the clear cases for MVS in Chart 10 and the cases that are clearly not qualified for MVS. This is the space occupied by the center footprint on the chart. This is a high-risk area where the company has relatively equal capability level to the level of risk for the investment.

In these cases, the organization needs to be truly honest with itself about its own capabilities. In the cases listed below that occupy this space, Lego's approach to Asia, while it had the ability to go "all-in" from the outset in Asia, this was not its initial plan until it gathered market demand data to clear the Fog of Forecasting from immediate short-term view.

Additionally, the Cuban Missile Crisis also occupies this space at the top right of our chart, in high stakes games played where the players have deeply entrenched experience. The odds of success in this space are 1:1, meaning that the chance of success is equal to the chance of failure.

These high-stakes games are where the precarious qualities of friction and chance that occupies our fate in life need to be deeply considered. Murphy's Law, "what can go wrong will go wrong", is not something to be taken lightly, and, although the relative risk is a "1" in this case, which are reasonable odds of success, the absolute risk being on the high-end (top right quadrant) of the scale should bring pause to those who play in the space of the top right corner of the C2CIR chart to consider a more minimally viable strategic approach.

By pursuing a minimally viable approach, organizations are pushing their ventures closer to the orange space, where, although capabilities are low, absolute risk level is low. Thus, although odds are still below one and the chance of failure is greater than the chance of success, the overall systemic risk to the organization is lowered and the consequences of failure are minimized.

Overall, however, this phased approach that would be required given a low C2CIR is not a "wait and see" approach, as some critics might claim.[193] They are real investments with real risk profiles, but these small bets allow for organizations to gain further capability and "intelligence" than they otherwise would have had.

What does stand out and what we have not discussed yet are instances when a Minimum Viable Strategy is not used in cases when we logically would think it should be, such as the case of Space X, depicted below. Elon Musk, as an entrepreneur, staked a large portion of his wealth on the belief that he had the capability of building a successful rocket company in an age when rocket companies were deeply entrenched players, heavily reliant on government contracts obtained through well-groomed relationships.

Elon, with no background in the industry, began building rockets to propel to space using capital from his own wealth to fund the venture. One would imagine that in such a case where a new organization completely lacks the capabilities to do something would take a phased approach to execution to minimize risk, but this was not the case for SpaceX. How could they? How does one build half a rocket? One doesn't.

Elon did not have a choice, really, in this scenario. His winning aspiration was to build a rocket company that could eventually be leveraged to send humans to Mars and, given the limitations of a phased approach and the ambition of his goal, he had no choice but to go all-in.

This reality is a testament to Elon as an entrepreneur, leader, and a manager who not only is willing to take large bets but also execute to a degree that allows for success despite the probability of success being much lower than the probability of failure. Indeed, failure did come as SpaceX's first attempts at launches failed and almost bankrupted the company in 2008.

It was the learnings from those failed launch attempts, however, that allowed for eventual success. Indeed, it shifted SpaceX on the C2CIR chart up as it grew its own capabilities over time to build and launch rockets. After the company's multiple experiences with rocket building and launching and its learning and improved financial position that has come with a steady stream of sales, SpaceX has shifted its C2CIR profile closer to the "boring" Ford factory scenario where rocket launching has almost become routine.[194]

But, again, the incredible risk taken by Elon and SpaceX cannot be overstated and stands as a testament to those who worked on the project and overcame the odds. This approach, however, is not for everyone. Entrepreneurs have the luxury to take risk because they have no alternative. There is no business without success, so they must succeed. Existing businesses, however, like Target and Lego, have viable, successful businesses. Thus, they do not have the same luxury that allows for risk taking as Elon had with SpaceX. Therefore, these entrenched players must consider more Minimally Viable alternatives when operating in the bottom right quadrant of the C2CIR chart.

Chart 10: Capability to Relative Capital Investment Chart

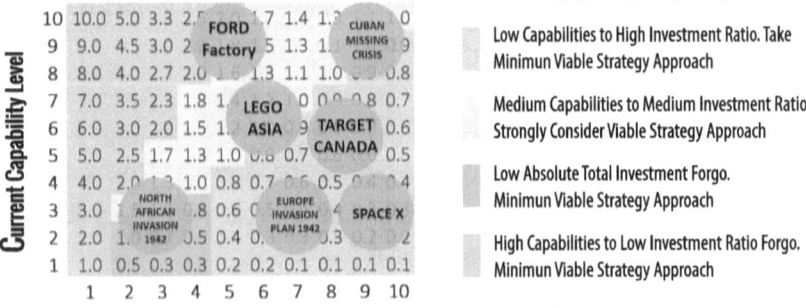

Low Capabilities to High Investment Ratio. Take Minimun Viable Strategy Approach

Medium Capabilities to Medium Investment Ratio. Strongly Consider Viable Strategy Approach

Low Absolute Total Investment Forgo. Minimun Viable Strategy Approach

High Capabilities to Low Investment Ratio Forgo. Minimun Viable Strategy Approach

Total Level of Relative Investment

Impact of Leadership

Developing a Minimum Viable Strategy is a different approach than many traditional strategic thinkers are accustomed to. It first involves recognizing your own weaknesses and limitations as an organization before coming to the conclusion that this is the right approach for the organization. This humility can be difficult for organizations to act upon if it has a strong history of hyper-growth and success, as I have witnessed at the Honest Company.

Later, as we will describe in the next chapter, it is the role of leaders to see things as they are, not as they want them to be. No one else in the organization holds the responsibility for this pragmatism more than those who are charged with leading the organization to future success, and the methods we recommend for leaders to take to do this are described in the next chapter.

ON LEADERSHIP

When beginning to write this chapter I realized that I faced quite a dilemma. How could I possibly prescribe methods to empower leaders to devise and implement a Minimum Viable Strategy when I am introducing it as a new concept for the first time. This prospect, as it seems, is a bit odd, and yet I believe it can be done.

I believe that a method of empowering leaders to devise a Minimum Viable Strategy can be prescribed because, as we have discussed in this book, this theory of strategy is part of an overall framework of strategy development, borrowed from Playing to Win, where leaders ask the following questions:

- What is our winning aspiration?
- Where do we want to play?
- How do we want to win?

These questions are the "heart of strategy" and, because it fits so well into this very framework, I feel that giving recommendations on how to empower leaders to devise and implement a Minimum Viable Strategy will be similar to the approach in how companies empower employees to develop a strategy in contemporary contexts. The difference is that the Minimum Viable Strategy approach attempts to push as much decision making down to those as close to the customer or to the operation as possible in instances when they are making non-existential related choices.

I do not wish, however, to propose that this book's pontification on leadership should be the bedrock of leadership principles or thought for all organizations. Books, articles, speeches, and theories on leadership are a dime a dozen and I've read, heard, seen, and listened to almost all of them.

I do, however, wish to propose principles I believe are essential to understanding when looking to execute a Minimum Viable Strategy. For knowing how to develop strategy is just step zero in a march of a thousand steps toward the end goal of winning, and no organization can win without leaders out front, pushing their teams despite the mundane, the difficult, and the hardships they may face together.

This chapter is divided into the following sections that go into further detail regarding the leadership principles I believe are necessary in understanding in order to successfully execute a Minimum Viable Strategy:

- Promoting decision making ownership and leadership down the chain of command;
- Training leaders to think strategically but act tactically;
- Leveraging Agile management to achieve goals;
- Organizing a team to achieve strategic goals;
- Learning the art and science of prioritization
- Training a team to take the extreme long-view
- Using 30-60-90 to align organizational priorities

Each principle section can stand on its own and often does, but together they form a larger means of thinking about how to 1) formulate a strategy and 2) execute a strategy. Organizations, indeed individuals can be great at 1 or 2 but fail at the combination of both. Truly remarkable leaders are good at both, and while the majority of this book has been spent on strategy development, it is the leadership component that delves into the strategy execution side to provide a rounded view of what is required to win. For winning does not sit in the academia ivory towers of Harvard Business School or within this book. Winning is achieved through sweat, grit, hard work, and determination from an organization driven by key leaders who push their teams to do more with less and leverage many of the same principles listed below in this chapter.

Promoting Decision Making Across the Organization

At the end of the day, getting to a Minimum Viable Strategy is about having true leaders within an organization. Because empowering, promoting, and developing leaders is so critical to an organization's ability to develop, not only a Minimum Viable Strategy, but a strategy in general, I will devote some time on the topic in this chapter on how, in general, a company should develop leadership in its own organization.

One of the best definitions of leadership I have encountered in my extensive exposure and study of the topic is the definition derived and published by the US Army. It states in Army Regulations Manual 600-100 that:

> *The Army defines leadership as influencing people by providing purpose, direction, and motivation, while operating to accomplish the mission and improve the organization.* [195]

I have had mixed feelings about high level discussions of leadership by those at the Honest Company who spoke of leadership but often lacked the skills necessary to understand the deeper complexities of their role and, thus, used such talk of leadership as a fallback for their own core competency versus trying to truly understand the deeper meaning of their work. But this is short-sighted thinking, and discussion of leadership, although lofty and high-minded at times, can be critical in strategy formulation when discussing the making of tough choices. It is leaders that conclusively make decisions and, at the end of the day, the best leaders will take responsibility for the success or failure of their team without passing the buck.

This is the heart of where strategy and leadership intersect. To move an organization forward, difficult decisions need to be made. Leaders will need to be willing to take risks and take responsibility for those risks and the plan formulated to avoid those. As such, discussions of how to create and empower such leaders for the sake of formulating and executing strategy is key to a holistic view of how strategy can enable an organization's success.

Implementing any strategy at any level of the organization is about empowering leaders to make difficult choices facing an organization. Leaders of organizations often wish to hold tough choices at the highest level of the organization as possible in order to prevent poor decision making from causing an organization to function sub-optimally.

This approach, however, often stifles an organization's prospects for progress and improvement and prevents innovative leaders from introducing creative means of solving problems. These innovative solutions are often the most important drivers of an organization's ability to adapt to the changing landscape of warfare or business competition.

American officers in World War II, the myth goes, often frustrated German generals because they did not follow their own field manuals and guides. Rather, they came up with more creative ways to overcome the enemy in difficult situations, thus causing chaos in the German lines because the Americans were acting in ways that were not anticipated. This level of independence is at the heart of innovation and, thus, at the heart of implementing a Minimum Viable Strategy.

In addition, holding decision-making at the highest level of an organization means that strategy implementation, development, and review happen less frequently than the changing landscape of business. All too often, the data show us that a shift in strategy is required more quickly than the bi-annual meetings for strategy review are held, and, even if these meetings are held, there is no guarantee of compromise on what next steps are for the company. More meetings are needed for that.

On the one hand, a Minimum Viable Strategy can be used at every level of an organization, but each level must be empowered with the appropriate level of decision making capabilities in order to create an environment where doing this is possible. As mentioned earlier in the book, this type of leadership empowerment is called "two-way" door decisions. These types of decisions are not existential for the company, are reversible, and can often be empowering to leaders who are seeking to find ways to make their own corners of the business or organization better.

A one-way door decision is often an existential decision made by an organization that almost always cannot be reversed. Examples of such decisions are to invade Normandy on D-Day in 1944 or for P&G to acquire Gillette. These decisions are often made at the top of an organization's decision-making hierarchy, as they should be since they are at the core of what an organization is and does.

As Jeff Bezos, advocate of the two-way and one-way door decision philosophy describes the tactic, "Type 1 (one-way door) decisions...are consequential and irreversible or nearly irreversible – one-way doors - and these decisions must be made methodically, carefully, slowly, with great deliberation and consultation."[196] Type 2 (two-way door decisions) can be reversed and, as Bezos claims, should be made much faster.[197]

High-level strategy formulation can, therefore, be deeply empowering to an organization as it can lay a foundation for a roadmap for the company and can be used as a playbook for others to execute upon. Strategy, therefore, helps to drive the ship as it sets a course or a heading for the ship and the strategic choices made by subordinate leaders within the organization are making the necessary adjustments to the sails under their guard to ensure the ship stays that course.

The goal, therefore, should be to allow leaders to make the decisions in regards to adjusting their sails with the objective of keeping the ship on its heading. These decisions should be "two-way", non-existential decisions. All of these decision-making capabilities should be pushed down to as low a level as possible to make the speed of decision making as quick as possible.

In order to trust such latitude with leaders below the executive level with such important decision making as strategy development, whether it's customer facing or not customer facing, one must ensure those leaders understand the framework from which the company derives its strategy. As stated in previous chapters, we have laid out a framework for the questions that need to be asked to develop a Minimum Viable Strategy. Those questions are:

1. What is the business's winning aspiration?

2. Where does the business want to play?

    a. How is this *where to play* answer different than where the business is currently playing?

    b. What factors are driving the differences, if any, for the change in course for where to play choices?

3. How does the business want to win?

    a. What are our *strategic hypothesis* based on our where to play and how to win choices?

    b. What are the specific activities the business performs today that make it successful?

i. What are the key performance indicators of success for those activities?

ii. How do we know those key performance indicators are measuring the right level of success?

iii. Are these key performance indicators for each activity the right level of success for our winning aspirational goal?

c. What are the specific activities the business must perform in the future in order to be successful against its currently formulated winning aspirational goal and where to play questions?

i. What are the key performance indicators for these activities that we must meet to win?

ii. How do we measure these key performance indicators regularly and accurately?

iii. Why do these key performance indicators tie back to winning for the business?

d. What are the minimum number of data points I need to validate in order to provide feedback to my where to play and how to win choices?

i. What are the minimum resources required to collect these data points for the business in order to drive better decision making with further capital investments?

Strategy development at the top levels of an organization will often answer these questions independent of higher direction. This means that their strategy is not necessarily nested within a higher strategy than their own, but is the "heading for the ship" that all strategies below will nest theirs to.

This concept was followed in Afghanistan when, as we were informed prior to deployment during our pre-deployment briefings, the overarching goal for ISAF (*International Security Assistance Force, the name of the force that the American Army fell under during the war*) was:

> *Our vision of success is clear: extremism and terrorism will no longer pose a threat to stability; Afghan National Security Forces will be in the lead and self-sufficient; and the Afghan Government will be able to extend the reach of good governance, reconstruction, and development throughout the country to the benefit of all its citizens. This declaration is supported by a medium-term, internal political-military plan - consistent with the Afghanistan Compact and the Afghan National Development Strategy - which will be updated regularly and against which we will measure progress.* [198]

In short, the goal of the American Army, as we understood it from this strategic "vision" was to build good governance.

It was the job of each sub-commander, given this overarching strategy, to formulate an appropriate strategy to achieve the greater objective of winning the war through a political-military plan. We attempted to achieve this at the district and local level in Afghanistan by partnering with local leaders, building capabilities for governance and security, and fighting the Taliban directly where our Afghan partners lacked the capabilities to do so.

By doing this, our strategy was "nested" with the overall strategy of "winning" in Afghanistan and supported the goals and vision of the strategy laid out by our higher command. This was key as by ensuring our strategy was "nested" it allows for more flexibility in strategy development at lower levels of the organization. We didn't ask permission or get approval for everything we did as long as our strategy achieved the greater objectives of the war.

Additionally, thinking of *what* should be an organization's Minimum Viable Strategy can be as challenging as determining *what process* should be used to find that strategy. Strategists often think of how a company can create sustained value over the long-term. This is, indeed, the starting point. Answering large *where to play* and *how to win* questions are critical to overcoming competition or, in the case of the military, other potential enemies.

However, this thinking often leads these same organizations to commit to large, "all-in" strategies before the organization is ready to commit to such a large-scale investment with an unknown outcome. Some would argue that the decision between going forward on an "all-in" and a Minimum Viable Strategy is about how much experience a particular business or organization has in a certain market or, in military terms, against such an enemy. How confident is the organization on relative success?

This line of questioning, however, might be detrimental as it was overconfidence that led Target Canada to its demise and almost led General Marshall to send the American Army to Northern Europe prematurely. To truly think in minimally viable terms, an organization must be frank about its own capabilities and conservative in its prospects for success. It must consider Murphy's Law (the thought that what can go wrong will go wrong) and assume that strategy execution will falter, get delayed, or end in failure. Assume, therefore, the worst.

How, then, given these assumptions, can the given organization mitigate risk? It can do this by looking for incremental approaches to achieving the desired end-state. What is the first step in our journey of 1000 miles towards our goal? Can we take that step in isolation without betting to farm? Will that first step give us the learnings we need to apply greater investments of human, physical, and monetary capital?

The method of thinking is to, therefore, look for ways to move the ball forward down the field of strategy in ways that you can fail. Just as Roosevelt knew that it was "OK" if the Army failed in Operation Torch as it wasn't an "all-in" strategy, so too should more organizations look for these opportunities to develop Minimum Viable Strategies that take incremental steps toward the greater end-state.

The benefits of pushing two-way door decisions down to lower leaders is that you will not only gain those leaders' trust [as they see you as an organization's leader are trusting them with a wide latitude of responsibility], but also a benefit is that this gives members of a team another opportunity to excel and differentiate themselves. This will be critical when analyzing work of these individuals for advancement, as the best people within an organization are the ones that think strategically and are capable of getting things done. Pushing two-way door decisions down the organization's hierarchy to junior leaders is an opportunity for employees within an organization to find these strategic thinking skills.

Pushing these two-way door decisions to junior leaders will also facilitate the rapid develop and execution of a Minimum Viable Strategy. Enabling leaders to make decisions, to try, to experiment, and potentially fail is the surest way to develop your team to grow as well as encourage them to move the ball forward aggressively against your competitors.

Jeff Bezos, founder and CEO of Amazon, decries companies that continue to make decision making for all decisions, no matter the scale, too overcome by paralysis by analysis. He claims that companies apply too "methodical" of a decision-making process for "bigger calls to less weighty decisions too often: 'The end result of this is slowness, unthoughtful risk aversion, failure to experiment sufficiently, and consequently diminished invention."[199]

As we have learned, strategy development takes effort on behalf of an organization to train its leaders to make critical decisions at every level regarding strategy. This strategy development at every level is called "nesting" strategies, and it is the job of senior leaders to ensure they are setting the "heading of the ship" as to allow for junior leaders to make impactful two-way door decisions to ensure they are achieving the desired end-goal for the organization.

Think Strategically, Act Tactically

If organizations are truly dedicated to building strategic thinking, it must train them on how to do that while also being able to allow for the day-to-day tactical execution of the business to succeed. Much of the ability to think strategically, to lose tunnel vision and to see the forest instead of the trees, takes a simple but valuable and hard to come by resource: time.

This time usually comes easy to what I coin as "Ivory Tower" strategic thinkers for organizations. These are individuals isolated from the day-to-day, unbeknownst of the frustrations or challenges required to overcome to make things actually work. They think about things from an academic standpoint, removed from the emotional baggage and sunk costs that typically weigh down and over-influence the decisions of organizations and prevent them from moving beyond what they are doing to what they should be doing.

Some disagree with having these academic-types influence strategies and that, in fact, some think the word "strategy" should not be in a job title. In one article on the online news journal Quartz, Kevin Delaney cites that the word "strategy" appears in 725,178 LinkedIn job titles.[200]

Delaney's arguments for this belief, that strategy should not be in job titles, are twofold. The first is that, because strategy and strategy execution are far different exercises, the faults of strategic thinking are that "they aren't rooted in the reality of operations. And operations people too often aren't invested in executing the plans that the strategy people craft for them."[201]

Indeed, Kevin quotes the eminent Southwest Airlines co-founder, no stranger to major corporate success against entrenched giants in the airline industry, who he cites as saying, "Strategy is overrated, simply doing stuff is underrated. We have a strategic plan. It's called doing things."[202]

The second reason Kevin says that the word strategy should not be in a job title is because the mere presence of this means that it devolves others in the organization from the responsibility of thinking strategically. These individuals without the word strategy in their job title assume that others with the word "strategy" in their job title will take care of the deep, long-term thinking.[203]

The alternative proposed by Kevin, and one that I agree with, is that organizations should promote and empower strategic thinking. The major problem with this anecdote, and one addressed by Kevin, is that it is extremely difficult to think strategically when also managing day-to-day operations.

Research has proven that human beings, while once thought to be great at handling multiple thought processes at once, are actually terrible at it and end up performing the multiple tasks being juggled worse than if they had focused on it solely.[204] Intuitively, I know this to be true based on my personal experiences in simply trying to play games between meetings on my phone.

The game I've played was developed by former two-time Defense Secretary Donald Rumsfeld called *Churchill Solitaire*, a card game that, as the former Secretary describes as requiring some strategic thinking skills and a game Churchill purportedly played " throughout World War II to improve his strategic thinking."[205] When in play between meetings or walking somewhere for a few minutes, I can get in a few moves here and there to keep my mind busy, but these moves are often poor choices that often don't consider the alternatives or consequences of those choices (characteristics of strategic thinking). These moves, made without deep, long-term thinking, but rather in short sprints are poor decisions that lead to poor outcomes, usually me losing. When I can sit down at the end of the day, however, and play without interruption, my ability to make more sound choices is enhanced because I am given time to analyze the impact of each move and, thus, the end result is almost always a higher performance.

How do we reconcile these two dichotomies, then? How do we get operational realities to be reflected in strategic thinking by involving those who are working in the day-to-day but remove them enough to get them to make sound choices that are emotionally removed from the baggage of historical choices the organization has made, whether in poor past experiences or sunk costs that will negatively influence future strategic choices?

The answer is to have both the academic-strategic thinkers and the organizational leaders to collaborate on strategy together, taking what will likely ultimately be different perspectives, creating a better strategic plan than the alternative of any one plan developed in isolation. This allows for the strategic thinkers to look at choices with deep thinking, removed from the emotional baggage of the past, the demands of the tactical choices, and the day-to-day that could prevent good choices from being developed.

This also allows for the organizational leaders to give input into the operational realities and ideas to strategy that will positively influence what the ultimate strategic direction is because it will be grounded in tactical soundness. These operational leaders, as I have seen at the Honest Company, can often be poorly influenced by historical sunk costs that require cold, unemotional analysis of a situation without skin in the game to make tough choices on, such as decisions to relocate distribution facilities which result in the displacement of dozens of employees. This is the purpose of strategic thinking as well, to be that cold perspective and think, not a of a particular project or department's success, but of the success of the business.

The end game, however, is to get buy-in from both operations and strategy folks, resulting in one strategy that is decided upon, which requires a single leader to choose in order to reinforce the strategic direction of the organization no matter whose ideas of that direction are ultimately chosen. But a single leader making the call is essential for getting buy-in and having clarity for the entire organization as a whole at the end of the day.

With this buy-in and influence from all levels of an organization, strategy can therefore be transferred to tactical execution because frontline leaders have had a hand in the formulation of strategy. By having this hand in strategy, they can realistically see how to execute upon that in their own worlds.

Leveraging Agile Management

While at the Honest Company, I saw the organization evolve, mature, and grow during my tenure as a member of the Operations team. One significant transformation I saw is how we tackled software development, how software engineers are organized, and how software development initiatives are prioritized. In the "Old Days", the President of the company, Sean Kane, would meet with engineers on a monthly basis to list and rank the initiatives he wanted tackled for that month after a whole host of various members of different business departments presented and pressed for the prioritization of other projects. Sean would then say, given these circumstances, we will work on X, leaving those who wanted Y worked on in the dark as to why their initiatives were left behind. This is often referred to as waterfall decision making.

This system works to a point, but the engineering team and company out-scaled that framework, and the team moved to smaller teams called "Squads" that paired a team of engineers with a business owner who would dictate priorities and outline requirements for those initiatives. When this transformation happened, I found myself the Product Owner of a "Squad" that handled operations initiatives called the Fulfillment and Order Management Squad. I was then given a crash course into technology management and was introduced to foreign terms such as Scrum, Grooming, Sprint Planning, Kanban, and others.

This was the beginning of a journey for me as I initially thought this method of organizing work was ridiculous. Coming from the Army and Operations methods of leadership, it was just too different than I was traditionally used to. While in the past, structured Gantt charts and other similar tools were used, this method of management, called "Agile", was more democratized, which, again, coming from the Army, made it foreign and an initially uncomfortable experience for me.

But, after seeing it in action first hand for almost a year, I can honestly say I am a believer in the methodology, and I began to think of ways that it could be employed for other uses beyond software development work. It is, I believe, a methodology that can be adapted in a way to manage strategic initiatives in the "day-to-day" grind of pressing for these strategic goals.

Agile has its roots in the scientific method way of thinking, which originated with "Francis Bacon's articulation of the scientific method in 1620," and with the Toyota Production System and the "lean thinking" employed in that system.[206]

Agile is a "structured process that uses self-governing teams to accelerate the development of new products and processes."[207] The goals of the agile methodology are to:[208]

1. Set priorities
2. Establish innovation teams
3. Assign leaders to teams
4. Remove impediments

The key to this leader who owns the agile team is that they:[209]

1. Own results
2. Set visions and roadmaps
3. Ensures communication between team and key stakeholders
4. Approves the team's work

An Agile team has between 3-9 members, including the leadership owner. These team members are multidisciplinary and have the in-house skills required to solve the problem at hand. In short, they should be autonomous operating cells for the business.

After developing a list of priorities for the business, teams typically rank order their list of priorities based on what deliveries the highest value to the business and to customers.[210] Before ideas become priorities, they must be vetted and scoped out to determine the specific work required and who needs to be involved to complete the work for the project.

Each priority is broken down into "modules" or sprints of work, usually lasting 1-2 weeks, where a clear goal is set for which individual tasks that makeup the goal will be completed in the said timeframe. Clear exit criteria are set for each task so the definition of "done" is agreed upon by all team members at the beginning of the sprint before work begins. Finally, teams typically have regular "methodologies for testing their results" after work is completed on a specific task, which is dependent upon the work to be completed.[211]

Work is typically tracked with tools such as JIRA that display on a "Kanban Board" progress for each member of the team as well as displays tasks in levels of priority so all members have a global view of task priorities for the team. By having a fixed "sprint", members of the team have a good understanding over time how much they can actually do in a certain amount of fixed time, or what their "velocity" of work is.[212] Before each sprint begins during sprint planning sessions, each task's level of effort is estimated based on the team member's understanding of the work required to complete the task.

Thus, "points" are assigned to the task and the "sprint" as a whole, giving team members an understanding if they are being too ambitious or not ambitious enough in terms of what they intend to accomplish over the course of the sprint. This helps to set realistic expectations for the team members and for the team as a whole. This system also allows for leaders to be comfortable with their own limitations of capacity and bandwidth, which can be a challenge in many organizations.

Updates are given daily at Scrum meetings, where every member of the team briefs the status of what they are specifically working on that day.

These meetings are intended to last no more than 15 minutes and is simply to ensure everyone is on task and deconflict any roadblocks that may be preventing the ball from moving forward that particular day.

These meetings came out of studies that suggested that "short daily team meetings increased group productivity dramatically."[213] Additionally, studies have shown that those who have used agile claim that the teams who employ these methods "get things done faster than teams using traditional processes."[214] To this argument I can attest as a witness to.

Agile management is important for strategists, especially Minimum Viable Strategists, to understand because of the constant feedback loop it employs, its methods of organizing teams (discussed in the next section) to achieve strategic goals, and its ability to be precise on a daily basis to determine the three P's: Person to Task, Priority to Task, Progress to Task. Unless teams are being specific in tying the strategic back to tactical, daily tasks and answering these three P's using the Agile management on a *daily basis*, the ball will not move forward toward the end-goal of winning in a meaningful way and on a regular cadence.

Agile provides teams not only a clear sense of how far they've come, but also how far they have left to go. Work is quantified and estimated in terms of duration of work, so all team members have a clear sense of, not only what is left to work on, but what will be worked on next. The ship is never left astray in port without a clear heading, thus, progress is never stifled.

Organizing a Team to Achieve Strategic Goals

The best "methods of management" cannot, in the long-run, create a winning team without the right structure in place to ensure decisiveness reigns. Further, the day-to-day monitoring and execution of strategy in the day-to-day is critical, as was discussed and dissected in the Agile approach to strategic execution. However, more often than not, the *way* an organization is structured to achieve its strategic goals is often overlooked, thus crippling its ability to execute upon the goals it sets for itself. One critical aspect of organizational structure that is important to achieving strategic goals is accountability. Having a single individual responsible for achieving a specific strategic end is a must for ensuring that the weight of responsibility and the burden of execution falls on a single person's shoulders. That one person should wake up and go to sleep every day thinking how they will move the ball forward that day and the next to achieve X, and X should be a strategic goal the company has set for itself to achieve in a measurable period of time.

Without the burden of responsibility, everyone feels "slightly" responsible in an organization and, thus, no one feels responsible. As former CIA head and Secretary of Defense Leon Panetta conveys when approaching the problem of organizing the search for Osama bin Laden in 2009 (quoted at length):

> At a meeting shortly after (a suicide bomber killed a number of CIA agents in Afghanistan by a lead promising information for Bin Laden's location) in the director's conference room back at Langley, we asked a roomful of top-ranking Agency officers, "Who here is in charge of finding Osama bin Laden?" Everybody raised his or her hand, thinking that was the answer we were looking for. The scene captured a big problem: Within CIA, everyone felt ownership of the hunt, but there was no senior official - accountable to the CIA director - who woke up every day and went to sleep every night working on the Bin Laden mission.215

To fix the problem, Panetta put a single individual in charge of the hunt, and, to show the level of importance that search was to the Director and to the Agency as a whole, that individual briefed Director Panetta "every Tuesday afternoon, even if he had nothing new to report."216 The results of the change are clear. After close to a decade of a failed search attempt, Bin Laden was finally captured in May of 2011, just over a year and a half after the team's restructuring.

The Art and Science of Prioritization

Now that responsibility and method of action (Agile) are in place, the team is organized, and decisions are pushed to the lowest levels, how do we determine what to work on? One of the most critical skills for leaders while setting strategy is being able to clearly prioritize what are the most important initiatives for an organization to do in order to execute the strategy.

While this was somewhat clear in the military, it became much less clear in a chaotic startup environment during my first year and a half at The Honest Company, where new ideas were constantly being discussed, debated, and meetings were held with large groups of people about these new ideas that often turned into little more than throwing spaghetti at a wall. The unfortunate part about these initiatives is the time and focus they removed from the organization.

What became evident only in retrospect is that it was not that there was too much to do and too little time to do it. This is probably true for any organization of any size and growth curve if they are truly interested in success. The truth is that the company lacked the discipline of prioritization, and leaders didn't reinforce what should and should not be debated or discussed at the expense of taking time and energy away from the focus.

When assessing young leaders, this is often one of the things I look for. I ask, "Can they prioritize in a way that makes sense for the business? Can they articulate tradeoffs and business impacts?" These are the qualities, I believe, on top of hard work, that truly separate leaders from the crowd. These are essential qualities because they are indicative of decision making capabilities.

When we say prioritization is an *art* and a science, we mean that priorities can be quantified in terms of impact (what are the top-line and bottom-line impacts) as well as qualitatively discussed in terms of customer impact that cannot be predicted precisely (how will the customer feel about this). These two must be balanced when we approach prioritization, for forgetting one (focusing on cost savings) can result in ignoring another (how does cost savings actually help customers, again?).

Leaders are ultimately responsible for balancing the scales here between the art and the science in order to outline clear priorities. But, at the end of the day, a single individual *must* decide and deliver those decisions to the team. The lack of a clear decision maker and clear decision causes resources to be spread across too many resources as the team tries to do everything versus focusing on the decisions as no decisions have been made.

Thus, the ability to create discernable, sensible priorities based on business and customer impact are critical leadership qualities, and any young leaders today looking to rise in an organization should seek to learn how their business leaders are prioritizing initiatives and the thought processes they put in place to make these calculations. This skill is incredibly valuable to a business and to individuals in helping to align organizational resources around common goals.

Ultimately, however, prioritization has its roots in the overall strategy developed by the organization. My ultimate fear of someone on my team is for them to be asked by my boss what they are working on and for them to answer that they are working on something that doesn't tie back to the over-arching company strategy. By providing a clear strategy and, consequently, guidance on what is important to achieve a "winning" structure within an organization, companies make it easier for leaders and team members to prioritize their own work based on this clear guidance.

I will not, however, pretend to say here that I have a clear understanding of how to prioritize or *how* to train team members on how to prioritize. This topic could occupy a chapter itself. It is important, and what I will assert here, is that leaders, despite the methodology for prioritizing, *must* decide on a clear direction to reduce the waffling of team members who are not given clear guidance and, thus, are spinning their wheels, waiting to be given direction.

On Training Organizations to Take the Extreme Long-View

Another lesson learned from the search for Bin Laden at CIA in my readings, and one that I've learned in my own experiences at the Honest Company, is the value of taking the extreme long view in strategy development and execution. For the Bin Laden search, Panetta had to instill in those working for him and those he worked for, namely the President, Congress, and the American people, that the hunt for Bin Laden would take time, effort, sweat, and grit. As he puts it, "We needed to address a problem that plagues so many managers: the tyranny of the inbox where the urgent replaces the important. Managers need to know when to take the long-view to keep a team focused on key priorities, even in the face of crises or distractions. Finding Bin Laden was a classic case of an important, but not always urgent, mission."[217]

Panetta addressed this problem by ensuring that there was regular attention to how the challenge of the hunt was being tackled, who was on the team, and the resources that team was allocated. Progress was always tracked in a regularized way through weekly briefings to the Director. This structured, disciplined approach ensured the team was held accountable and the Director stayed abreast of progress and could, thus, brief the President on progress as well. By taking the long-view, disciplined approach, the team was able to maintain relevance as well as keep their eye on the ball, even if the ball was potentially years from reaching.

During my second year at the Honest Company, we transitioned from putting out fires on a daily basis to taking a strategic, long-view towards our operational challenges. In mid-2015, we started to take a more strategic view of our long-term distribution strategy versus putting out the daily operational fires of running a rapidly growing startup and all of the logistical problems behind doing that. I was on the team that led the charge in conducting the study that would eventually turn into a 5-year plan for building out our operational capabilities.

This was a long-term view that the company had not taken before in approaching operations, but we knew that to be successful and to scale appropriately for the long-term, we not only needed to think in long-term contexts but also dedicate resources to executing that strategy. The team I was a part of at Honest has been dedicated to executing that 5-year operational strategy and all of the day-to-day that goes along with executing such a strategy.

This was an important move for the company, and a signal that it cared deeply about its ability to scale operationally. It was also a signal that it intended to mature as a company and move away from putting out daily operational fires to becoming operationally boring, which is really the goal of any CPG company looking to be respected from a logistics standpoint.

How does one transition an organization to focus on the long-term while also fighting the battles of today? This is the heart of strategy, for the process of formulating the strategy is the first step in acknowledging that the organization does need to and will take a concerted approach to the long-term.

Regularly approaching strategy development and execution is the key to organizational change, and to lift the eyes of those focused on the targets in front of them to those out further than their immediate front requires deliberate action on behalf of leaders to sit folks down and talk about the long-term. Strategy formulation doesn't just happen; it happens deliberately, and it is the role of leaders to ensure that they make it happen through deliberate action and through bringing people together. Nothing in business or war happens by accident, but is the result of leaders taking charge when they are in charge.

Training Strategy Development and Execution

Leadership traits that combine the ability to execute in tandem with the ability to think strategically, as the Harvard Business Review identified in an article quoted earlier in the book, are often rare. Leaders that can both formulate and execute a strategy are not easily often found in today's business climate. "In a 2013 survey of nearly 700 executives across a variety of industries" executives were asked to "rate the effectiveness of the top leaders of their companies. How many excelled at strategy? How many excelled at execution?"[218] The results of the survey show that only 8% of leaders rated were good at both strategy and execution and a dismal 35% were neutral or bad at both. [219]

What this survey tells us is that finding high caliber leaders that can both think strategically and act tactically is rare. Perhaps this is a perception problem and leaders are a bit more skilled than this survey indicates or these leaders are victims of circumstance, stifled by a staggering economy or industry. But, inevitably, as is the case with all situations such as this, the truth is probably somewhere in-between.

Thus, the conclusion that leaders are often not great as both strategy and execution in general probably holds. The following sections, this book hopes, will provide guidance into how to translate the strategy in previous chapters into execution that will result in a winning strategy.

Gaining Organizational Alignment Using 30-60-90 Goals

We've talked at length thus far in this chapter about a number of leadership platitudes, something that I typically try to avoid because they often come off as too vague or too nebulous for the harsh realities of day-to-day competitive execution in war, commerce, or any other human endeavor. But, perhaps platitudes are a good starting point for greater understating of the nuts and bolts of leadership, of translating the strategic into the tactical. Given this potential, this possibility that it is better to begin with a platitude and drill down into the actuality of how it translates to the physical, real-world of leading living, breathing human beings, I will attempt to explain yet another, and perhaps the most critical, leadership principle that should be studied, learned, and executed by organizational leaders looking to steadily execute a strategy holistically across an organization: alignment.

Alignment, as defined by Jonathan Trevor and Barry Vacore in "A Simple Way to Test Your Company's Strategic Alignment" is when all members of a team (for them a business but for us any organization) are "arranged in such a way as to best support the fulfilment of its long-term purpose."[220] The following are what we believe to be steps in how to achieve that alignment based on previous experience in day-to-day operating activities:

Step 1: Communicate the Strategy Up and Down

The most important step for any strategic alignment plan is to clearly communicate the strategy to each level of the organization emphatically with clear timetables for achievement. This should be done by both senior executives to as large a group as possible then, again, at smaller department level meetings, which have leaders that can present their nesting strategies to their smaller organizations and who can articulate clearly how that particular segment of the business is aligned with the overall organizational objectives.

Step 2: Prioritize Left and Right (the X and Y Dilemma)

Step 1 was the easy part of strategy. Sitting in a room, drafting cool slides, and presenting these slides to the team and telling them to boldly go where no teams have gone before is very easy relative to the remaining things that need to happen to execute strategy. The difficult part is actually getting teams' efforts to align to meet that strategy.

Nothing in the modern work environment can be done in a vacuum. Almost all major initiatives that will have meaningful impact to organizational achievement are cross-functional and require some resource dedication from multiple teams or departments. But how, then, does the prioritization of initiatives stack up across teams?

What if I, the VP of Operations, need initiative X to be a top priority to execute and succeed in creating a winning departmental strategy that will nest nicely will the overall organizational strategy, but the VP of Marketing sees, however, that initiative Y for his department is more important? What if we both need some overlapping attention to both X and Y for both, neither department can do X or Y at the same time effectively and in a timely manner, but neither department wants to be the one to blink on X or Y and, hence, lose relative organizational influence in getting his or her initiatives prioritized.

This is ultimately the large gorilla in the room, the prisoner's dilemma played out in bureaucratic and office politics day after day. This turf war causes organizations to be "incapable of delivering its strategy", thus, making "the strategy effectively worthless" and the organization's "purpose will go more or less unfulfilled."[22] This is where leadership truly comes into play.

At the end of the day, competing organizational department heads, such as the X and Y dilemma we described above, requires an arbiter, a decider, someone to say this is what we are going to do definitively as a company because X aligns with our strategy and is a priority for the business now while Y will come later. Once priorities are agreed to and communicated, the supporting leaders of a business should be driven to execute those stated priorities to the fullest measure.

Step 3: Sync Prioritization Time Tables (30-60-90 Day Goals)

These decisions of prioritization also require the alignment of timetables for when organizations will tackle certain key initiatives together in a cross-functional, collaborative way. At Honest, we initially thought creating large road maps, laid out week by week would work by individual departments and then creating a road map of road maps would create a global picture and then we could find pockets of time to sync resources that way.

But this became cumbersome and difficult to manage and maintain. We moved away from the road map of road maps that went out 6 months to 18 months and, instead, created simple plans based on 30-day increments, or, 30-60-90-day goals that synced up all departments timetables for getting stuff done.

All teams working on initiatives were, thus, held to a timetable of getting these goals done that start and ended on the month and, thus, created deadlines that were relatively in sync with the rest of the business. Executives could then easily say that priority X is a priority for this 30 days and we will focus the business on priority X and priority Y will come in 60 days.

This easily understood means of measuring time and syncing up of resources made it easier for executives to make deliberate, definitive, and decisive decisions on what needed to be done now. If there were competing priorities, then stacking those priorities relative to each other in a sense of time for when each should be planned to be done was easy. The 30-60-90-day planning cycle, though simplistic for a growing startup, worked.

The act of "syncing" cannot be understated in terms of its importance. Organizations past a certain point of size are incredibly fluid in terms of activities and projects being tackled, and there are varying degrees of relative importance that some departments assign to an issue relative to another. It is critical that organizations ensure everyone, to the extent possible, has a similar view in terms of relative importance of priority for initiatives in order to align resources on specific, targeted goals and projects. This takes deliberate planning and a strong leadership mentality of steering the ship where appropriate.

Executing Minimum Viable Strategy - the 1% Principle

Minimum Viable Strategy, as you have learned, is an iterative approach to strategic thought, development, and execution. It requires tough, smart, determined leaders willing to take the extreme long-view on both strategic development and execution, not allowing themselves to be beholden to the daily grind of the mundane but bring their entire selves to bear on moving the ball forward with their teams daily, yard by yard.

Thus, with Minimum Viable Strategy execution, we believe in the 1% principle as codified by Dave Brailsford, General Manager and Performance Director of Team Sky, a British pro cycling team.[222] The idea that Brailsford used to improve his team was "aggregation of marginal gains", or "the 1 percent margin for improvement in everything you do."[223]

By taking this view on improvement, Brailsford began to improve on the mundane and the overlooked by traditional cycling team managers. He focused on the big stuff like nutrition and training, of course, but he also looked at different sleeping methods for cyclists to improve their performance during training periods, different methods for "washing hands to avoid infection."[224]

When implementing this approach Brailsford, expected to win the Tour De France in five years, but instead they won in three. These marginal gains, while not necessarily recognizable to the naked eye, added up *in the long-run.*[225]

Chart 11: Aggregation of Marginal Gains

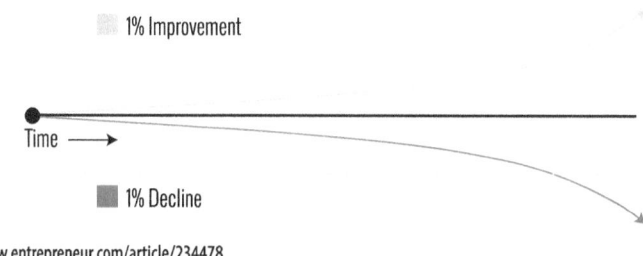

1% Improvement

Time ⟶

1% Decline

https://www.entrepreneur.com/article/234478

As *Entrepreneur Magazine* describes in covering this story, the process also works backwards, against the performer. Gone unnoticed, the small decisions we make that impact our daily improvement for the worse add up over time, aggregating themselves to large declines in improvement.[226]

In the Army, the saying went that the best military units do routine tasks and drills routinely, and thus become masters at maintaining the basic skills and executing the basic tasks required to be an exceptional unit. Being routine about executing the mundane, even small, unsexy things such as weapons' maintenance, is critical to maintaining a well-oiled military unit. It is difficult, however, to inspire people to do the routine, the mundane excellently. This, in the end, is where true leadership comes into play.

The 1% improvement principle, or improving on the small stuff, which often is codified by the daily routine tasks conducted by organizations, is at the heart of what makes strategy translate to the everyday. It is, in the end, the leaders of organizations that move this ball forward daily in advance of either stunning victory or obvious defeat.

How this is executed is through syncing priorities and executing project management on a daily basis through agile management techniques and routinizing data collection and forecast review sessions that seek to look at these marginal gains and improve upon them daily and incrementally.

Tying this All Together

We have covered a lot of ground in this chapter on "Empowering Leaders". We have discussed:

- How to promote leadership by pushing decisions as low as possible in the organizational chart (one-way vs. two-way door decisions)

- How to train on strategy develop and properly nest strategies in an organization

- How to think in minimally viable terms as a strategist

- How to translate the strategic to the everyday

- How to use Agile management techniques to execute on strategy daily

- How to organize a team in order to create sole responsibility for strategy execution

- How to teach prioritization to young leaders and identify those who have the skill to conduct prioritization activities

- How to train organizations to take the extreme long-view, the proper forecasting horizon for strategy development

- How to gain organizational alignment and sync priorities across an organization

- How to execute a Minimum Viable Strategy through the marginal gains approach

This chapter on leadership is perhaps as much about "management" as it is about leadership and what tactics and techniques can be used to formulate and execute strategy. This is true, but good leadership requires good, organized management skills that can move an organization forward in the right direction, and in this chapter, we've attempted to lay out ways that leaders can organize their teams around a formulated strategy to be prepared to execute on that strategy both daily and in the long-run.

But beyond management and using tools such as Agile and 30-60-90 Day goals, organizations require an immense amount of motivation to keep their eye on the ball. The daily grind wears the human out, and often we do not see our improvements to an organization when we track them minutely on a daily basis, much like watching a newborn grow to be a toddler (you don't notice the difference in height or weight on a daily basis, only in retrospect when looking at photos).

It's the job of the leader to motivate, to remind people how far they've come, and to encourage them that, despite having come this far, there is still more to do. It is this capability to lift people up when they need it and press them to keep going that is the ultimate role, not of a "management", but of leaders that is so critical to proper strategy execution.

WHEN IS AN MVS NOT APPROPRIATE?

While in many cases a Minimum Viable Strategy approach is appropriate to collect strategic insights on certain pieces of data before committing large amounts of resources to a particular endeavor, not all situations are appropriate for a Minimum Viable Strategy. In these cases, the timeline required for success is so abbreviated that the company or organization only has a single opportunity for success or failure. It must, therefore, commit all of its resources and effort to the single goal of success in that particular endeavor through an "all-in" strategy.

And yet, in other cases, an organization has already collected the strategic data required to feel comfortable in doubling down its investment in an "all-in" strategy, given that type of strategy is required for success. For example, one of the case studies reviewed earlier in this book elaborated on Franklin Roosevelt's Minimum Viable Strategic approach towards the opening of the North African Front with Operation Torch. During this campaign, the Army and other US forces learned a considerable amount about themselves and the Germans, which was later applied to an "all-in" campaign with D-Day and Operation Overload.

By the time 1944 came about, the Army learned what it needed from Torch and other campaigns, such as those in Sicily and Italy, to apply to Overload. In addition, it had no choice but to approach Overlord with an "all-in" style campaign because it was that level of investment that was required to make the beach landings successful due to the expected German resistance in Northern France and Rommel's now infamous and, at the time, thought impenetrable Atlantic wall.   Or, as James Winik so eloquently described the scene of June, 1944:

> "By late spring, all would be in readiness. The only thing left would be for the man in the trailer, General Eisenhower, to give the final order for the assault. For Roosevelt, Eisenhower, and the Allies, there was no real contingency planning. As the general put it, 'We cannot afford to fail.' Overlord was all or nothing."[227]

There will be other times that the Minimum Viable Strategic approach is not appropriate at any point in the planning process. In a different context, but still retaining our focus on war, the American Army of the late 20th and 21st Century is not likely to take a Minimum Viable Strategy approach when seeking to take on an enemy combatant around the world in a conventional conflict. The level of confidence in the force and expertise of the men and women who served in uniform today gives strategic planners the confidence needed to plan larger engagements that in another time would bring about concern about the sheer size of the investment of troops in a single campaign. The American Army in Desert Storm is a perfect example of a confident American Army capable of conducting all-in desert operations with little regard for considering minimally viable options because of the high quality of training, technology capabilities, and vast force superiority over the enemy.

Does this same line of thinking, however, not apply to Target with their Canadian endeavor one might ask? Were they not completely confident in their capabilities as to have confidence in their ability to execute in Canada almost exactly what they were doing in the United States? Were they not a successful retail operation and, thus, to extend just beyond the border should have been almost a natural extension of their US operation? Some might argue that the US and Canadian markets are so comparable that it was fair for Target to have confidence in their ability to succeed under these conditions.

As strategists, however, we should know better. We should always question assumptions, make them transparent, and ensure that they are known to all who are committing to a particularly aggressive strategy. It is fine, however, to be aggressive in business and in war, but aggression must be focused, deliberate, and with purpose.

Aggression must also not put an entire organization at risk by being sloppy. It is great to be aggressive in battle, young Lieutenants joining the US Army Infantry as green officers learn, but exceptional tactics and precision on the battlefield are better. Aggression makes up for a lack of this skill, and aggression results, inevitably, in sloppy frontal assaults that cause more losses than they particularly should in many cases.

Thus, with Target expanding to Canada, there were assumptions abound and, indeed, the approach was more in the fashion of a frontal assault than one of precision. Assumptions about Canadian customers, their profile as a consumer, and Target's choice of a third-party logistics provider to be able to ramp up operations as quickly as Target could open stores were all assumptions that eventually crippled Target's Canadian launch. Thus, Target overestimated their "capabilities" when assessing risk, to their detriment.

It is clear, therefore, that a more phased approach involving a Minimum Viable Strategy would have given Target more breathing room to fail and more flexibility to determine what an optimal Canada operation looks like for the retailer. However, how does one know when a Minimum Viable Strategy is appropriate and when an "all-in" strategy should be preferred?

To come to the right conclusions, we must ask ourselves a series of questions to lead our strategic choices in the right direction. Such questions should include:

1. Does my organization have time to execute a Minimum Viable Strategy?

2. Does my organization have the discipline to execute a Minimum Viable Strategy?

3. Does my organization have a strategy at all that everyone executes against?

   a. We ask this question because "all-in" strategies typically don't require a "strategy" per se to be executed over the long-term but, rather, a significant capital investment that will show success or failure in the medium to short-term.

4. Does the organization have the information it requires to measure its capabilities and the progress of those capabilities over the long-term?

It is important, therefore to consider the "closeness" of the strategy for expansion or the strategy for the new undertaking to what you have done before or are doing currently to gauge whether it requires a Minimum Viable Strategy or not. In international business theory, this is sometimes referred to as the CAGE framework when understanding if a new market is similar to the market you are currently operating in. The CAGE framework analyzes cultural, administrative, geographic, and economic differences between a business's current market and its expected market to determine the viability of market expansion to the new market.

A similar approach can be used to determine if a Minimum Viable Strategy is required to undertake in strategy. This framework is called the DIST framework, which looks at if a business currently has the discipline required to execute a measured approach to strategy, if it has the capabilities to collect the information required to execute a Minimum Viable Strategy, if an organization has a current strategy framework to build the Minimum Viable Strategy off of, and if the organization has time required to execute a disciplined Minimum Viable Strategy.

A lack of any of these variables for a particular organization will often result in poor results when executing an MVS and, therefore, a different approach should be considered. A Minimum Viable Strategy approach is not, as is said at Ranger School in the US Army, for the faint or the weak at heart. It is for those willing to take a hard look at the data, be creative about phased solutions, and execute with precision through the daily grind of the mundane.

As we have learned, a Minimal Viable Strategy is not appropriate for all situations. In some cases, an organization may already have the data and experiences required to execute an "all-in" strategy, or it might not otherwise have an alternative option. Also, an organization may or may not meet the criteria necessary internally to execute a Minimum Viable Strategy, disqualifying it, not from needing a Minimum Viable Strategy, but from being able to execute it properly at all.

Finally, an organization may not have the time to executive a Minimum Viable Strategy, which is true in many technology industries, as some mentors have told me, since the fast pace at which innovation is "copied" precludes taking a measured approach. While I'm not entirely convinced, as I will outline in my section on the theory of Blitzscaling, that technology companies are under the gun to stay in front of their competitors on all fronts at all times, I see the merits in the argument that in a rapidly copying market there are constraints to leveraging the Minimum Viable Strategy approach (though a strong counter-argument may be if that is a wise market to be *playing* in to begin with).

Harry's, Inc

Harry's, a New York City based startup attempting to disrupt the men's razor and shave industry, has placed itself uniquely in the marketplace to serve a specific customer need: high quality razors at a reasonable price that come regularly in the mail through a subscription service. Harry's faces large odds and the deep pockets of entrenched players such as Gillette.

Full disclosure: I have been a regular Harry's customer for years and have shunned away from a direct competitor of Harry's, Dollar Shave Club (acquired by Unilever in 2016), as the Harry's razor was of much higher quality, which I required during my time in the Army as I was required to shave daily. But my positive customer experience is a result of their all-in strategy, which I will describe here and which also flies in the face of my proposal for Minimum Viable Strategy.

As reported in an Inc. magazine article highlighting the company's major strategic shift during a time of dread and uncertainty amongst startups in May of 2016, Jeff Raider, a co-founder of Harry's, attempted to ease the worries of the startup's group of loyal employees by saying "Last year was the year of the unicorn...This is the year of the cockroach."[228]

The message that Raider was trying to communicate was that times were changing, the euphoria was dying in the market, and reality was soon going to be setting in. Raider and his fellow employees could take comfort in the fact, however, that the financials and the strategy that Harry's had taken was leading it in the right direction and that it was, as he put it, "making real money."[229] He reminded the timid group that the company had hard assets and that it had its own factory producing its own razors.[230]

In the year 2014 Harry's officially acquired Feintechnik, a razor manufacturer located in a small German town named Eisfeld, three hours from Frankfurt. Feintechnik, at the time of acquisition, was owned by a European private equity firm and was making razors for "dozens of mostly European retailers and distributors."[231]

After an exhaustive search of the best high-end razor manufacturers that took them on a tour of razors produced in such places as Egypt and Japan, they finally stumbled on Feintechnik, which was producing a high-quality razor in Europe using the "gothic arch cut, which sharpens the steel on both sides into a parabolic edge, giving the blade both remarkable sharpness and strength."[232]

It took five months for Raider to convince Feintechnik to become a Harry's supplier in May of 2012.[233] However, it was, ultimately, not a typical supplier relationship that the brash Harry's founders were looking for. Their visions were grander.

The typical startup play is to minimize risk and maximize return by relying on suppliers and reducing overhead, thus utilizing investor capital on growing top line revenues and growth. Dollar Shave Club, after all, relies on outside suppliers for manufacturing similar to other growing consumer brand startups.

The grand plans for Harry's, however, are far different than Dollar Shave Club and require a different approach to properly differentiate itself in the marketplace. It was, as Jeff Raider sees it, *not* an option for Harry's not to go big on manufacturing and vertical integration. It was about a "distinct competitive advantage" that owning the manufacturing provided to Harry's in the long-run, allowing the company not to be beholden to suppliers and potentially face them as competitors, a situation Dollar Shave Club was faced with by its own supplier.

By the time the founders raised the cash, $122.5M in total, to acquire Feintechnik, they had been in the razor business for a mere ten months and were putting all of the cards on the table by becoming a vertically integrated company at such a young age and with such little experience in actually running a razor manufacturing plant.[234] Not only has the Harry's team purchased an existing manufacturing plant, but they have, in recent years, expanded production capacity aggressively with plans to expand the existing plant while having already built a second one after raising an additional $171 million to fund the campaign.[235]

All of this has been, ultimately, in pursuit of a single goal: to quite literally "own the manufacturing" of high end razors given that there were "only a few manufacturers in the world that can make what it sells - high-end razor blades- at scale".[236] It seems, given the current status of the business, that Harry's can at least say it is on its way to achieving that goal.

But the greater issue for us, Minimum Viable Strategists, is to analyze if the decision made sense strategically given all we know about strategy and our inclination to tend towards paths that don't require formulating "all-in" strategies. Before we begin this analysis, however, we must ask ourselves if it was, indeed, "all-in".

To answer this question, we must first answer one fundamental question: Could Harry's sell their newly acquired plant if they failed miserably at running the business at a price reasonably close to their acquisition price to recoup the investment and turn to suppliers for their razor needs? The answer to this is, if they failed at running Feintechnik, both the success of Harry's and the value of the plant would be reduced. Thus, it is unlikely their investment would be recouped in a substantial quantity enough to make up for the loss and it's unlikely that Harry's itself would have survived long if they failed and if the founders were focused on saving their plant from demise. Therefore, Harry's had no choice but to succeed in their "all-in" venture. Failure would have been their demise.

But we are left with the question of choices: should they have staved off this decision, relied on suppliers for a longer period of time to use their capital on growing their customer base versus acquiring a plant, and later have gone deep on vertical integration after they experienced growth and maturity over a number of years? This question goes to the heart of strategy and is, in fact, a wholly existential question for Harry's: Does Harry's even exist if it's not vertically integrated? If they are not vertically integrated, are they just another player in the market, relying on suppliers who can, in turn, produce the same razors for other potential Harry's competitors, making the Harry's razor a commodity, succumbing to being how Dollar Shave Club was to its own supplier?

It is clear, then, that Harry's required vertical integration given that its sustainable competitive advantage was to not be a commodity player but to provide a unique product in the market place. Thus, it's reasonable to conclude that the "all-in" strategy pursued by the Harry's founding team was a sound choice.

But, we must, as strategist, refer to our analytic model for conducting this analysis as well. The model we will use, the DIST model as described earlier, will answer the following questions:

1) Did Harry's have the discipline required to execute a Minimum Viable Strategy?

2) Did Harry's have the information required?

3) Did it have the appropriate long-term strategy in place?

4) Did it have the *time* required to execute a Minimum Viable Strategy?

While looking at this basic framework, we can reasonably conclude that the Harry's team likely had the discipline, information, and long-term vertical integration strategy in place, they lacked the time to execute a Minimum Viable Strategy as a scrappy startup vying for a place to call their own in an increasingly disrupted industry. This time was a constraint because of competitors whom were quickly adapting to the changing business models of Dollar Shave Club and others.

It is reasonable to assume that, had Harry's delayed its decision to vertically integrate, it would have lost the opportunity to acquire their high-end manufacturer (it would have been purchased by a competitor). This denial strategy could have spelled demise for Harry's if they had been forced to switch suppliers mid-stride, causing a reduction in blade quality and, consequently, a reduction of their brand equity. Their manufacturer became, in consequence of Harry's market position, a strategic asset that they needed to ensure they did not lose access to over the long-term. Thus, they found themselves in a position where they needed to immediately secure that strategic resource in a quick-changing marketplace where decision by competitors, because of the quickly changing landscape, become increasingly hard to predict.

Blitzscaling

What we wish to avoid here, however, is the notion that all startups get a "pass" on strategy and rather can execute "growth-at-all-costs" methodologies on a time-constrained based argument or something of the like. This is problematic, and it is a point that needs to be addressed directly. Indeed, it is this author's wish to address the topic of "Blitzscaling" head on as it contradicts almost all notions of Minimum Viable Strategy and is, therefore, in opposition to our proposed methods of strategy formulation in this book. Blitzscaling is "what you do when you need to grow really, really quickly. It's the science and art of rapidly building out a company to serve a large and usually global market, with the goal of becoming the first mover at scale."[237]

Blitzscaling is a course taught by LinkedIn founder Reid Hoffman at Stanford University, aptly named Technology-Enabled Blitzscaling.[238] Hoffman coins the term "Blitzscaling" because of the all-in approach to startup scaling that it takes as, once the decision is made to scale rapidly, there is no turning back, similar to tactics as the German Army used in World War II to rapidly invade neighboring nations using a tactic called the blitzkrieg.[239]

Hoffman uses the term Blitzscaling to reference building up organizational capacity to bring a product to a larger market, as opposed to scaling revenues or customer base.[240] The decision to go "all-in" and scale typically and most logically happens after the startup has "ironed out the product-market fit" and enough data has been drawn from experience to justify the massive scaling moves.[241]

Hoffman addresses the inherent problems with this approach directly. He acknowledges that, while Blitzscaling, a lot of things in the organization won't work smoothly and that the organization won't be able to tackle all of the problems at once. They will need to address each problem one at a time. But the fundamental flaw in Hoffman's logic comes with his reasoning behind fixing problems when he says, "You fix the things that will get investors to give you more cash. The lift that capital provides means you have a longer time in the air to get things right. You're unlikely to get your plan to fly on your first capital lift or even your second."[242] He then says that, despite the chaos that comes with Blitzscaling for the team members of the organization, the "thing that keeps these companies together - whether it's PayPal, Google, eBay, Facebook, LinkedIn, or Twitter - is the sense of excitement about what's happening and the vision of a great future."[243]

Such thinking can be seen at companies like Spotify. Although based abroad, the music provider has a large US presence. As of 2016, it was reported that, despite continued losses, Spotify's average annual salary has continued to climb. It continues to add staff to compete in a hyper-competitive industry and continues to pay more for the limited and valuable engineering resources so valuable to scaling a software company. As stated by the company, "We depend on key personnel to develop great products and services, as well as operate our business, and if we are unable to retain, attract, and integrate qualified personnel, our ability to successfully grow our business could be harmed."[244]

This delusion can also be seen in recent IPO filings by companies such as Twilio, whose sales have growth threefold over the last two years to 2015. However, like Spotify, the company "lost about $36 million last year."[245] At the time of this writing in 2016, it is one of the few tech companies to file for and execute IPO, and even its unit economics do not seem to be working *quite just yet.*

Even yet, despite Twilio's unworkable unit economics to date, its IPO had a "stellar first day performance" and was a "huge sigh of relief for Silicon Valley."[246] Some are, however, questioning its stock price and ballooning stock price post-IPO, despite it not turning a profit in 8 years.[247]

Further, Silicon Valley seems to be obsessed with the growing valuation of technology companies whose continued funding and ballooning value has led to a category for such companies: the unicorn. One recent example is Snapchat, whom just raised $1.8 billion, resulting in a $20 billion valuation as of May 2016. As Quartz has put it, "Snapchat's valuation isn't based on the company's making money, but on rapid growth and constant usage."[248]

According to a pitch deck obtained by the tech news outlet TechCrunch, Snapchat's revenues were merely $59 million in revenue in 2015. However, in April of 2016, Snapchat "told investors it was attracting 10 billion views a day."[249] But, as it seems, this has yet to transition to cold, hard cash to justify the incredible multiple of its current valuation.

Chart 13: Spotify's Earnings; from Quartz

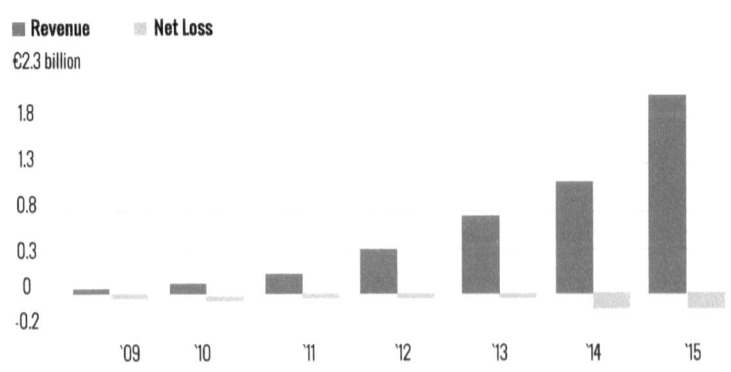

http://qz.com/691188/spotifys-average-salary-keeps-rising-even-as-its-losses-mount/

Chart 13: Spotify's Payroll and Headcount; from Quartz

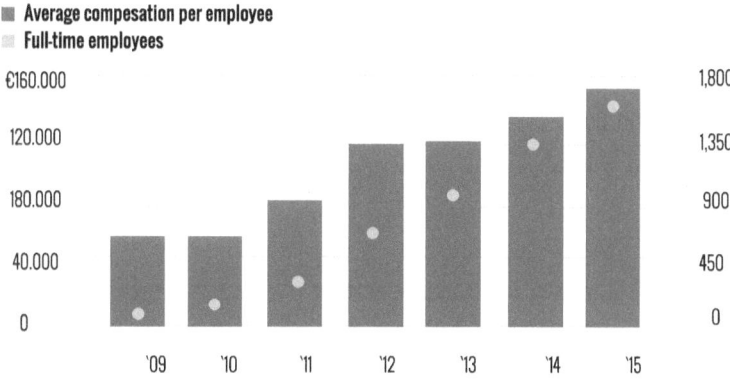

- Average compesation per employee
- Full-time employees

http://qz.com/691188/spotifys-average-salary-keeps-rising-even-as-its-losses-mount/

The problem persists, not only in Silicon Valley, but also in other technology startup hubs, and extends beyond mere over-valuations. The obsession with valuation at the expense of sound business fundamentals has negatively influenced society to see paper wealth as the end goal and something to be desired and respectful of, despite all of its misgivings and false assumptions.

For example, Elizabeth Holmes, once reported to be the richest self-made woman in America, valued at nearly $4.5 billion, is now considered have a grand total of $0 of that value after Forbes "downgraded its estimation of Elizabeth Holmes' wealth" to nothing.[250] In reality, the flurry of articles proclaiming Holmes to be worth $4.5 billion prior to the downgrade failed to report that she never really had the fortune to begin with because it was on the whole almost entirely made up of shares she owned in her startup Theranos.

Holmes shares in Theranos, however, were illiquid, not capable of being sold on a public market because Theranos is still a private company. This made Holmes a "paper billionaire."[251] The regulatory troubles with Theranos and its product performance in mid-2016 caused Forbes to downgrade the business value and, thus, Holmes' wealth.

The overall problem, however, is the valuation phenomena and the unicorns that make it up are fundamentally causing America and other nations obsessed with the startup culture to have returning tendencies of irrational exuberance from previous technology bubbles that are not grounded in fundamental economic principles. Founders are building companies to be paper billionaires in the hopes of going public with no regard for long-term fundamentals, and the obsession with Homes' wealth that never existed fueled the craze.

History should be a lesson that valuations that makeup the reports of vast founder wealth are often poor indicators of what businesses who acquire them are actually willing to pay and are, thus, moving targets. In June of 2016, Bed Bath & Beyond acquired One Kings Lane, a struggling online furniture retailer, for a quantity listed as "not material" by Bed Bath & Beyond. One Kings Lane was once valued at $900 million in 2014, another victim of the over-valuation of companies with poor economics, as I saw on the frontlines when in 2015 Honest occupied the One Kings Lane space that it acquired prior to 2015 in hopes that its hyper growth would continue. The winds did not continue to move in its favor, the large warehouses remained empty, and we were happy to take advantage of their woes. Thus, the forever entrenched mantra in Honest Operations comes full circle: Don't be One Kings Lane.

My inherent and fundamental problem with Hoffman's Blitzscaling is that it works while the music is still playing and capital from investors is still flowing. But, as we will address in future chapters, this could lead entrepreneurs to succumb to *Chancellorsville Syndrome*: the idea that past success is indicative of future success, or, in this case, that because you received funding in the past, you will get funding in the future and that scaling at all costs is the only way to win.

The Blitzscaling method makes sense if you believe that time is a constraint, as was in the Harry's case, and in order to be the first to grow to scale for the market you must hasten that pace at all costs. But this is a false truth. The

Harry's case was an investment in a strategic asset with hard value for the long-term. It was not hiring enormous staff to worsen the fundamental unit economics but, if anything, improved Harry's unit economics. The Blitzscaling methodology is ultimately a prisoner's dilemma between organizations that truly believe, because of people like Hoffman, that scaling is a race, but, as we have seen, it can lead to a race to the bottom.

As long as the music continues to play, companies like Spotify and Snapchat will survive. However, if it ever stops for both the industry and liquidity dries up, startups like Spotify, following the gospel of Hoffman, will ask, as German generals famously did of one another after World War I, "How did it all happen?"

Indeed, the signs are there. I recollect a trip to Las Vegas while at the Honest Company where we were looking potential distribution space during a phase of growth for the company, much of the decision driven by increased unit economic forecasts because of increased costs in California, our then existing operational geography. We gazed upon the Vegas strip while driving back to the Aria hotel and our real estate agent said, "All these people. It's so much busier now than it used to be. But the winter is coming." We all expected some form of recession was to come very soon.

Jason Calcanis, angel investor, would report the same thing, going so far as to say that the reason fewer startups without fundamental workable unit economics weren't seeing additional funding rounds is because investors see the winter approaching and want to bet on existing winners.[252] The winter, or recession as he was referring to, would show signs of creeping in, and the music would begin to slow, especially as I write this with the recent British decision to leave the EU and the signs of economic slowness as a product of the decision.

One such technology startup, Buffer, has witnessed the music begin to slow and had to make tough choices regarding the organizational staff after following a similar Blitzscaling path that led to over-hiring. In a post by co-founder

Joel Gascoigne, it is identified that Buffer hired more quickly than they were growing as their over-aggressive forecasts and "proudness" of the size of their company over profitability caused them to succumb to irrationality and to keep hiring, only to be forced to lay-off 10 employees instead of running out of money and, hence, needing to raise more capital.[253]

Buffer is now taking the narrow and untrodden path toward focusing on profitability. Unfortunately, the consequences were felt by the employees whom were let go in the process, but the co-founders are cutting their salaries, as is reported, to contribute towards the march toward profitability.[254]

But Buffer isn't the only startup hearing the music slow down. Birchbox, a "pioneer in subscription beauty sales" pulled back aggressive growth plans in mid-2016. The company "paused an expansion into overseas markets such as China according to former employees. It has also cut roughly 50 to 300 employees and consolidated from two floors onto one at its New York headquarters."[255]

Like Buffer, Birchbox is now focusing on profitability. "It is all about showing how you can operate this business profitably and it has forced us to completely change the way we operate, the way we spend money," CEO and co-founder Katia Beauchamp reports.[256] Unfortunately, as was the case with Buffer, the employees of Birchbox were the victims of irrational exuberance and a focus on valuation over profitability.

It is my opinion that, with Blitzscaling, Hoffman is peddling the Delusion of Silicon Valley: that capital is infinite, that profits don't matter, and that to win big you need to play big. As we have seen both in recent years and throughout history, these fundamental assumptions of Blitzscaling are not always true. Capital is not always infinite and sometimes investors will say no. Markets can take a turn south, other investment opportunities promising better returns come into play, or sales drop off and investors no longer believe your product to be the true future of the industry.

In fact, many investors are already beginning to preach the call for profits to avoid "sharky" type deals in a low liquidity marketplace. Bill Gurley, a partner at a Silicon Valley VC firm, explains that, "in Silicon Valley boardrooms, where 'growth at all costs' had been the mantra for many years, people began to imagine a world where the cost of capital could rise dramatically, and profits could come back in vogue. Anxiety slowly crept into everyone's world."[257]

While other venture capitalists "pooh-poohed his warnings", these VC's who don't believe in the bubble said that they would not invest in companies that weren't spending cash at enormous rates because that indicated that those particular startups "don't have enough ideas about what valuable things to do with more money."[258] These investors were preaching a market share grab strategy, urging founders to grow to $100M in revenue as quickly as possible, and shoot for an IPO or an acquisition as to allow for the investors to liquidate their holdings.[259]

The fundamental problem is that, at that particular scale, "unicorns" become a difficult acquisition target (unicorns being startups that are valued at over $1B). At that point, there is a "limit to how much venture investors are willing (and able) to keep these cash-guzzling startups afloat", as Gurley states, and an IPO may be the only viable option to stay afloat without having to turn to sharks with "dirty term sheets".[260]

Gurleys solution to the problem, to avoid having to IPO at a low valuation or turn to dirty term sheets is to pursue profits and to avoid "spending $5 to make $1", as the CEO of unicorn startup Gusto explained.[261] But profit making is hard and takes skills that are fundamentally different than simply executing a "spend-to-win" strategy that unicorns have been chastised by investors to pursue in the 21st Century.[262]

But the benefits of profitability are clear. In one analysis, when looking at startups coached during Series A funding in '05 and '07, who were instructed to grow at all costs and had high access to capital, to those in '09 and '10 who were forced to be more cash efficient, the failure rate differences found between the two vastly different eras of startups was stark. The "failure rate approximately halved in '09 despite continued difficult funding dynamics."[263]

While cash-flow break even isn't the goal of the Venture Capitalists who funded startups, nor is it probably the goal of those who are starting these firms, it is important to understand that, to some degree, the unit economics of a business need to make sense. Growth can mask these fundamental economics when the noise of growth masks the inherent problems with the business model, and this fundamental truth needs to be understood from the beginning: that, at some level of scale, a business needs to make money. Perhaps it would be wise, then, to follow the advice of another major startup influencer, Guy Kawasaki, who said:

> *Eat what you kill. Take the risk of foregoing sales and jeopardizing your service reputation by not scaling until sales are in hand. I've never seen a company fail because it couldn't scale fast enough, and I've never seen a company ship on time. You may be the first, but the trend is not your friend.*[264]

Thus, conclusively, the previous subtitle of this book was *The Anti-Silicon Valley Theory* for clear reasons. While the Valley (which I've never truly worked in, only tangentially at startups with offices there and with a spirit of "the Valley") practices MVP (Minimum Viable Product), it dismally fails to practice Minimum Viable Strategy, leaving a plethora of destruction in the wake of "growth at all costs". This section of the book isn't meant to undermine the tremendous work that goes into scaling a startup, but rather hopes to be a voice of reason in a growing crowd of delusional entrepreneurs that don't think in terms of fundamental unit-economics and only come to grips with those basic principles when it's too late and the staff has to suffer.

Google, The Source of the Problem?

This idea of Blitzscaling, the idea of 20% time for employees to spend 1 out of their 5-day work weeks on their own self-directed projects, napping pods, and other Silicon Valley sourced ideas of how to grow a successful company has its roots in the un-replicable success of Google. Google has seen an incredible amount of growth and actual profit due to its highly successful search engine plus advertising business model, which has allowed it to almost magically print money since the inception of this revenue stream. The story of Google, with its unique work environment and incredible profit margins is a remarkable feat in business execution, steady market share domination of the search engine market, and continuous, steady growth in other business segments, many subsidized from the profits of the core advertising business.

But Google is hard to replicate, and many businesses believe that, by replicating Google's practices, they can become as successful and profitable. But this is, inherently, a false belief. I was shocked one day in an Honest Company-wide meeting to hear someone ask for napping pods, despite the fact that we were wholly unprofitable at the time, though we had a plan we were executing to in order to achieve profitability. I thought to myself, "Isn't that why we have coffee machines!"

There were yet other stories, too, at Honest: engineers putting puzzles together instead of coding at work, people playing ping-pong. Perhaps it is the Puritanism, Army mindset, or Operations focus in me, but I couldn't help but want to tell folks to stop playing games and get to work.

I've come to think that my generation has been led to believe that it is OK to be unprofitable, to take naps, to request 20% time to work on vanity projects, and other things because Google had done it, is wildly successful, and now all the other unprofitable Silicon Valley startups are doing it. Why not us? These characteristics were especially true of our engineering team, whom often pined for the culture of Google and other Valley startups, but failed to grasp the fact that they worked at a CPG company, that margins were tight, and that the company needed to be incredible lean to be competitive over the long-term. I wished, in many interactions with these types of employees, that the executives would denounce the slow creep of the culture of glut which is probably an inevitable part of a culture shift for successful startups which cannot be staved off on the whole without direction from the top of the organization.

Perhaps it is also improper for a mere manager in the trenches at one unicorn based in Los Angeles to be poking holes into the theories of the founder of another as, by all measures, Hoffman can be deemed more successful, at least financially, than I up to today. Despite this, I cannot agree, however, in Hoffman's assertion that startups should scale their organizations at all costs, at lightning speed, and hope that this strategy, knowing it will not return profits, will convince investors to give more when the day comes that cash runs dry.

I imagine myself trying to convey this "business strategy" to the local gas station owner in my small Louisiana hometown whom I used to sell pecans to by the pound every fall to see if, at a fundamental business level, Hoffman's strategy would make sense to the average person, thinking that perhaps I'm missing something. In no scenario can I imagine myself telling Hoffman's story to that gas station owner and have it make sense to him as a small, rural business owner, which is perhaps a measuring stick for common business sense.

As I have seen, and witnessed firsthand on the front-lines of such an organization that did this, scaling organizations, building teams, and hiring people is incredibly challenging. People do not scale like software, and at the smallest sense of a slow in growth, what was once seen as a sound decision to grow the team as if the company were a $2B company suddenly looks like short sightedness. This slowed growth, which *will* happen, not if, brings about, not executives looking to fill chairs with bodies, but with the counting of heads on org-charts and, if done correctly by managers, the scrutiny of each individual's contributions to the team within the organization. For, after the music ends, comes the organization audits and, inevitably, the culling.

It is, fundamentally, I believe, about the unit economics of business that needs to eventually work in the favor of the enterprise in order to be competitive *over the long-run*. If the unit economics do not make sense, then the business will fail and competitors will triumph. Blitzscaling does not put the onus on unit economics but, rather, on scaling for the benefit of the valuation of the business. The valuation, after all, is how the founders cash out at acquisition or IPO. This is a short-term model of business building and one that is clouding the judgements of many a unicorn in the marketplace, for after the music stops and the cash to supplement poor unit economics stops coming in, then those that lose out, probably more than the founders, are the employees, who ultimately will be the ones whom will be on the short end of the string of layoffs that inevitably will follow in an effort to make unit economics make sense.

The Need for Leaders

I began down this path during a chapter meant to set out when Minimum Viable Strategy is not appropriate for companies like Harry's to explaining why some are now following it for false reasons (Blitzscaling) and, consequently, taking a jab at the Valley's irrational exuberance mindset with a purpose in my mind. That purpose is about the need for leadership.

It is clear that Silicon Valley is in need of real leadership, of managers willing to make tough choices in the face of those who would otherwise guide them down a less prosperous path. Even Silicon Valley itself recognizes this fact, as Don Faul, Chief Operating Officer at Athos, points out when he said, "The biggest scarcity in the Valley is great leaders."[265]

The Valley has sought to make up for this deficit by bringing on leaders with real, hard experiences who can make these tough choices, such as Navy SEALs and Army Rangers. The thought is that these units' experience with leading small, elite teams to success, despite being given tough objectives is just what the Valley needs to make a turnaround in various business units. The "decentralized decision making" in these teams is comparable to how Silicon Valley operates and, thus, the fit seems to be clear.

This may be a mask, however, for greater systemic problems. While it is commendable that the Valley is hiring veterans to make a real change in smaller teams, the leadership needs to come, ultimately, from the top in order to drive a company to see profitability and long-term competitiveness as a core part of the business objectives. This means founders, CEOs, COOs, and other executive level officers needs to look, not at their own net worth in terms of their company stock price, but for how the company will compete and be of value to its employees and customers for the foreseen and unforeseen future.

The Second Gilded Age

At a higher level, perhaps we are more generally living in what some describe as a Second Gilded Age. This is in reference to the age in the late 19th Century that, what some observers see as a time of growth and prosperity, was also a time of great social and political turmoil and disparity for many parts of America.

I say this because the concepts of Blitzscaling has put many companies and consequently the economy as a whole at risk of being gold on the outside but hollow on the inside, driven by a focus on un-profitable growth and valuations versus stable metrics that "boring" firms used to track their performance like profitability. While it is true that startups and entrepreneurship can create jobs and boost employment, if those jobs are in firms with fundamentally flawed business models, it could create more woe than not in instances when those firms have to downscale to stay afloat. In addition, many of these employers also create jobs that are low-skilled work and, consequently, pay low wages and aren't taking advantage of all of the skillsets that the current work force has gained through increased education access.

In the end, Dan Lyons, author of *Disrupted*, who chronicled his time at HubSpot in a groundbreaking book on aged employees in the tech industry, may be right when he describes the effects of poor economics on employees when companies like "Zynga and Groupon are losing hundreds of millions of dollars, yet their founders have become billionaires."[266] After decrying Reid Hoffman's LinkedIn for losing money three of the last ten years of its operations, even as late as 2015, and noting Hoffman's net worth is nearly $5 billion despite this fact, Mr. Lyons identifies that, under such unbalanced effects when the bubble of these startups bursts, the founders and their billions will be saved by the employees, who join these startups for the opportunity but will be left feeling the most pain when the music stops.[267]

But what does all of this have to do with strategy? Is it all just one person's rant? Perhaps, but strategists need to be acutely aware of their own tendencies toward personal hubris, and they need to recognize that it is their responsibility to see things as they are not as they want them to be. By giving a clear-eyed view of some fundamental economic factors that are causing this hubris in our current market, it is my goal to provide some level-headedness that, I hope, will be imbued upon the reader to provide steadiness to make strategy.

On Time

Conclusively and clearly, we can see that, indeed, a Minimum Viable Strategy approach is not the best approach in all circumstances. When firms lack the information, the discipline, an overarching strategy, or the time, this approach can either be premature or not fast enough. More often than not, the primary constraint is that of time.

This approach takes time and discipline to see through, to acquire a sense of success on the measured approach that the organization is taking toward progress and winning. Thus, if the organization has the time, it can be a winning strategic construct to follow for all the reasons mentioned previously. If the organization does not have the time, it can be detrimental.

But it is easy, as we have seen with Blitzscaling, to trick one's self into thinking that time is of a greater constraint than it may be. In 1942, could not a coherent argument be made for the constraints of time in favor of a European invasion? Did time not make itself to be the primary factor in the argument favoring missile strikes and invasion against Cuba in 1962? Was time not the reason Lego pursued diversification in order to stave off against the digital onslaught that was taking over the child's living room?

These would have been and were fair arguments, and in some cases the calls were heeded, such as with Lego, but in others leaders re-looked at the circumstances their organizations faced and pushed against the expert advice to buy their organizations more time, in small ways, through pursing a Minimum Viable Strategy in order to build capabilities, keep options open, and reduce systemic risk to the organization. Leaders must be frank with themselves and their teams about the true constraints and effects of time.

Is time really a factor? Was it a real factor for Harry's as we have argued? Counterfactuals are difficult if not impossible to ascertain in these cases that we have seen, but clear arguments can be made for either side of the table. What is clear is that, in almost all cases where a Minimum Viable Strategy was not pursued, retrospectively it is apparent that the organization bit off more than it could chew and that a measured approach was the more viable alternative. In that case and in that scenario, we should consider defaulting ourselves as leaders to a heuristic that leads us to look at scenarios through the lens of minimally viable options first before looking for the decisive victories or all-in strategies.

By defaulting to this heuristic, we will then assume that a measured approach is always the *right* one until a preponderance of factual evidence can prove otherwise. This approach puts the burden of evidence on the "all-in" strategy that has systemic implications versus a measured approach.

CONCLUSION

We seek to now conclude our discussion on strategy, its minimum viable aspects, and how we pursue and identify those aspects to not only seek results, but also to seek a greater understanding of our own organization and, perhaps, ourselves. What can we say that has not already been said? What can we hope to accomplish in these last few precious pages of writing that we have not already done so as, even in so few pages as we have written so far, we have covered and have said and done so much.

Perhaps we should begin to conclude with a warning to the strategist. After reading such promising tomes that foresee progress through thought and planning, one might be excited with the prospect of never ending success that will almost definitely come with simply laying out a plan that will be read well, consumed by many, and executed upon flawlessly.

This, however, cannot be farther from reality. There are specific faults of strategists that I have encountered and will seek to define and thwart for those who choose to be warned and, therefore, wish to take the higher but more dubious and more tenuous path.

The Armchair General

The first fault of strategists that I encounter most frequently is the fault of execution. The fault of execution lies with the armchair general. He who lays out a plan and seeks to find others to execute or he who takes pride in the print rather than the work to see the strategy through to success is the subject of our discussion. I encounter these strategists frequently in my time as an MBA student as many management consultants looking for a position at The Honest Company have often reached out to me in search of a position at a "cool" company but come to the table with the perspective of an armchair general.

It is no fault of their own, but rather the culture imbued upon them not only by the management consulting companies they have come from such as Bain or McKinsey but also from the way of working at their MBA programs. Indeed, our capstone project at UCLA Anderson involved this very form of armchair general strategy as we wrote a 50-page US Market Entry Strategy business plan which we handed to a Brazilian software development firm. After we were done with our slick B-Plan and beautifully designed 15-page PowerPoint presentation, which we presented and got many congratulations from the company and faculty on, we peaced out as the company was left to execute our "hopefully well-thought-out plan".

And, thus, these very same students believe they will come work at a startup, put together a 50-page business plan whom someone in the firm will execute upon. While these positions do exist at companies such as Honest, these individuals are few and, at least at Honest, all worked together at Goldman Sachs. They drive strategy at the highest level of the company. But, yet, there is strategy at every level of the company as each department must formulate its strategy, nested in the greater strategic goals of the over-arching company's strategy.

In addition, these strategists from Goldman Sachs who now work in the finance department, though incredibly smart and driven, are not executors.

They do not drive the strategy to fruition in the company. This is done by different parts of the organization, and it was the job of the team I was a part of to take that 10-year strategy developed by the finance guys and nest our operational strategy to be in line with the overall company strategy.

Our team of operational strategists not only took the strategy and created an operations strategy from it, but we also executed the very strategy that we formulated. Whether this was procuring warehouses, negotiating new shipping carrier deals, or implementing new technology to service our customers in a new way, we never saw our jobs as the "armchair generals" who wrote strategy and expected others to execute upon that strategy.

Thus, it is my personal belief from this experience that the best strategists are those that are doing the execution in a deep way. This is also a critical part, I believe, of Minimum Viable Strategy theory since, as we have discussed, the data points collected drive strategy formulation over short periods of time. Those closest to the data and to the real-world experiences are best equipped to make course corrections to strategy as different variables come into play over the course of strategy execution. These course corrections typically cannot wait for the quarterly strategy review for the "set-it-and-forget-it" strategists to review, make a decision, and have someone else execute, only to wait for the following quarter to get feedback.

Thus, Minimum Viable Strategy requires people of action, people who can drive results, and people who can conceptualize how to turn high-minded rhetoric into actionable things. These are the real strategists who drive a company to success by being close to the work, making small course corrections as necessary, and then formulating follow-on strategy based on first-hand experiences. These are strategists that also have a deep understanding of tactics in addition to strategy, which is hard to do if one goes straight from college to working in management consulting at McKinsey.

This is not to discredit the academic, but rather to place more emphasis on the executer than is given credit for today. The credit seems to lie, in today's business climate, with those who reside in ivory towers, dictating strategy without knowing how to execute. While, as mentioned before in this book, I think there is a role for strategic work from an academic standpoint, the emphasis should not be with the armchair general nor should the best talent be placed in this group for the company. Companies should invest their talent resources in the executors of strategy to the fullest extend available resources allow for.

Chancellorsville Syndrome

In one of my favorite books, James McPherson, frequent author on the American Civil War, walks readers through the battlefield of Gettysburg in *Hallowed Grounds*. I love reading the tales of heroism, of critical points of the battle that could have swayed it in either direction for either the North or the South, and the heroism on both sides. I especially enjoy reading about the West Point graduates who fought against each other in the battle and were personal friends from the Academy, an aspect of the battle that gives it a personal touch to graduates of the institution.

In the book, McPherson ponders what went wrong for the South during Gettysburg. When what appears to be a Southern victory on July 1st turned out to be a disaster in the making for Lee's army come 3 July, many have looked at the historical record to determine what decisions were made, why they were made and what could have been done different to drive different outcomes.

One of the hypothesis of McPherson is that the blunder of Pickett's Charge, a frontal assault made by the Confederacy that ended in disaster for the South and, thus, was a major reason for the loss of the battle for the Southern Armies. This was a decision made directly, in effect, by Lee, whom McPherson says was coming off of the victory at Chancellorsville with high confidence in that, by using similar tactics at Gettysburg that were used at Chancellorsville, his men would win the day.[268]

We often read, for those of us whom are investors, that previous returns are no guarantee of future success. This is also true of victory in battle, but yet it appears to historians and appeared to observers that during the Battle of Gettysburg that decisions were made, not from cold logic and sound judgement by Lee, but clouded by a sense that, despite the overwhelming evidence to the contrary, his men would be victorious if only they were given the chance to win. This clouded judgement, masked by the lingering feelings of previous accomplishment through past victory, is coined as "Chancellorsville Syndrome" by McPherson.[269]

Chancellorsville Syndrome is, in effect, the inability to make sound judgements for future strategy because previous victories have overshadowed the cold facts of the present. The realities of previous success that were true and led to those victories may not be relevant to the success of present activities and, therefore, what was once thought of as a "sure thing" dives to defeat because the enemy or the circumstances or the competition are underestimated, whom, because of previous defeats, over prepare for future encounters and, thus, perform at a higher level than in previous instances of engagement.

We can see this, not only in some of the case studies we have reviewed in this book, but also in our everyday lives. Did Target not think that a Canadian launch was a sure bet? Did Lego not think, after the resounding success of their Lego Star Wars line, that sales would continue to climb as aggressively in the future as they did in the past? The examples of Chancellorsville Syndrome are easily recognizable in our everyday lives, and it is something that strategists must always be aware of as strategy for future activities are formulated.

We suffered this even at The Honest Company, where resounding success for some product launches caused us to assume we could compete in many unrelated product categories. When results were not as expected, we wondered why did we underperform? Was it that we underperformed, or did Chancellorsville Syndrome creep in, causing our ambitious forecasts to be a bit higher than what a cold, factual analysis would have predicted?

It is often difficult to identify the existence of this syndrome in the present, but it is a factor that we, as strategists, must be fully aware of while formulating and debating strategy. Kennedy got around this, in many ways, by appointing a designated "Devil's Advocate" in debate, played by Bobby Kennedy, whom, despite the overwhelming majority of EXCOMM in favor of invasion, sought to debunk the proposal by looking for cracks in the argument. This strategy turned out to sway the course of the debate to a more reasonable solution that did not have false assumptions baked into it as was the case with Bay of Pigs. Thus, such a Devil's Advocate role defined in decision-making groups may be a fine solution to prevent Chancellorsville Syndrome from having negative impacts on strategic formulation in your organization.

Not Getting Buy-In

When I began taking my International Business Strategy class as part of my MBA program at UCLA Anderson, I used the capstone project of the course as an opportunity to develop an "international strategy" for the Honest Company. This, as mentioned before, is where the foundations for what I would later call a Minimum Viable Strategy were developed. When I presented the deck to my Vice President, there was intrigue, but there were greater expectations at the time for a full-bore launch into China and that was top of mind for everyone at the company versus a model to test the data before this launch. Much of the China strategy was driven by a single founder, Brian Lee, and everyone was marching to the beat of a single drum in that regard, as they should have been.

It took almost a full year of lunches, short 15-minute conversations by the water cooler, or 30-minute presentations on the idea to small groups to get people to start talking about the potential of a Minimally Viable International Strategy for the brand and, finally, a GO decision by the executives to pursue the idea beyond the slideshow was made. The reason behind the gaining of steam for the idea was the very question about a risky push into China in advance of actual collection of data, the fundamental principles of a Minimal Viable Strategy.

Thus, it was not an idea that was "so good" folks went crazy about it when it was first introduced. Thus, over that year, as I kept pursuing the idea in small bits, I realized a couple of things. The first is that getting "buy-in" on strategy is typically as much work, if not more work, than actually developing the strategy. Without "buy-in" from smaller groups that eventually turn into bigger groups, it will be difficult for any idea to gain traction and, consequently, become an effective strategy.

It was a painful yet extremely valuable learning experience for myself, whom, as mentioned before, came from the Army, an organization where "buy-in" isn't really required but demanded through orders from commanding officers. The concept of "buy-in" from a strategist's perspective is an art more than a science and, as strategists who typically think in mathematical terms, this can be difficult to grasp conceptually and there can be heuristic flaws where strategists assume that if the numbers make sense, everyone will "buy-in". This, however, as I have learned is not always the case. Rationality does not always supersede emotion; indeed, it rarely does in any organization.

Thus, strategists are left with the concept of "buy-in" to help persuade people in their organization that the proposed strategy is a fitting one. Often, strategists seek to gain "buy-in" from the very top, as I did with a minimally viable international strategy proposal, which I sent to my Vice President. But these are often the most difficult folks to get "buy-in" from as change is often difficult to sell as an idea in isolation. Thus, "buy-in" must be gained from mid-level individuals first before it should be pursued at a higher level. This "mid-level" buy-in gets the engines of talk going around the company in favor of such a strategy and, thus, those mid-level folks become advocates for such a strategy. The more advocates whom are in favor across the organization, the more convincing the argument for such a strategy will be to higher executive levels of the organization.

Getting "buy-in", even from a top-down perspective on strategy is also critical as well. While the above example was more "bottom's-up", executives who seek to define strategy should also get alignment from all levels of the organization as well as feedback on the proposed strategy. This feedback will allow for all members of a business to feel as if they, too, own the plan and that everyone in the company is in the same boat working toward a greater goal rather than just "doing what they are told."

Losing Operational Discipline

The common sense amongst MBA students when assessing how particular career paths rank against one another is that finance and strategy are usually at the top of the food chain, marketing and sales somewhere in the middle, and operations is at the bottom. Even Michael Porter says that operational effectiveness is the baseline for performance of organizations and is not inherently strategy.

As someone who works in operations, I'd like to take a moment to reflect on this and perhaps, in some way, bring operations a bit higher on the pyramid and make it return to a prominent place among academics and young professionals. While I agree that operations are not inherently strategy, it cannot be ignored by strategists either. Operational discipline is inherently necessary for survival, as Lego learned in the early 2000's and Target learned during its launch into Canada. Strategic thought in the absence of operational thinking is doomed to fail.

But operations require a tremendous amount of physical effort. It requires leaders to follow the Japanese management philosophy of Genchi Genbutsu, or to go and see. Operations requires leaders to be on the front lines of sometimes less than desirable work environments, which is harder than sitting at a desk in front of an excel spreadsheet in an air-conditioned office on a business campus. It can be physically, mentally, and emotionally uncomfortable, often involving spending lots of time in hot or cold warehouses.

This daunting task of "doing stuff" doesn't appeal to consultants and bankers or finance folks who'd rather live in Microsoft Excel. It requires a comfort with the gritty side of the business. Thus, organizations that lose sight of the importance of operational discipline because it's uncomfortable to focus on operational discipline end up paying for it in the long-run.

Again, it is my belief that, to the detriment of many organizations, operations are too often downplayed and seen as "less important" than strategy or finance. On the contrary, as I've made the case before, operations should be held up as the pinnacle of where talent should be allocated to and resourced as operational discipline and innovation can make or break and organization.

Murphy's Law

Finally, at the conclusion of this book about strategy, we look a bit ahead to determine the utility of such a book in the future of business and in war. Is such a principle fitting of CEOs, Presidents, and Generals in an age of almost unlimited data manipulation and storage, of nuclear weapons, of powerful forces that can swiftly project overwhelming power anywhere in the world in a matter of hours? We are bombarded with the conceptual philosophy of the first mover advantage, of growth at all costs for companies, of "Shock and Awe" against our enemies, and are, thus, left to wonder if an approach such as one with minimal viability has a place in our world today.

In an age such as this, one may come to believe that this approach does not have a place in our world. However, I would counter-argue that the age-old principles that I learned at the Academy, namely Murphy's Law, or "what can go wrong will go wrong", and that "the plan is only good until the first shot is fired", still ring true in both the business world and in the sphere of human conflict.

Given we know that these principles exist, we also accept that forecasts are increasingly inaccurate over the horizon of time and that, although we can spend much time pontificating on the response of the market, it is often difficult to project just how a company will perform in a new market. It is with these truths of uncertainty in mind and the knowledge that we should always expect the worst to go wrong if it can that we should approach strategy formulation and execution.

We do not suggest that timidity rule the day in execution of strategy; but, rather, that companies and armies should consider the options and formulate strategy against placing all of their chips on the table in a single, decisive engagement, market strategy, or product. It is preferable to, instead, take a data-centric approach around growth and the execution of strategy and seek strategies that do not bet the house on unknowns.

The execution of Minimally Viable Strategies should be executed with vigor and aggression, with the full intent of proving hypothesis true or false in as short a time with as few resources as possible in order to move forward to the next data collection task as part of the overall execution of the strategy. It is the aggressive pursuit of truth, therefore, that the strategy proposes companies seek to engage their resources in for the long-term.

It is, in the final analysis, the truth that armies and companies seek. They seek truth about their companies, their products, their strengths and weaknesses, and their capabilities. The truth is what this book proposes that leaders pursue in a rigorous and structured way without putting the entire organization at risk in pursuit of that truth.

Once this truth is found, however, it is freeing to the mind of a leader, knowing that the rest of the road map he or she has laid out for their organizations has either been proved or disproved by factual knowledge instead of conjecture. This truth is freeing in decision making when contributing more resources to an engagement or a cause. Finally, it is this truth we urge you, the leader, to seek through discipline and rigor.

EPILOGUE

At the completion of this book in the winter of 2016, at the end of the tumultuous presidential election cycle, I began to think of the faults of this book. There are many, of course, but one that stuck out to me was this book's lack of appeal to the raw, unshielded human emotions that drives much of our decision making as people. I focus here on the need for data-driven decisions, as many companies these days are trying to do, but by doing so perhaps I am missing out on a critical aspect of what drives and creates our humanity. One can argue that the strategy employed by the winning Republican candidate in 2016 was not necessarily a data-driven strategy but an emotion driven strategy, and it was a strategy that was employed and executed upon to success.

After considering this deeply, I acknowledge and recognize this fact and realize that, by not appealing to the human emotions that are so frequently driving decisions, perhaps this book will not find its way into the hearts of people as others that do appeal to those emotions otherwise will. This is fine for me, as my objective is to strip away the emotions and reveal clear-eyed thinking.

But is there a place for emotion? Of course. When the time comes to make the hard decisions and you have arrived at a critical juncture where that decision becomes existential, then emotion will play a part. Will you fight or perish? There is no longer data to consider. When you are a lieutenant on the beaches of Normandy leading soldiers into battle, data is gone and you are simply left with the raw, human emotion of fear, courage, and anger. Which you choose is not a data driven decision, but one that comes from who you are as a person and whom you seek to be.

Thus, despite being data driven, it is important to note here the significance that human emotion and the human spirit take part in how history plays out and how plans are executed against and are felt for, either rationally or irrationally. This is something that strategists must always bear in mind and know when to look past data at the raw human variables of life in the universe.

Finally, I'd also like to end this book with a final warning. I departed the Honest Company in the late summer of 2016 to join another startup in Denver, Colorado. At the time of my departure, it was clear that a malaise was settling over the company and, to no one's surprise, in December of 2016 the Honest Company laid off 15% of its staff. Many observers claimed that the move was inevitable, as the Honest Company staffed itself and saw itself as a tech startup despite having the margins and scalability of a consumer products company. Indeed, Honest lost an acquisition play to Unilever, who instead acquired Seventh Generation because the operating principles that Seventh Generation employed were more sound: lower corporate staffing with comparable revenues.

All too often in startup circles I hear "If we cut marketing spend, we'd be profitable tomorrow." This is something I heard at Honest too, but the fundamental truth is that this isn't long-term thinking. Can an online company that survives based on getting a certain number of new customers every month really employ a long-term strategy of becoming profitable, eventually, but cutting marketing spend to near-zero? This is hope without a plan (I don't believe in hope, only plans), and was an attitude that I was happy to depart from for the Rocky Mountain culture of the grit required to become sustainable, not lofty self-prescribed visions of your own grandeur.

Honest did not employ a Minimum Viable Strategy, or any clear strategy for that matter, and continues to suffer those consequences while it searches for profitability and an exit. Alternatively, in Denver, I found the anti-Silicon Valley mentality: where profitability matters and lavishness in office designs is an expression of abundance that is blinding to underlying problems. Perhaps this is a difference in geography: the grit of the Rockies versus the glamor of the Hollywood Hills. Regardless, one works for business in perpetuity while the other does not.

It is in the Rockies that I found the approach to scaling methodically that I was looking for, hopefully for the long-run. With all the lessons taken from my experiences in war, the military academy, business school, startup life, I can say this: the things that were true yesterday are typically the same fundamental things that will be true tomorrow. Fundamentals matters, risk can and should be mitigated, and people are bad at doing new things for the first time. Given all of these factors, I hope you, the reader, have found a useful tool in MVS to employ in order to ensure you don't bet the house on doing stuff you've never done before.

A SHORT READING LIST

Below is a list of books I recommend be read by anyone, strategist or not, interested in learning more about the world, history, strategy, business, or other topics I think worth of someone hoping to be or in a leadership position. I've also included commentary regarding why each is on this list and why, from my perspective, it is worth your time to read. It's a short list, but potent in takeaways for strategists.

1. *Eisenhower In War and Peace* – One of the greatest leaders of the modern age, Dwight D. Eisenhower comes to life in this book. His systematic methods of management (he invented the Chief of Staff role and played a major role in other executive reorganizations in the West Wing) are case studies in how organizations should be run methodically.

2. *Playing to Win* – Mentioned many times in this book as the founding principles we base Minimum Viable Strategy construct on, this book is the starting point for any serious business strategist looking to understand how companies like P&G continue to win year in and year out.

3. *Superforecasting* – Forecasting probabilities is hard, but organizations can become better at predictability, which is the key to operational discipline. This book offers some insight into the qualitative and quantitative methods to become better forecasters. Understanding probabilistic thinking is key to understanding Minimum Viable Strategy.

4. *The Week the World Stood Still* – This book is based on the transcribed audio tapes from the EXCOMM deliberations during the Cuban Missile Crisis. This is perhaps the best account of any presidential cabinet level deliberations during a serious national security crisis every recorded in history. The insight into actual words said and how deliberations play out in real time is crucial for anyone interested in organizational and behavioral psychology or for any leader for that matter.

5. *Moneyball* – The ultimate sports-data book and behavioral psychology book. Michael Lewis tells an incredible story of the Oakland Athletics' journey to success as the poorest team in baseball through using data to build a winning bench. Anyone interested in data-driven decisions should read this book.

A NOTE FROM THE AUTHOR

"Thanks for Reading the Book"

I hope the book inspires startups and other organizations to take a new approach to strategy formulation by implementing a methodology that involves reducing existential risk, testing strategic hypothesis, and using data from this method to make better, deliberate choices about strategy.

ABOUT JOHN

John is a West Point graduate, veteran of the war in Afghanistan, has obtained his MBA from UCLA, and has worked for high-growth startups such as The Honest Company in Santa Monica, CA.

Learn more about John and his other writings at:
MINIMUMVIABLESTRATEGY.com

CONSCIOUS WRITING

Based on our experience with the Conscious Capitalism movement, we are taking similar principles and applying them to what we term the **Conscious Writing** initiative at Minimum Viable Strategy.

For every copy of the book sold, one dollar will be donated to UNICEF Education Programs. Few things are more important in life than being granted the opportunity for a quality education.

By partnering with UNICEF, we are striving towards achieving that goal of a quality education for everyone who is exposed to the greatest level of need. Writing is as much about education and learning as anything else, and it is fitting that through writing we can work together with UNICEF to achieve better outcomes for those who need our assistance.

NOTES

[1] "The Electoral College Blind Spot | FiveThirtyEight." 23 Jan. 2017, https://fivethirtyeight.com/features/the-electoral-college-blind-spot/.

[2] A Death in the Class of 9/11 - TIME." http://content.time.com/time/nation/article/0,8599,1540856-4,00.html.

[3] "The peculiar traits of great Amazon leaders: Frugal, innovative and ...." 13 May. 2015, https://www.geekwire.com/2015/the-peculiar-traits-of-great-amazon-leaders-frugal-innovative-and-body-odor-that-doesnt-smell-like-perfume/.

[4] Tetlock, Philip, and Dan Gardner. Superforecasting the Art and Science of Prediction. Random House Books, 2016. Page 214.

[5] Ietlock, Philip, and Dan Gardner. Superforecasting the Art and Science of Prediction. Random House Books, 2016. Page 214.

[6] Tetlock, Philip, and Dan Gardner. Superforecasting the Art and Science of Prediction. Random House Books, 2016. Page 244.

[7] Tetlock, Philip, and Dan Gardner. Superforecasting the Art and Science of Prediction. Random House Books, 2016. Page 244.

[8] "One Kings Lane sold for less than $30 million after being ... - Recode." 23 Aug. 2016, https://www.recode.net/2016/8/23/12588428/one-kings-lane-flash-sales-acquisition-price-bed-bath-beyond.

[9] Lafley, A. G., and Roger L. Martin. Playing to Win: How Strategy Really Works. Boston, MA: Harvard Business Review, 2013. Print.

[10] Freedman, Lawrence. Strategy: A History. New York: Oxford UP, 2015. Page IX.

[11] Freedman, Lawrence. Strategy: A History. New York: Oxford UP, 2015. Page X.

[12] Ghemawat, Pankaj. "Competition and Business Strategy in Historical Perspective." SSRN Electronic Journal (n.d.).

[13] Freedman, Lawrence. Strategy: A History. New York: Oxford UP, 2015. Audio Book. Chapter 4, position 1:56:22.

[14] Freedman, Lawrence. Strategy: A History. New York: Oxford UP, 2015. Page IX.

[15] Beard, Mary. SPQR: A History of Ancient Rome. New York: Liveright Corporation, a Division of W.W. Norton, 2016. Audio Book. Chapter 4, position 27:41.

[16] Beard, Mary. SPQR: A History of Ancient Rome. New York: Liveright Corporation, a Division of W.W. Norton, 2016. Audio Book. Chapter 4, position 27:41.

[17] Ghemawat, Pankaj. "Competition and Business Strategy in Historical Perspective." SSRN Electronic Journal (n.d.). Page 37.

[18] Ghemawat, Pankaj. "Competition and Business Strategy in Historical Perspective." SSRN Electronic Journal (n.d.). Page 38.

[19] Ghemawat, Pankaj. "Competition and Business Strategy in Historical Perspective." SSRN Electronic Journal (n.d.).Page 38.

[20] Ghemawat, Pankaj. "Competition and Business Strategy in Historical Perspective." SSRN Electronic Journal (n.d.). Page 40.

[21] Ghemawat, Pankaj. "Competition and Business Strategy in Historical Perspective." SSRN Electronic Journal (n.d.).Page 39.

[22] Ghemawat, Pankaj. "Competition and Business Strategy in Historical Perspective." SSRN Electronic Journal (n.d.).Page 39.

[23] Ghemawat, Pankaj. "Competition and Business Strategy in Historical Perspective." SSRN Electronic Journal (n.d.).Page 38.

[24] Ghemawat, Pankaj. "Competition and Business Strategy in Historical Perspective." SSRN Electronic Journal (n.d.).Page 38.

[25] Ghemawat, Pankaj. "Competition and Business Strategy in Historical Perspective." SSRN Electronic Journal (n.d.).Page 41.

[26] Leinwand, Paul, and Cesare Mainardi. Strategy That Works: How Winning Companies Close the Strategy-to-execution Gap. Boston, MA: Harvard Business Review, 2016. Print. Page 205.

[27] Porter, M. E. "What Is Strategy?" Harvard Business Review 74, no. 6 (November–December 1996): 61–78.R

[28] Leinwand, Paul, and Cesare Mainardi. Strategy That Works: How Winning Companies Close the Strategy-to-execution Gap. Boston, MA: Harvard Business Review, 2016. Print. Page 205.

[29] Reeves, Martin, Knut HaanÃ¦s, and Janmejaya Sinha. Your Strategy Needs a Strategy: How to Choose and Execute the Right Approach. Boston, MA: Harvard Business Review, 2015. Print.

[30] Reeves, Martin, Knut HaanÃ¦s, and Janmejaya Sinha. Your Strategy Needs a Strategy: How to Choose and Execute the Right Approach. Boston, MA: Harvard Business Review, 2015. Print. Page 28.

[31] Collis, David. "Lean Strategy." Harvard Business Review. N.p., 09 June 2016. Web. 03 Aug. 2017.

[32] Collis, David. "Lean Strategy." Harvard Business Review. N.p., 09 June 2016. Web. 03 Aug. 2017.

[33] Collis, David. "Lean Strategy." Harvard Business Review. N.p., 09 June 2016. Web. 03 Aug. 2017.

[34] Collis, David. "Lean Strategy." Harvard Business Review. N.p., 09 June 2016. Web. 03 Aug. 2017.

[35] "Why Amazon is the Best Place in the World to Fail" The Organge County Register pg. 5 Business Section by Jena McGregor The Washington Post

[36]http://www.fool.com/investing/general/2016/02/15/is-this-the-real-reason-why-amazoncom-wants-its-ow.aspx

[37] Collins, James C., and Morten T. Hansen. Great by Choice: Uncertainty, Chaos, and Luck: Why Some Thrive despite Them All. New York, NY: HarperCollins, 2011. Print.

[38] Collins, James C., and Morten T. Hansen. Great by Choice: Uncertainty, Chaos, and Luck: Why Some Thrive despite Them All. New York, NY: HarperCollins, 2011. Print.

[39] Collins, James C., and Morten T. Hansen. Great by Choice: Uncertainty, Chaos, and Luck: Why Some Thrive despite Them All. New York, NY: HarperCollins, 2011. Print.

[40] Collins, James C., and Morten T. Hansen. Great by Choice: Uncertainty, Chaos, and Luck: Why Some Thrive despite Them All. New York, NY: HarperCollins, 2011. Page 87.

[41] Collins, James C., and Morten T. Hansen. Great by Choice: Uncertainty, Chaos, and Luck: Why Some Thrive despite Them All. New York, NY: HarperCollins, 2011. Page 87.

[42] Leinwand, Paul, and Cesare Mainardi. Strategy That Works: How Winning Companies Close the Strategy-to-execution Gap. Boston, MA: Harvard Business Review, 2016. Page 14.

[43] On Strategy. Boston, MA: Harvard Business Review, 2010. Page 125, Blue Ocean Strategy chapter.

[44] On Strategy. Boston, MA: Harvard Business Review, 2010. Page 125, Blue Ocean Strategy chapter.

[45] On Strategy. Boston, MA: Harvard Business Review, 2010. Page 125, Blue Ocean Strategy chapter.

[46] On Strategy. Boston, MA: Harvard Business Review, 2010. Page 132-133, Blue Ocean Strategy chapter.

[47] On Strategy. Boston, MA: Harvard Business Review, 2010. Page 134, Blue Ocean Strategy chapter.s

[48] On Strategy. Boston, MA: Harvard Business Review, 2010. Page 138, Blue Ocean Strategy chapter.

[49] "Learning Curve Analysis." Pearsons. Web. http://wps.pearsoned.co.uk/wps/media/objects/8970/9185376/65767_30_Suppl.pdf

[50] "Learning Curve Analysis." Pearsons. Web. http://wps.pearsoned.co.uk/wps/media/objects/8970/9185376/65767_30_Suppl.pdf

[51] "WHY DID THE RAF BOMB CITIES?" National Archives. United Kingdom, n.d. Web. http://www.nationalarchives.gov.uk/education/worldwar2/theatres-of-war/western-europe/investigation/hamburg/sources/docs/7/

[52] Wayne, William J. AbernathyKenneth. "Limits of the Learning Curve." Harvard Business Review. N.p., 01 Aug. 2014. Web. 07 Aug. 2017.

53 Wayne, William J. AbernathyKenneth. "Limits of the Learning Curve." Harvard Business Review. N.p., 01 Aug. 2014. Web. 07 Aug. 2017.

54 Wayne, William J. AbernathyKenneth. "Limits of the Learning Curve." Harvard Business Review. N.p., 01 Aug. 2014. Web. 07 Aug. 2017.

55 Wayne, William J. AbernathyKenneth. "Limits of the Learning Curve." Harvard Business Review. N.p., 01 Aug. 2014. Web. 07 Aug. 2017.

56 Mauboussin, Michael, Dan Callahan, and Darius Majd. "The Base Rates Book." Credit Suisse, 26 Sept. 2016. Web. https://research-doc.credit suisse.com/docView?language=ENG&format=PDF&source_id=csplusresearchcp&document_id=1065113751&serialid=Z1zrAAt3OJhElh4iwlYc9JHmliTCIAR-Gu75f0b5s4bc%3D

57 Zweig, Jason. "Some of the Wisest Words Ever Spoken About Investing." The Wall Street Journal. Dow Jones & Company, 25 Nov. 2016. Web. 07 Aug. 2017.

58 Mauboussin, Michael, Dan Callahan, and Darius Majd. "The Base Rates Book." Credit Suisse, 26 Sept. 2016. Web. https://research-doc.credit suisse.com/docView?language=ENG&format=PDF&source_id=csplusresearchcp&document_id=1065113751&serialid=Z1zrAAt3OJhElh4iwlYc9JHmliTCIAR-Gu75f0b5s4bc%3D

59 Zweig, Jason. "Some of the Wisest Words Ever Spoken About Investing." The Wall Street Journal. Dow Jones & Company, 25 Nov. 2016. Web. 07 Aug. 2017.

60 "Asset Prices Are High across the Board. Is It Time to Worry?" The Economist, The Economist Newspaper, 7 Oct. 2017, www.economist.com/news/leaders/21730019-ultra-loose-monetary-policy-coming-end-it-best-tread-carefully-asset-prices-are.

61 Graham, Benjamin. The Intelligent Investor: the Definitive Book on Value Investing. Harper, 2006. Page 512.

62 "Here's an Explanation of Ben Graham's Concept of 'Margin of Safety'." Business Insider, Business Insider, 10 Feb. 2016, www.businessinsider.com/ben-grahams-concept-margin-of-safety-2016-2.

63 Shurkin, Michael. "The French Way of War."POLITICO Magazine. N.p., 17 Nov. 2015. Web. 07 Aug. 2017.

64 Shurkin, Michael". The French Way of War."POLITICO Magazine. N.p., 17 Nov. 2015. Web. 07 Aug. 2017.

65 Shurkin, Michael. "The French Way of War."POLITICO Magazine. N.p., 17 Nov. 2015. Web. 07 Aug. 2017.

66 Goldberg, Jeffrey. "The Obama Doctrine." The Atlantic. Atlantic Media Company, 17 Mar. 2016. Web. 07 Aug. 2017.

67 "The Birth of an Obama Doctrine." The Economist. The Economist Newspaper, 28 Mar. 2011. Web. 07 Aug. 2017.

68 Goldberg, Jeffrey. "The Obama Doctrine." The Atlantic. Atlantic Media Company, 17 Mar. 2016. Web. 07 Aug. 2017.

69 "John F. Kennedy: Book Review by Senator John F. Kennedy of." The American Presidency Project. N.p., n.d. Web. 07 Aug. 2017. http://www.presidency.ucsb.edu/ws/?pid=25937.

[70] "John F. Kennedy: Book Review by Senator John F. Kennedy of." The American Presidency Project. N.p., n.d. Web. 07 Aug. 2017. http://www.presidency.ucsb.edu/ws/?pid=25937.

[71] "John F. Kennedy: Book Review by Senator John F. Kennedy of." The American Presidency Project. N.p., n.d. Web. 07 Aug. 2017. http://www.presidency.ucsb.edu/ws/?pid=25937.

[72] Snyder, Glenn H.. "Deterrence, Defense, and Disengagement". World Politics 14.2 (1962): 393–403.

[73] Snyder, Glenn H.. "Deterrence, Defense, and Disengagement". World Politics 14.2 (1962): 393–403.

[74] "The Return of Von Clausewitz." The Economist. The Economist Newspaper, 09 Mar. 2002. Web. 07 Aug. 2017.

[75] "The Return of Von Clausewitz." The Economist. The Economist Newspaper, 09 Mar. 2002. Web. 07 Aug. 2017.

[76] "The Return of Von Clausewitz." The Economist. The Economist Newspaper, 09 Mar. 2002. Web. 07 Aug. 2017.

[77] "The Return of Von Clausewitz." The Economist. The Economist Newspaper, 09 Mar. 2002. Web. 07 Aug. 2017.

[78] "The Return of Von Clausewitz." The Economist. The Economist Newspaper, 09 Mar. 2002. Web. 07 Aug. 2017.

[79] "The Return of Von Clausewitz." The Economist. The Economist Newspaper, 09 Mar. 2002. Web. 07 Aug. 2017.

[80] "How the Weak Vanquish the Strong." The Economist. The Economist Newspaper, 19 Jan. 2013. Web. 07 Aug. 2017.

[81] "How the Weak Vanquish the Strong." The Economist. The Economist Newspaper, 19 Jan. 2013. Web. 07 Aug. 2017.

[82] Ryan, Cornelius. A Bridge Too Far. London: Hodder, 2007. Audible audio version. Chapter 15, 13.33

[83] Ryan, Cornelius. A Bridge Too Far. London: Hodder, 2007. Audible audio version. Chapter 15, 14:00.

[84] Lewis, Michael. The Undoing Project: A Friendship That Changed Our Minds. New York: W.W. Norton, 2017. Audible audio version. Chapter 2, 35:59.

[85] Lewis, Michael. Moneyball: The Art of Winning an Unfair Game. New York: W.W. Norton, 2013. 18. Print.

[86] Lewis, Michael. Moneyball: The Art of Winning an Unfair Game. New York: W.W. Norton, 2013. 18. Print.

[87] Lewis, Michael. Moneyball: The Art of Winning an Unfair Game. New York: W.W. Norton, 2013. 18. Print.

[88] Lewis, Michael. Moneyball: The Art of Winning an Unfair Game. New York: W.W. Norton, 2013. 18. Print.

[89] Lewis, Michael. Moneyball: The Art of Winning an Unfair Game. New York: W.W. Norton, 2013. Audible audio version. Chapter 5, 30:00.

[90] Lewis, Michael. Moneyball: The Art of Winning an Unfair Game. New York: W.W. Norton, 2013. Audible audio version. Chapter 5, 30:00.

[91] Johnson, Keith. "What Kind of Game Is China Playing?" The Wall Street Journal. Dow Jones & Company, 11 June 2011. Web. 07 Aug. 2017.

[92] Nougayrède, Natalie. "The Best Lesson China Could Teach Europe: How to Play the Long Game | Natalie Nougayrède." The Guardian. Guardian News and Media, 23 Oct. 2015. Web. 07 Aug. 2017.

[93] Powell, Bill. "China's Not-So-Secret Game Plan." Newsweek. N.p., 21 Mar. 2016. Web. 08 Aug. 2017.

[94] Powell, Bill. "China's Not-So-Secret Game Plan." Newsweek. N.p., 21 Mar. 2016. Web. 08 Aug. 2017.

[95] Carlson, Benjamin. "Why Big American Businesses Fail in China." CNBC. CNBC, 27 Sept. 2013. Web. 08 Aug. 2017.

[96] Haas, Julian. Birkinshaw, Martine. "Increase Your Return on Failure." Harvard Business Review. N.p., 10 May 2016. Web. 08 Aug. 2017.

[97] Haas, Julian. Birkinshaw, Martine. "Increase Your Return on Failure." Harvard Business Review. N.p., 10 May 2016. Web. 08 Aug. 2017.

[98] Haas, Julian. Birkinshaw, Martine. "Increase Your Return on Failure." Harvard Business Review. N.p., 10 May 2016. Web. 08 Aug. 2017.

[99] "Trial and Error Is No Way to Make Strategy." 2015. 13 Oct. 2015 <https://hbr.org/2015/04/trial-and-error-is-no-way-to-make-strategy>

[100] "Playing To Win: How Strategy Really Works - HBR." 2014. 13 Oct. 2015 <https://hbr.org/books/playing-to-win>

[101] "Why a Strategy Is Not a Plan." The Economist. The Economist Newspaper, 02 Nov. 2013. Web. 08 Aug. 2017.

[102] "Why a Strategy Is Not a Plan." The Economist. The Economist Newspaper, 02 Nov. 2013. Web. 08 Aug. 2017.

[103] Haas, Julian BirkinshawMartine. "Increase Your Return on Failure." Harvard Business Review. N.p., 10 May 2016. Web. 08 Aug. 2017.

[104] Hamilton, Nigel. The Mantle of Command: FDR at War, 1941-1942. London: Biteback, 2016. Print. Page 328.

[105] Hamilton, Nigel. The Mantle of Command: FDR at War, 1941-1942. London: Biteback, 2016. Print. Page 328.

[106] Hamilton, Nigel. The Mantle of Command: FDR at War, 1941-1942. London: Biteback, 2016. Print. Page 345.

[107] Hamilton, Nigel. The Mantle of Command: FDR at War, 1941-1942. London: Biteback, 2016. Print.

[108] Hamilton, Nigel. The Mantle of Command: FDR at War, 1941-1942. London: Biteback, 2016. Print.

[109] Hamilton, Nigel. The Mantle of Command: FDR at War, 1941-1942. London: Biteback, 2016. Print. Page 329.

[110] Hamilton, Nigel. The Mantle of Command: FDR at War, 1941-1942. London: Biteback, 2016. Print.

[111] Hamilton, Nigel. The Mantle of Command: FDR at War, 1941-1942. London: Biteback, 2016. Print.

[112] "Military Science." WPI. N.p., n.d. Web. 08 Aug. 2017. <http://www.wpi.edu/academics/military/prinwar.html>.

[113] Hamilton, Nigel. The Mantle of Command: FDR at War, 1941-1942. London: Biteback, 2016. Print.

[114] Hamilton, Nigel. The Mantle of Command: FDR at War, 1941-1942. London: Biteback, 2016. Print. Page 349.

[115] McPherson, James M. Tried by War: Abraham Lincoln as Commander in Chief. Waterville, ME: Thorndike, 2009. Audible. Chapter 1, position 1:17:05

[116] McPherson, James M. Tried by War: Abraham Lincoln as Commander in Chief. Waterville, ME: Thorndike, 2009. Audible. Chapter 2, position 4:24.

[117] Hamilton, Nigel. The Mantle of Command: FDR at War, 1941-1942. London: Biteback, 2016. Print. Page 353.

[118] Stern, Sheldon M. The Week the World Stood Still: Inside the Secret Cuban Missile Crisis. Stanford, CA: Stanford U, 2007. Print. Page 43.

[119] Stern, Sheldon M. The Week the World Stood Still: Inside the Secret Cuban Missile Crisis. Stanford, CA: Stanford U, 2007. Print. Page 45.

[120] Newhouse, John. "13 Days That Almost Shook the World." The New York Times. The New York Times, n.d. Web. 08 Aug. 2017.

[121] Jordan Michael Smith Globe Correspondent October 21, 2012. "Cuban Missile Crisis: In 1962, Did a Mistake save the World? - The Boston Globe." BostonGlobe.com. N.p., 21 Oct. 2012. Web. 08 Aug. 2017.

[122] Tuchman, Barbara Wertheim. The Guns of August. New York: Ballantine, 1990. Print.

[123] Stern, Sheldon M. The Week the World Stood Still: Inside the Secret Cuban Missile Crisis. Stanford, CA: Stanford U, 2007. Print.

[124] Stern, Sheldon M. The Week the World Stood Still: Inside the Secret Cuban Missile Crisis. Stanford, CA: Stanford U, 2007. Print. Page 28.

[125] "JFK Tapes » Curtis LeMay on the Cuban Missile Crisis and Blockade." The Fourteenth Day: JFK & the Aftermath of the Cuban Missile Crisis. N.p., 10 May 2016. Web. 08 Aug. 2017.

[126] Tetlock, Philip, and Dan Gardner. Superforecasting the Art and Science of Prediction. London: Random House, 2016. Print. Page 55.

[127] "The Cuban Missile Crisis, 1962." The Cuban Missile Crisis | Wyzant Resources. N.p., n.d. Web. 08 Aug. 2017. <https://www.wyzant.com/resources/lessons/history/hpol/jfk/cuban>.

[128] Menezes, David Wood, Tarika. "Target Corporation: The Canadian Decision." Harvard Business Review, hbr.org/product/target-corporation-the-canadian-decision/W15334-PDF-ENG.

[129] Menezes, David Wood, Tarika. "Target Corporation: The Canadian Decision." Harvard Business Review, hbr.org/product/target-corporation-the-canadian-decision/W15334-PDF-ENG.

[130] Menezes, David Wood, Tarika. "Target Corporation: The Canadian Decision." Harvard Business Review, hbr.org/product/target-corporation-the-canadian-decision/W15334-PDF-ENG.

[131] Menezes, David Wood, Tarika. "Target Corporation: The Canadian Decision." Harvard Business Review, hbr.org/product/target-corporation-the-canadian-decision/W15334-PDF-ENG.

[132] Menezes, David Wood, Tarika. "Target Corporation: The Canadian Decision." Harvard Business Review, hbr.org/product/target-corporation-the-canadian-decision/W15334-PDF-ENG.

[133] Menezes, David Wood, Tarika. "Target Corporation: The Canadian Decision." Harvard Business Review, hbr.org/product/target-corporation-the-canadian-decision/W15334-PDF-ENG.

[134] Menezes, David Wood, Tarika. "Target Corporation: The Canadian Decision." Harvard Business Review, hbr.org/product/target-corporation-the-canadian-decision/W15334-PDF-ENG.

[135] Menezes, David Wood, Tarika. "Target Corporation: The Canadian Decision." Harvard Business Review, hbr.org/product/target-corporation-the-canadian-decision/W15334-PDF-ENG.

[136] Menezes, David Wood, Tarika. "Target Corporation: The Canadian Decision." Harvard Business Review, hbr.org/product/target-corporation-the-canadian-decision/W15334-PDF-ENG.

[137] Menezes, David Wood, Tarika. "Target Corporation: The Canadian Decision." Harvard Business Review, hbr.org/product/target-corporation-the-canadian-decision/W15334-PDF-ENG.

[138] Menezes, David Wood, Tarika. "Target Corporation: The Canadian Decision." Harvard Business Review, hbr.org/product/target-corporation-the-canadian-decision/W15334-PDF-ENG.

[139] Menezes, David Wood, Tarika. "Target Corporation: The Canadian Decision." Harvard Business Review, hbr.org/product/target-corporation-the-canadian-decision/W15334-PDF-ENG.

[140] Menezes, David. Wood, Tarika. "Target Corporation: The Canadian Decision." Harvard Business Review, hbr.org/product/target-corporation-the-canadian-decision/W15334-PDF-ENG.

[141] Menezes, David Wood. Tarika. "Target Corporation: The Canadian Decision." Harvard Business Review, hbr.org/product/target-corporation-the-canadian-decision/W15334-PDF-ENG.

[142] Pirouz, Dante. Hong, Steven. "Target Canada." Harvard Business Review, https://hbr.org/product/target-canada/W14656-PDF-ENG#.

[143] Ap. "Target Pulling out of Canada." CBS News, CBS Interactive, 15 Jan. 2015, www.cbsnews.com/news/target-pulling-out-of-canada/.

[144] Ap. "Target Pulling out of Canada." CBS News, CBS Interactive, 15 Jan. 2015, www.cbsnews.com/news/target-pulling-out-of-canada/.

[145] Robertson, David Chandler., and Bill Breen. Brick by Brick: How LEGO Rewrote the Rules of Innovation and Conquered the Global Toy Industry. Random House Business Books, 2014. Audible. Chapter 2, Position 8:00.

[146] Robertson, David Chandler., and Bill Breen. Brick by Brick: How LEGO Rewrote the Rules of Innovation and Conquered the Global Toy Industry. Random House Business Books, 2014. Page 7.

[147] Robertson, David Chandler., and Bill Breen. Brick by Brick: How LEGO Rewrote the Rules of Innovation and Conquered the Global Toy Industry. Random House Business Books, 2014. Page 18.

[148] Robertson, David Chandler., and Bill Breen. Brick by Brick: How LEGO Rewrote the Rules of Innovation and Conquered the Global Toy Industry. Random House Business Books, 2014. Page 18.

[149] Robertson, David Chandler., and Bill Breen. Brick by Brick: How LEGO Rewrote the Rules of Innovation and Conquered the Global Toy Industry. Random House Business Books, 2014. Audible. Chapter 4, Position 9:00.

[150] Robertson, David Chandler., and Bill Breen. Brick by Brick: How LEGO Rewrote the Rules of Innovation and Conquered the Global Toy Industry. Random House Business Books, 2014. Audible. Chapter 4, Position 9:30.

[151] Robertson, David Chandler., and Bill Breen. Brick by Brick: How LEGO Rewrote the Rules of Innovation and Conquered the Global Toy Industry. Random House Business Books, 2014. Audible. Chapter 4, Position 10:00.

[152] Bigus, Darren. Meister, Paul. "Lego Group: Building Strategy." Harvard Business Review, hbr.org/product/lego-group-building-strategy/W11169-PDF-ENG.

[153] Bigus, Darren. Meister, Paul. "Lego Group: Building Strategy." Harvard Business Review, hbr.org/product/lego-group-building-strategy/W11169-PDF-ENG.

[154] Robertson, David Chandler., and Bill Breen. Brick by Brick: How LEGO Rewrote the Rules of Innovation and Conquered the Global Toy Industry. Random House Business Books, 2014. Audible. Chapter 4, Position 23:30.

[155] Robertson, David Chandler., and Bill Breen. Brick by Brick: How LEGO Rewrote the Rules of Innovation and Conquered the Global Toy Industry. Random House Business Books, 2014. Page 7.

[156] Robertson, David Chandler., and Bill Breen. Brick by Brick: How LEGO Rewrote the Rules of Innovation and Conquered the Global Toy Industry. Random House Business Books, 2014. Audible. Chapter 4, Position 35:00.

[157] Robertson, David Chandler., and Bill Breen. Brick by Brick: How LEGO Rewrote the Rules of Innovation and Conquered the Global Toy Industry. Random House Business Books, 2014. Audible. Chapter 4, Position 51:00.

[158] Robertson, David Chandler., and Bill Breen. Brick by Brick: How LEGO Rewrote the Rules of Innovation and Conquered the Global Toy Industry. Random House Business Books, 2014. Audible. Chapter 4, Position 18:00.

[159] Robertson, David Chandler., and Bill Breen. Brick by Brick: How LEGO Rewrote the Rules of Innovation and Conquered the Global Toy Industry. Random House Business Books, 2014. Audible. Chapter 5, 56:30.

[160] Robertson, David Chandler., and Bill Breen. Brick by Brick: How LEGO Rewrote the Rules of Innovation and Conquered the Global Toy Industry. Random House Business Books, 2014. Audible. Chapter 5, 10:11.

[161] Robertson, David Chandler., and Bill Breen. Brick by Brick: How LEGO Rewrote the Rules of Innovation and Conquered the Global Toy Industry. Random House Business Books, 2014. Audible. Chapter 5, 10:11.

[162] Robertson, David Chandler., and Bill Breen. Brick by Brick: How LEGO Rewrote the Rules of Innovation and Conquered the Global Toy Industry. Random House Business Books, 2014. Audible. Chapter 5, 14:35.

[163] "The LEGO Group: Envisioning Risks in Asia Harvard Case Solution & Analysis."TheCaseSolutions. com, www.thecasesolutions.com/the-lego-group-envisioning-risks-in-asia-780.

[164] Robertson, David Chandler., and Bill Breen. Brick by Brick: How LEGO Rewrote the Rules of Innovation and Conquered the Global Toy Industry. Random House Business Books, 2014. Audible. Chapter 5, 56:00.

[165] Robertson, David Chandler., and Bill Breen. Brick by Brick: How LEGO Rewrote the Rules of Innovation and Conquered the Global Toy Industry. Random House Business Books, 2014. Audible. Chapter 5, 56:30.

[166] Robertson, David Chandler., and Bill Breen. Brick by Brick: How LEGO Rewrote the Rules of Innovation and Conquered the Global Toy Industry. Random House Business Books, 2014. Audible. Chapter 5, 56:30.

[167] "The Lego Case Study, by John Ashcroft and Company, Case Studies in Corporate Strategy. "The Lego Case Study, www.thelegocasestudy.com/.

[168] Mikes, Anette, and Dominique Hamel. "The LEGO Group: Envisioning Risks in Asia (A)." The LEGO Group: Envisioning Risks in Asia (A) - Case - Harvard Business School, 15 Nov. 2012, www.hbs.edu/ faculty/Pages/item.aspx?num=43619.

[169] Meister, Darren. Bigus, Paul. "The Lego Group: Building Strategy" Harvard Business Review, https:// hbr.org/product/lego-group-building-strategy/W11169-PDF-ENG#

[170] Mikes, Anette, and Dominique Hamel. "The LEGO Group: Envisioning Risks in Asia (A)." The LEGO Group: Envisioning Risks in Asia (A) - Case - Harvard Business School, 15 Nov. 2012, www.hbs.edu/ faculty/Pages/item.aspx?num=43619.

[171] Mikes, Anette, and Dominique Hamel. "The LEGO Group: Envisioning Risks in Asia (A)." The LEGO Group: Envisioning Risks in Asia (A) - Case - Harvard Business School, 15 Nov. 2012, www.hbs.edu/ faculty/Pages/item.aspx?num=43619.

[172] Mikes, Anette, and Dominique Hamel. "The LEGO Group: Envisioning Risks in Asia (A)." The LEGO Group: Envisioning Risks in Asia (A) - Case - Harvard Business School, 15 Nov. 2012, www.hbs.edu/ faculty/Pages/item.aspx?num=43619.

[173] Mikes, Anette, and Dominique Hamel. "The LEGO Group: Envisioning Risks in Asia (A)." The LEGO Group: Envisioning Risks in Asia (A) - Case - Harvard Business School, 15 Nov. 2012, www.hbs.edu/ faculty/Pages/item.aspx?num=43619.

[174] Mikes, Anette, and Dominique Hamel. "The LEGO Group: Envisioning Risks in Asia (A)." The LEGO Group: Envisioning Risks in Asia (A) - Case - Harvard Business School, 15 Nov. 2012, www.hbs.edu/ faculty/Pages/item.aspx?num=43619.

[175] Mikes, Anette, and Dominique Hamel. "The LEGO Group: Envisioning Risks in Asia (A)." The LEGO Group: Envisioning Risks in Asia (A) - Case - Harvard Business School, 15 Nov. 2012, www.hbs.edu/ faculty/Pages/item.aspx?num=43619.

[176] Mikes, Anette, and Dominique Hamel. "The LEGO Group: Envisioning Risks in Asia (A)." The LEGO Group: Envisioning Risks in Asia (A) - Case - Harvard Business School, 15 Nov. 2012, www.hbs.edu/ faculty/Pages/item.aspx?num=43619.

[177] Mikes, Anette, and Dominique Hamel. "The LEGO Group: Envisioning Risks in Asia (A)." The LEGO Group: Envisioning Risks in Asia (A) - Case - Harvard Business School, 15 Nov. 2012, www.hbs.edu/ faculty/Pages/item.aspx?num=43619.

[178] Mikes, Anette, and Dominique Hamel. "The LEGO Group: Envisioning Risks in Asia (A)." The LEGO Group: Envisioning Risks in Asia (A) - Case - Harvard Business School, 15 Nov. 2012, www.hbs.edu/faculty/Pages/item.aspx?num=43619.

[179] Mikes, Anette, and Dominique Hamel. "The LEGO Group: Envisioning Risks in Asia (A)." The LEGO Group: Envisioning Risks in Asia (A) - Case - Harvard Business School, 15 Nov. 2012, www.hbs.edu/faculty/Pages/item.aspx?num=43619.

[180] Staff, Fast Company. "How Lego Became The Apple Of Toys." Fast Company, Fast Company, 8 July 2017, www.fastcompany.com/3040223/when-it-clicks-it-clicks.

[181] Staff, Fast Company. "How Lego Became The Apple Of Toys." Fast Company, Fast Company, 8 July 2017, www.fastcompany.com/3040223/when-it-clicks-it-clicks.

[182] Mikes, Anette, and Amram Migdal. "The LEGO Group: Envisioning Risks in Asia (B)." The LEGO Group: Envisioning Risks in Asia (B) - Supplement - Harvard Business School, 10 Dec. 2013, www.hbs.edu/faculty/Pages/item.aspx?num=45944.

[183] Colvin, Geoff. "Jim Collins: In His Own Words." Fortune.com, Fortune, 30 July 2014, fortune.com/2011/09/30/jim-collins-in-his-own-words/.

[184] Lafley, A. G., and Roger L. Martin. Playing to Win: How Strategy Really Works. Harvard Business Review Press, 2013.

[185] Haas, Julian Birkinshaw, Martine. "Increase Your Return on Failure." Harvard Business Review, 10 May 2016, hbr.org/2016/05/increase-your-return-on-failure.

[186] Staff, Investopedia. "Hurdle Rate." Investopedia, 13 Mar. 2015, www.investopedia.com/terms/h/hurdlerate.asp.

[187] Haas, Julian Birkinshaw, Martine. "Increase Your Return on Failure." Harvard Business Review, 10 May 2016, hbr.org/2016/05/increase-your-return-on-failure.

[188] Tillmanns, Martin ReevesClaire LovePhilipp. "Your Strategy Needs a Strategy." Harvard Business Review, 21 Mar. 2016, hbr.org/2012/09/your-strategy-needs-a-strategy.

[189] Iyer, George Stalk Jr.Ashish, et al. "How to Hedge Your Strategic Bets." Harvard Business Review, 18 Apr. 2016, hbr.org/2016/05/how-to-hedge-your-strategic-bets.

[190] Iyer, George Stalk Jr.Ashish, et al. "How to Hedge Your Strategic Bets." Harvard Business Review, 18 Apr. 2016, hbr.org/2016/05/how-to-hedge-your-strategic-bets.

[191] Iyer, George Stalk Jr.Ashish, et al. "How to Hedge Your Strategic Bets." Harvard Business Review, 18 Apr. 2016, hbr.org/2016/05/how-to-hedge-your-strategic-bets.

[192] Iyer, George Stalk Jr.Ashish, et al. "How to Hedge Your Strategic Bets." Harvard Business Review, 18 Apr. 2016, hbr.org/2016/05/how-to-hedge-your-strategic-bets.

[193] Iyer, George Stalk Jr.Ashish, et al. "How to Hedge Your Strategic Bets." Harvard Business Review, 18 Apr. 2016, hbr.org/2016/05/how-to-hedge-your-strategic-bets.

[194] Space X recently lost a rocket due to an explosion as late as September 2016 after this writing. While their position has indeed moved closer to Ford, it still has space to grow to become a routine player without incident.

[195] "Army Regulation 600-100: Army Leadership." 8 Mar. 2007, www.apd.army.mil/epubs/DR_pubs/DR_a/pdf/web/r600_100.pdf.

[196] "Amazon CEO Jeff Bezos Shares Thoughts on Corporate Culture, Decision-Making and Failure." Los Angeles Times, Los Angeles Times, www.latimes.com/business/la-fi-0410-on-leadership-bezos-20160410-story.html.

[197] "Amazon CEO Jeff Bezos Shares Thoughts on Corporate Culture, Decision-Making and Failure." Los Angeles Times, Los Angeles Times, www.latimes.com/business/la-fi-0410-on-leadership-bezos-20160410-story.html.

[198] Nato. "ISAF's Strategic Vision - Declaration by the Heads of State and Government of the Nations Contributing to the UN-Mandated NATO-Led International Security Assistance Force (ISAF) in Afghanistan." NATO, www.nato.int/cps/en/natolive/official_texts_8444.htm.

[199] "Amazon CEO Jeff Bezos Shares Thoughts on Corporate Culture, Decision-Making and Failure." Los Angeles Times, Los Angeles Times, www.latimes.com/business/la-fi-0410-on-leadership-bezos-20160410-story.html.

[200] Delaney, Kevin J. "No One Should Have the Word 'Strategy' in Their Job Title." Quartz, Quartz, 12 May 2016, qz.com/680887/no-one-should-have-the-word-strategy-in-their-job-title/.

[201] Delaney, Kevin J. "No One Should Have the Word 'Strategy' in Their Job Title." Quartz, Quartz, 12 May 2016, qz.com/680887/no-one-should-have-the-word-strategy-in-their-job-title/.

[202] Delaney, Kevin J. "No One Should Have the Word 'Strategy' in Their Job Title." Quartz, Quartz, 12 May 2016, qz.com/680887/no-one-should-have-the-word-strategy-in-their-job-title/.

[203] Delaney, Kevin J. "No One Should Have the Word 'Strategy' in Their Job Title." Quartz, Quartz, 12 May 2016, qz.com/680887/no-one-should-have-the-word-strategy-in-their-job-title/.

[204] Hamilton, Jon. "Think You're Multitasking? Think Again." NPR, NPR, 2 Oct. 2008, www.npr.org/templates/story/story.php?storyId=95256794.

[205] Barnes, Julian E. "Strategy and Tactics: Tackling Donald Rumsfeld's Churchill Solitaire." The Wall Street Journal, Dow Jones & Company, 25 Jan. 2016, blogs.wsj.com/speakeasy/2016/01/25/strategy-and-tactics-tackling-donald-rumsfelds-churchill-solitaire/.

[206] Takeuchi, Darrell K. RigbyJeff SutherlandHirotaka. "The Secret History of Agile Innovation."Harvard Business Review, 20 Apr. 2016, hbr.org/2016/04/the-secret-history-of-agile-innovation.

[207] Rigby, Darrell K., et al. "A Quick Introduction to Agile Management." Harvard Business Review, 18 Apr. 2016, hbr.org/video/4846148015001/a-quick-introduction-to-agile-management.

[208] Rigby, Darrell K., et al. "A Quick Introduction to Agile Management." Harvard Business Review, 18 Apr. 2016, hbr.org/video/4846148015001/a-quick-introduction-to-agile-management.

[209] Rigby, Darrell K., et al. "A Quick Introduction to Agile Management." Harvard Business Review, 18 Apr. 2016, hbr.org/video/4846148015001/a-quick-introduction-to-agile-management.

[210] Rigby, Darrell K., et al. "A Quick Introduction to Agile Management." Harvard Business Review, 18 Apr. 2016, hbr.org/video/4846148015001/a-quick-introduction-to-agile-management.

[211] Rigby, Darrell K., et al. "A Quick Introduction to Agile Management." Harvard Business Review, 18 Apr. 2016, hbr.org/video/4846148015001/a-quick-introduction-to-agile-management.

212 Rigby, Darrell K., et al. "A Quick Introduction to Agile Management." Harvard Business Review, 18 Apr. 2016, hbr.org/video/4846148015001/a-quick-introduction-to-agile-management.

213 Takeuchi, Darrell K. RigbyJeff SutherlandHirotaka. "The Secret History of Agile Innovation."Harvard Business Review, 20 Apr. 2016, hbr.org/2016/04/the-secret-history-of-agile-innovation.

214 Takeuchi, Darrell K. RigbyJeff SutherlandHirotaka. "The Secret History of Agile Innovation."Harvard Business Review, 20 Apr. 2016, hbr.org/2016/04/the-secret-history-of-agile-innovation.

215 Bash, Leon E. PanettaJeremy. "The Former Head of the CIA on Managing the Hunt for Bin Laden." Harvard Business Review, 2 May 2016, hbr.org/2016/05/leadership-lessons-from-the-bin-laden-manhunt.

216 Bash, Leon E. PanettaJeremy. "The Former Head of the CIA on Managing the Hunt for Bin Laden." Harvard Business Review, 2 May 2016, hbr.org/2016/05/leadership-lessons-from-the-bin-laden-manhunt.

217 Bash, Leon E. PanettaJeremy. "The Former Head of the CIA on Managing the Hunt for Bin Laden." Harvard Business Review, 2 May 2016, hbr.org/2016/05/leadership-lessons-from-the-bin-laden-manhunt.

218 Kleiner, Paul LeinwandCesare MainardiArt. "Only 8% of Leaders Are Good at Both Strategy and Execution." Harvard Business Review, 6 Apr. 2016, hbr.org/2015/12/only-8-of-leaders-are-good-at-both-strategy-and-execution.

219 Kleiner, Paul LeinwandCesare MainardiArt. "Only 8% of Leaders Are Good at Both Strategy and Execution." Harvard Business Review, 6 Apr. 2016, hbr.org/2015/12/only-8-of-leaders-are-good-at-both-strategy-and-execution.

220 Varcoe, Jonathan TrevorBarry. "A Simple Way to Test Your Company's Strategic Alignment."Harvard Business Review, 18 May 2016, hbr.org/2016/05/a-simple-way-to-test-your-companys-strategic-alignment.

221 Varcoe, Jonathan TrevorBarry. "A Simple Way to Test Your Company's Strategic Alignment."Harvard Business Review, 18 May 2016, hbr.org/2016/05/a-simple-way-to-test-your-companys-strategic-alignment.

222 Clear, James. "This Person Improved Every Tiny Thing by 1 Percent and Here's What Happened." Entrepreneur, 12 June 2014, www.entrepreneur.com/article/234478.

223 Clear, James. "This Person Improved Every Tiny Thing by 1 Percent and Here's What Happened." Entrepreneur, 12 June 2014, www.entrepreneur.com/article/234478.

224 Clear, James. "This Person Improved Every Tiny Thing by 1 Percent and Here's What Happened." Entrepreneur, 12 June 2014, www.entrepreneur.com/article/234478.

225 Clear, James. "This Person Improved Every Tiny Thing by 1 Percent and Here's What Happened." Entrepreneur, 12 June 2014, www.entrepreneur.com/article/234478.

226 Clear, James. "This Person Improved Every Tiny Thing by 1 Percent and Here's What Happened." Entrepreneur, 12 June 2014, www.entrepreneur.com/article/234478.8

227 Winik, Jay. 1944: FDR and the Year That Changed History. Thorndike Press, a Part of Gale, Cengage Learning, 2016. Page 81.

[228] Warner, Bernhard. "Why This Shaving Startup Made a $100 Million Gamble on a 100-Year-Old Factory." Inc.com, Inc., www.inc.com/magazine/201605/bernhard-warner/harrys-razors-german-factory.html?linkId=24006668.

[229] Warner, Bernhard. "Why This Shaving Startup Made a $100 Million Gamble on a 100-Year-Old Factory." Inc.com, Inc., www.inc.com/magazine/201605/bernhard-warner/harrys-razors-german-factory.html?linkId=24006668.

[230] Warner, Bernhard. "Why This Shaving Startup Made a $100 Million Gamble on a 100-Year-Old Factory." Inc.com, Inc., www.inc.com/magazine/201605/bernhard-warner/harrys-razors-german-factory.html?linkId=24006668.

[231] Warner, Bernhard. "Why This Shaving Startup Made a $100 Million Gamble on a 100-Year-Old Factory." Inc.com, Inc., www.inc.com/magazine/201605/bernhard-warner/harrys-razors-german-factory.html?linkId=24006668.

[232] Warner, Bernhard. "Why This Shaving Startup Made a $100 Million Gamble on a 100-Year-Old Factory." Inc.com, Inc., www.inc.com/magazine/201605/bernhard-warner/harrys-razors-german-factory.html?linkId=24006668.

[233] Warner, Bernhard. "Why This Shaving Startup Made a $100 Million Gamble on a 100-Year-Old Factory." Inc.com, Inc., www.inc.com/magazine/201605/bernhard-warner/harrys-razors-german-factory.html?linkId=24006668.

[234] Warner, Bernhard. "Why This Shaving Startup Made a $100 Million Gamble on a 100-Year-Old Factory." Inc.com, Inc., www.inc.com/magazine/201605/bernhard-warner/harrys-razors-german-factory.html?linkId=24006668.

[235] Warner, Bernhard. "Why This Shaving Startup Made a $100 Million Gamble on a 100-Year-Old Factory." Inc.com, Inc., www.inc.com/magazine/201605/bernhard-warner/harrys-razors-german-factory.html?linkId=24006668.

[236] Warner, Bernhard. "Why This Shaving Startup Made a $100 Million Gamble on a 100-Year-Old Factory." Inc.com, Inc., www.inc.com/magazine/201605/bernhard-warner/harrys-razors-german-factory.html?linkId=24006668.

[237] Sullivan, Tim. "Blitzscaling." Harvard Business Review, 24 Aug. 2016, hbr.org/2016/04/blitzscaling.

[238] Sullivan, Tim. "Blitzscaling." Harvard Business Review, 24 Aug. 2016, hbr.org/2016/04/blitzscaling.

[239] Sullivan, Tim. "Blitzscaling." Harvard Business Review, 24 Aug. 2016, hbr.org/2016/04/blitzscaling.

[240] Sullivan, Tim. "Blitzscaling." Harvard Business Review, 24 Aug. 2016, hbr.org/2016/04/blitzscaling.

[241] Sullivan, Tim. "Blitzscaling." Harvard Business Review, 24 Aug. 2016, hbr.org/2016/04/blitzscaling.

[242] Sullivan, Tim. "Blitzscaling." Harvard Business Review, 24 Aug. 2016, hbr.org/2016/04/blitzscaling.

[243] Sullivan, Tim. "Blitzscaling." Harvard Business Review, 24 Aug. 2016, hbr.org/2016/04/blitzscaling.

[244] Wong, Joon Ian. "Spotify's Average Salary Keeps Rising-Even as Its Losses Mount." Quartz, Quartz, 24 May 2016, qz.com/691188/spotifys-average-salary-keeps-rising-even-as-its-losses-mount/.

[245] Tech Startup Twilio Files to Go Public." CNNMoney, Cable News Network, money.cnn.com/2016/05/26/technology/twilio-ipo/index.html?sr=fbmoney052616twilio-ipo0918PMStoryLink&linkId=24914961.

[246] Truong, Alice. "The Most Hyped Tech IPO of 2016 Is Living up to Expectations." Quartz, Quartz, 23 June 2016, qz.com/715364/the-most-hyped-tech-ipo-of-2016-is-living-up-to-expectations/.

[247] Truong, Alice. "The Most Hyped Tech IPO of 2016 Is Living up to Expectations." Quartz, Quartz, 23 June 2016, qz.com/715364/the-most-hyped-tech-ipo-of-2016-is-living-up-to-expectations/.

[248] Kar, Ian. "Snapchat Just Raised $1.8 Billion, Bringing It to a Reported $20 Billion Valuation."Quartz, Quartz, 26 May 2016, qz.com/693205/snapchat%C2%ADjust%C2%ADraised%C2%AD1%C2%AD8%C2%ADbillion%C2%ADbringing%C2%ADit%C2%ADto%C2%ADa%C2%ADreported%C2%AD20%C2%ADbillion%C2%ADvaluation/.

[249] Kar, Ian. "Snapchat Just Raised $1.8 Billion, Bringing It to a Reported $20 Billion Valuation."Quartz, Quartz, 26 May 2016, qz.com/693205/snapchat%C2%ADjust%C2%ADraised%C2%AD1%C2%AD8%C2%ADbillion%C2%ADbringing%C2%ADit%C2%ADto%C2%ADa%C2%ADreported%C2%AD20%C2%ADbillion%C2%ADvaluation/.

[250] Commentary. "Only in Silicon Valley Could Elizabeth Holmes Lose $4.5 Billion She Never Had to Begin With." Quartz, Quartz, 15 June 2016, qz.com/707143/only-in-silicon-valley-could-elizabeth-holmes-lose-4-5-billion-she-never-had-to-begin-with/.

[251] Commentary. "Only in Silicon Valley Could Elizabeth Holmes Lose $4.5 Billion She Never Had to Begin With." Quartz, Quartz, 15 June 2016, qz.com/707143/only-in-silicon-valley-could-elizabeth-holmes-lose-4-5-billion-she-never-had-to-begin-with/.

[252] Coren, Michael J. "It's Time for Startups to Grow up and Get a Business Model." Quartz, Quartz, 22 June 2016, qz.com/712909/its-time-for-startups-to-grow-up-and-get-a-business-model/.

[253] Gascoigne, Written by Joel, and Joel Gascoigne Read more. "Tough News: We've Made 10 Layoffs. How We Got Here, the Financial Details and How We're Moving Forward." Open, 22 June 2016, open.buffer.com/layoffs-and-moving-forward/.

[254] Gascoigne, Written by Joel, and Joel Gascoigne Read more. "Tough News: We've Made 10 Layoffs. How We Got Here, the Financial Details and How We're Moving Forward." Open, 22 June 2016, open.buffer.com/layoffs-and-moving-forward/.

[255] Safdar, Khadeeja. "Birchbox, a Pioneer in Subscription Beauty Sales, Scales Back." The Wall Street Journal, Dow Jones & Company, 15 June 2016, www.wsj.com/articles/birchbox-retrenches-amid-rapid-rise-in-competition-cash-squeeze-1465983002.

[256] Safdar, Khadeeja. "Birchbox, a Pioneer in Subscription Beauty Sales, Scales Back." The Wall Street Journal, Dow Jones & Company, 15 June 2016, www.wsj.com/articles/birchbox-retrenches-amid-rapid-rise-in-competition-cash-squeeze-1465983002.

[257] Bort, Julie. "Silicon Valley Startups Are Terrified by a New Idea: Profits." Business Insider, Business Insider, 21 Apr. 2016, www.businessinsider.com/valley-unicorns-terrified-by-profits-2016-4.

[258] Bort, Julie. "Silicon Valley Startups Are Terrified by a New Idea: Profits." Business Insider, Business Insider, 21 Apr. 2016, www.businessinsider.com/valley-unicorns-terrified-by-profits-2016-4.

[259] Bort, Julie. "Silicon Valley Startups Are Terrified by a New Idea: Profits." Business Insider, Business Insider, 21 Apr. 2016, www.businessinsider.com/valley-unicorns-terrified-by-profits-2016-4.

[260] Bort, Julie. "Silicon Valley Startups Are Terrified by a New Idea: Profits." Business Insider, Business Insider, 21 Apr. 2016, www.businessinsider.com/valley-unicorns-terrified-by-profits-2016-4.

[261] Bort, Julie. "Silicon Valley Startups Are Terrified by a New Idea: Profits." Business Insider, Business Insider, 21 Apr. 2016, www.businessinsider.com/valley-unicorns-terrified-by-profits-2016-4.

[262] Bort, Julie. "Silicon Valley Startups Are Terrified by a New Idea: Profits." Business Insider, Business Insider, 21 Apr. 2016, www.businessinsider.com/valley-unicorns-terrified-by-profits-2016-4.

[263] Holcomb, Tim. "Cash-Flow Breakeven: Controlling Your Own Destiny." VC With Me, vcwithme.co/2016/05/31/cashflowbreakevencontrollingyourowndestiny/.

[264] Kawasaki, Guy. "10 Mistakes Every Entrepreneur Needs to Stop Making." Business Insider, Business Insider, 3 Mar. 2015, www.businessinsider.com/mistakes-entrepreneurs-make-2015-3.

[265] Staley, Oliver. "What Silicon Valley Wants from Navy SEALs and Army Rangers." Quartz, Quartz, 28 May 2016, qz.com/689368/what-silicon-valley-wants-from-navy-seals-and-army-rangers/.

[266] LYONS, DAN. DISRUPTED. ATLANTIC Books, 2017. Page 27.

[267] LYONS, DAN. DISRUPTED. ATLANTIC Books, 2017. Page 125-126.

[268] MCPHERSON, JAMES M. HALLOWED GROUND: A Walk at Gettysburg. CRESTLINE, 2017.

[269] MCPHERSON, JAMES M. HALLOWED GROUND: A Walk at Gettysburg. CRESTLINE, 2017.

Copyright © 2017 John Childs

All rights reserved.

Published in the United States in Partnership with Amazon Create Space.

No portion of this book may be reproduced in any form without permission from the publisher, except as permitted by U.S. copyright law. For permissions, use the contact form at http://minimumvaiblestrategy.com to learn more.

Create Space books are available at special discounts for bulk purchases, for sales promotions, or corporate use. Special editions or signed copies can be obtained through the Minimum Viable Strategy website at http://minimumviablestrategy.com through the contact page.

Library of Congress Cataloging-in-Publication Data is available upon request.

ISBN-13:
978-1535376358

ISBN-10:
153537635X

www.ingramcontent.com/pod-product-compliance
Lightning Source LLC
Chambersburg PA
CBHW021404170526
45164CB00002B/493